KT-154-260

 touring

on the road

FRANCE

Produced by AA Publishing

Revised second edition 1995, published in this format 1997
Reprinted December 1997, August 1998, April 1999,
Revised third edition 2000
First published January 1991

Edited, designed and produced by AA Publishing.

© The Automobile Association 1997, 2000
Maps © The Automobile Association 1997, 2000

Distributed in the United Kingdom by AA Publishing, Norfolk
House, Priestley Road, Basingstoke, Hampshire, RG24 9NY.

A CIP catalogue record for this book is available from the British
Library.

ISBN 0 7495 2286 0

All rights reserved. No part of this publication may be
reproduced, stored in a retrieval system, or transmitted in any
form or by any means – electronic, photocopying, recording or
otherwise – unless the permission of the publishers has been
obtained beforehand.
This book may not be lent, resold, hired out or otherwise
disposed of by way of trade in any form of binding or cover other than that in which it is published, without the prior consent of
the publisher.

The contents of this publication are believed correct at the time
of printing. Nevertheless, the publishers cannot accept responsi-
bility for errors or omissions or for changes in details given in this
guide or for the consequences of any reliance on the information
provided by the same. Assessments of attractions and so forth
are based upon the author's own experience and, therefore,
descriptions given in this guide necessarily contain an element of
subjective opinion which may not reflect the publisher's opinion
or dictate a reader's own experience on another occasion.
We have tried to ensure accuracy in this guide, but things do
change and we would be grateful if readers would advise us of
any inaccuracies they may encounter.

Published by AA Publishing, (a trading name of Automobile
Association Developments Limited, whose registered office is
Norfolk House, Priestley Road, Basingstoke, Hampshire, RG24
9NY. Registered number 1878835).

Colour separation: Daylight Colour Art, Singapore

Printed and bound by G. Canale & C. S.P.A., Torino, Italy

Front cover: *near Pertuis, Vaucluse*
Inset: *sunset over Le Mont-St-Michel*

Opposite: *lace coiffe, Pont l'Abbé*

CONTENTS

ABOUT THIS BOOK

This book is not only a practical touring guide for the independent traveller, but is also invaluable for those who would like to know more about the country.

It is divided into 6 regions, each containing between 3 and 5 tours which start and finish in major towns and cities considered to be the best centres for exploration.

Each tour has details of the most interesting places to visit en route. Panels catering for special interests follow some of the main entries – for those whose interest is in history, wildlife or walking, and those who have children. There are also panels which highlight scenic stretches of road and which give details of events, crafts and customs. The simple route directions are accompanied by an easy-to-use tour map at the beginning of each tour, along with a chart showing how far it is from one town to the next in kilometres and miles. This can help you to decide where to take a break and stop overnight. (All distances quoted are approximate.)

Before setting off it is advisable to check with the information centre (addresses are given after the symbol $\boxed{i}$ at the end of town entries) at the start of the tour for recommendations on where to break your journey and for additional information on what to see and do, and when best to visit.

Tour Information
See pages 162–73 for addresses, telephone numbers and opening times of the attractions mentioned in the tours, including telephone numbers of tourist offices.

Accommodation
See pages 159–61 for a list of recommended hotels for each tour.

Business Hours
Banks: normal banking hours are 9am–noon and 2–4pm weekdays and they are closed either Mondays or Saturdays, all Sundays and public holidays. Banks close at noon on the day before a national holiday, and all day on Monday if the holiday falls on a Tuesday.

Post offices: main post offices are open 8am–7pm on weekdays, and 8am–noon on Saturdays, though some small offices may close for lunch. Stamps may also be bought in tobacco shops (*tabacs*) or cafés marked with a red cigar sign. Letter boxes are yellow.

Credit Cards
International credit cards are accepted widely throughout France, though not so much in rural areas. They are not accepted at some petrol stations.

Currency
The unit of currency is the Euro; during the transitional period for full change-over (until December 2001), the franc will continue to be used as a 'sub-unit' of the Euro and a dual pricing system will operate. In January 2002, Euro bank notes and coins will be introduced. Bank notes will come in denominations of 5, 10, 20, 50, 100, 200 and 500; coins will come in denominations of 1, 2, 5, 10, 20 and 50 centimes, 1 and 2 Euros. Currently the franc is divided into 100 centimes. Coins are in denominations of 10, 20 and 50 centimes, and 1, 2, 5, 10 and 20 francs; notes are in denominations of 20, 50, 100, 200 and 500 francs. Most French banks no longer accept Eurocheques.

Customs Regulations
Since 1 January 1993 there is no limit on the importation into one EU country of tax-paid goods purchased in another, provided they are for personal use. However, all EU customs authorities have fixed indicative limits on alcohol and tobacco. Beyond these limits the importer must be able to prove that they are for personal use.

Electricity
220 volts (50 cycles AC), with the standard continental two- (or three-) pin round plug, making an adaptor essential for British and American appliances.

Embassies
British Embassy: 35 rue du Faubourg St Honoré, 75008 Paris Cedex 08 tel: (1) 44 51 31 00.
Canadian Embassy: 35 avenue Montaigne, 75008 Paris tel: (1) 44 33 29 00.
US Embassy: 2 avenue Gabriel, 75008 Paris Cedex 08 tel: (1) 47 05 07 99.

Emergency Telephone Numbers
Police tel: 17
Fire tel: 18
Ambulance tel: 15.

Entry Regulations
No visas are required for nationals of EU countries (except Turkey), Andorra, Australia, Bermuda, Brazil, Brunei, Canada, Chile, Croatia, Cyprus, Czech Republic, Hungary, Iceland, Israel, Japan, Liechtenstein, Malaysia, Malta, Mexico, Monaco, New Zealand, Norway, Paraguay, Poland, San Marino, Singapore, Slovakia, Slovenia, South Korea, Sweden, Switzerland, Vatican City, Uragua and USA. Visas are required for all others. Check, though, with a travel agent or the French Government Tourist Office, since visa policy is subject to review.

BORDERS®

BORDERS®

BORDERS®

BORDERS®

BORDERS
BOOKS MUSIC AND CAFE
98 Buchanan Street
Glasgow G1 Scotland

STORE: 0283   REG: 02/44 TRAN#: 5387
SALE   22/05/2001 EMP: 07436

INSIGHT POCKET GD KENYA
     6058357   QP T   6.99
FRANCE TOURING GD
     6092305   QP T   9.99

 2 Items   Total   16.98
            MASTERCARD   16.98
ACCT # /S 5454600144181
           AUTH: 022972
NAME: LANG/MARLYN A.MRS

CUSTOMER COPY

22/05/2001 03:24PM

THANK YOU FOR SHOPPING AT BORDERS
PLEASE ASK ABOUT OUR SPECIAL EVENTS

Vat No: 650072731

Health Matters

There are no special health requirements or regulations. Visitors other than EU citizens, where reciprocal medical services may be available, are advised to take out medical insurance.

Motoring

For information on all aspects of motoring in France see pages 158–59.

Public Holidays

1 January – New Year's Day
Easter Monday
1 May – Labour Day
8 May – VE Day
6th Thursday after Easter – Ascension Day
2nd Monday after Ascension – Whitsun
14 July – Bastille Day
15 August – Assumption Day
1 November – All Saints' Day
11 November – Remembrance Day
25 December – Christmas Day

Roche Tuilière and Roche Sanadoire, near Le Mont-Dore in the Auvergne

Telephones

Insert coin after lifting the receiver; the dialling tone is a continuous tone. For local calls use a 1 franc coin. Most booths now take phonecards (*télécartes*). Buy them for 40FF, 60FF or 97.50FF from post offices, tobacconists and newsagents.

For international calls dial 00, wait for a new tone, then dial the national code, followed by the local code, omitting the initial 0, and then the number.

Time

France follows Greenwich Mean Time (GMT) plus one hour, with clocks put forward for a further hour from late March to late September.

Tourist Offices

Where no address is given for a separate tourist information office, enquire at the *Mairie* (mayor's office) the *Hôtel de Ville* (town hall) or perhaps the *Syndicat d'Initiative* office. In some places the tourist offices open only seasonally, and the *Mairie* or *Hôtel de Ville* will handle enquiries out of season.

Useful Words

The following words and phrases may be helpful.

English	French
I need petrol	*j'ai besoin d'essence*
my car has broken down	*ma voiture est en panne*
oil	*huile*
the road for	*la route pour*
traffic lights	*les feux*
tyres	*les pneus*
after	*après*
behind	*derrière*
before	*avant*
here	*ici*
left	*à gauche*
near	*près*
opposite	*en face*
right	*à droite*
straight on	*tout droit*
there	*là*
where?	*où?*
where is?	*où est?*
I do not understand	*je ne comprends pas*
do you speak English?	*parlez-vous Anglais?*
help!	*au secours!*
how much is it?	*ça coute combien?*
I'm sorry	*pardon*
thankyou	*merci*

NORMANDY & BRITTANY

Normandy has rebuilt itself since World War II into a region of cheerful holiday resorts, attractive farmlands and archetypal rustic villages. Here and there, you will pick up eerie echoes of an earlier invasion which went from Normandy across the English Channel. The original Normans were Norsemen – Vikings who swept down from Scandinavia and, in the 10th century, created the dukedom of Normandy. William the Conqueror was Duke of Normandy, with a legal claim to the English throne, long before he invaded England in 1066. From that point on, the histories of Normandy and England intertwined.

The Normandy coastline is a succession of resorts. Look for the seafood restaurants in the fishing ports. Inland, the livestock farms supply a cuisine which is rich in butter, cheeses, cream and hefty helpings of meat. Apples and pears are major crops. The wooded farmlands of Normandy create some of the most beautiful landscapes in northern France.

Brittany becomes more Breton as you move further west. A wonderful coastline and an airy, high-level interior are linked by a wooded middle district which could easily be in Devon or Cornwall.

Waves of colonists from Britain started arriving in the 5th century. Britain and Brittany, Briton and Breton are all from the same basic word; but the close connection was lost long ago.

Bretons, particularly in the west, retain a feeling of 'apartness' from the rest of France, and you will not be long there before being aware of something Celtic in the air. Traditional costumes and religious processions, not always as well supported as they have been in the past, underline the differences in culture and background.

In both Brittany and Normandy, regional nature parks are very well organised, with wildlife reserves, museums of traditional ways of life and places where you can see products such as bread and cider being made in the old pre-industrialised way.

Caen

You cannot miss William the Conqueror's influence on Caen, which has risen again from the devastation of 1944. Its centrepiece is the château of the dukes of Normandy. Inside this massive fortress, founded by William in 1060, you will find the Musée des Beaux-Arts with its splendid collection of French and Italian paintings, and the Musée de Normandie, devoted to archaeology, history and traditional life. William also endowed the monastery of the Abbaye aux Hommes, just as his wife built the original convent of the Abbaye aux Dames. William's tomb is in the Church of St-Étienne at the Abbaye aux Hommes, which now serves as Caen's Hôtel de Ville.

The Musée de la Nature here concentrates on the wildlife of coast and country. The Mémorial-Musée pour la Paix has impressive displays and audio-visual presentations charting the rise of Facism, the collaboration of the Resistance and the D-Day landings through to the present day.

Dieppe

Like Caen, Dieppe has erased most of the scars of World War II. Its harbour area includes ferry, freight, fishing and pleasure ports. Morning fish stalls are set up by the roadside.

The best view of Dieppe is from the 15th-century hillside château. It houses a fine museum and art gallery with extensive maritime rooms and a glorious collection of ivories, including a full-rigged ship with billowing sails.

Rennes

Rennes is the historic and flourishing provincial capital of Brittany. The River Vilaine runs through it, but, from the tourist office in the Quai Lamartine, there is no water to be seen. Here, the Vilaine has been roofed over to provide a car park.

Another quay, this time named after the writer Émile Zola, is the address of the Musée des Beaux-Arts, with its rich display of paintings, drawings, engravings and sculptures, many confiscated from religious houses during the Revolution. Rubens,

Opposite: Le Mont-St-Michel, steeped in magic and history
Above: brightly painted fishing boats in the harbour at Dieppe ·

Gaugin, Sisley, Boudin and Picasso are all represented. In the same building is the Musée de Bretagne, which traces the history of Brittany from prehistoric times.

Quimper

Quimper is more Breton than Rennes. The Musée Breton is here, completely refurbished. The pleasant old quarter centres on a square dominated by the twin spire of the cathedral, St-Corentin. Here is an architectural curiosity: the 15th-century nave is accidentally out of alignment with the 13th-century choir.

Quimper's Musée des Beaux-Arts, totally renovated to include audio-visual presentations, is well provided with 17th-century Flemish paintings. In the same era, Quimper itself began the production of the glazed pottery for which it is still famous. Factories and ceramic artists' workshops welcome visitors.

Legacy of D-Day

Normandy is a land of apples and cider, of spacious sands, of lovely inland *bocage* country with hedges and tree-lined fields, but behind the peaceful present-day scenes the region hides a past once devastated by the D-Day landings in June 1944, when the huge invasion force of Operation Overlord stormed the German defences.

3 DAYS • 456KM • 283 MILES

i Place du Canada, Caen

▶ *Leave Caen on the D513 as for Cabourg. Go left on the D37, then take the D514 as for Ouistreham to Pegasus Bridge.*

❶ Pegasus Bridge,
Normandy
In the eastern sector of the D-Day landings, the years of planning and training came down to one amazingly audacious feat. Just after midnight on the morning of 6 June 1944, three gliders with no room for a conventional approach suddenly crash-landed beside this ugly but vital little tilting bridge on the Caen–Ouistreham canal. British troops poured out and after four minutes' fierce fighting secured the bridge. They held it until reinforcements arrived, most decisively the Commandos led by Lord Lovat, who reached here exactly two-and-a-half minutes behind schedule after fighting their way inland from Sword Beach.

Three columns in the scrubland southeast of the bridge show where the gliders landed. On the west side, a museum tells the story of that dramatic engagement and on summer evenings there is a *Son et Lumiere* presentation. In November 1993 the original bridge was replaced by something more appropriate to modern traffic.

▶ *Take the D35 to Douvres then follow the 'Bayeux' signs. Go right on the D79 to Courseulles-sur-Mer, then right on the D12 and follow signs to Arromanches-les-Bains.*

❷ Arromanches, Normandy
Without massive supplies, the D-Day landings could not have developed into an advance across the whole of France. Arromanches was the scene of one of the greatest engineering feats of the war – the building, from thousands of tons of prefabricated parts shipped across the Channel, of Port Winston, the giant Mulberry (artificial) harbour. It threw a 5.7km (3½-mile) breakwater round the sea approaches to Arromanches, from which pontoon bridges reached to the shore, and was operational within 12 days.

Today, Arromanches is a busy but unremarkable little resort on a bay between all but vertical cliffs. A viewpoint on the eastern cliff overlooks the many sections of the artificial harbour which remain offshore. On the seafront, the lively and well-presented Musée du Débarquement illustrates, with working models, films and photographs the creation and operation of 'the key to the liberation of France'.

i Place du Groupe Lorraine

BACK TO NATURE
....

In the busy resort of Courseulles, part of Juno Beach on D-Day, the Maison de la Mer features aquariums with seahorses and conger eels, and a splendid display of shells.

▶ *Leave Arromanches-les-Bains for Bayeux on the D516.*

❸ Bayeux, Normandy
Most of the fine historic buildings here, recently restored, survived the 1944 campaign. You can stroll through old streets and over narrow bridges, admiring the gleaming stonework of the mills on the

The Café Gondrée,
Pegasus Bridge

Bayeux's splendid Norman Gothic Cathedral of Notre Dame

River Aure. On the ring road, the Musée de la Bataille de Normandie is 'guarded' by British, American and German tanks. Everything in Bayeux, however, pales in importance beside the priceless 11th-century tapestry, displayed in the Centre Guillaume le Conquérant, with its lively scenes of the Norman Conquest of England. Weavers and lace-makers still have studios in the town.

Alongside the cathedral, the Musée Baron Gérard shows paintings, lacework and ceramics. It opens from a little court-yard shaded by the famous 'liberty tree', planted according to the Revolutionary calendar (France's official calendar from 1793–1805) on 10 Germinal of the year V – otherwise 30 March, 1797.

i *Pont St Jean*

▶ *Leave Bayeux on the **D6** to Port-en-Bessin-Huppain. Go left on the **D514** for Plage d'Omaha.*

❹ Plage d'Omaha, Normandy

Most side roads to the right of the D514 here reach memorials above the Americans' principal D-Day landing beach, although signs for the Plage d'Omaha lead to a holiday camp area. Look for Wn 62, a high-set German strongpoint above the shoreline. There are American monuments here as well as explanations of the D-Day action and the fearsome German defences.

The American military cemetery for the men lost during the landings is close by, and there is a Musée Omaha,

displaying military vehicles, weapons, uniforms and insignia. There are exhibits on the planning and accomplishing of the D-Day landings.

FOR HISTORY BUFFS

Turn right off the D514 after Omaha Beach for Pointe du Hoc, to learn about the desperate struggle of the American Rangers to scale the cliffs on D-Day. Later, the landings were re-staged here for the film *The Longest Day*.

▶ *Continue on the **D514** then go right on the **N13** as for Cherbourg and continue to Valognes.*

❺ Valognes, Normandy

In its 17th- to 19th-century heyday, Valognes was 'the Versailles of Normandy'. Aristocratic families owned town houses here, and there was a high-flying social life. The bombardments of 1944 wrecked the centre, which has been rebuilt, and destroyed part of the Church of St Malo. A modern reinforced concrete nave and tower stand beside the 14th-century chancel.

However, several of Valogne's mansions survived. The elegant 18th-century Hôtel de Beaumont is open to visitors. The Hôtel de Thieuville houses the Musée de l'Eau de Vie et des Vieux Métiers, whose two main subjects are brandy and leatherwork. An annexe has

FOR HISTORY BUFFS

Ste-Mère-Église near Utah Beach was the first French town liberated on D-Day. A museum to the 82nd US Airborne Division describes the action and how it is commemorated, and explains why the figure of a paratrooper hangs from the church tower every summer.

displays on the French Revolution with some unusual themes, such as the role of scientists in Revolutionary times.

Close at hand the Musée du Cidre et du Calvados, once a dyer's workshop, then a barracks and then a smithy, covers five centuries of cider-making and distilling.

[i] *Place du Château*

▶ *Leave Valognes for Barneville-Carteret on the D902.*

BACK TO NATURE

Until early this century, the huge sand dunes north of the Cap de Carteret were moved steadily inland by the wind, engulfing roads and a mill. You can see how, classified as a nature reserve, they have now been stabilised by the planting of marram grass thickets. Look for birds such as Dartford warblers and stonechats as well as numerous lizards.

▶ *Leave Barneville as for La Haye-du-Puits on the **D903**, then keep right on the **D650**. Go straight on along the **D20**, to Bréhal, then right on the **D971** and into Granville.*

7 Granville, Normandy
Granville grew from a fortified town on a promontory rock, and, thanks to the contortions of history, it was first fortified by the English against the French! The story of the town is illustrated in the Musée du Vieux Granville, just inside the

6 Barneville-Carteret, Normandy

These two little towns, administratively linked together, form a family holiday resort with excellent sands, a spectacular rocky headland and a very sheltered tidal river harbour. This is a pleasant walking and watersports area, and summer ferries sail to the Channel Islands. Make for the lighthouse on Cap de Carteret, a wonderful viewpoint towards Jersey, Sark, Herm and, on the northern horizon, Alderney.

Take care in the sea. Every year people ignore the notices warning that, while the town beaches have a lifeguard service, the quieter one north of the Cap does not. There, it

is all too easy for youngsters and less strong adult swimmers to be taken well out of their depth.

[i] *10 rue des Ecoles*

RECOMMENDED WALKS

At Barneville-Carteret, start from either of the beaches flanking the Cap de Carteret along the exhilarating Sentier des Douaniers (the Excisemen's Path), which contours the lichen-clad cliffs and passes the site of an 18th-century coastal gun battery.

The beach at Barneville-Carteret, north of Cap de Carteret

preserved drawbridge gateway of the Haute Ville (High Town).

The 15th-century Notre Dame Church stands among the alleyways here; a good aquarium includes shell and mineral collections; and a scenic path follows the cliffs below the lighthouse, with views of the low-lying Chausey archipelago. Ferries sail to La Grande Île, with its château built by motor magnate Louis Renault.

On no account miss Granville's Jardin Public. Its lush lawns, pine trees and beautifully laid-out flower beds surround the pink-and-white villa once owned by couturier

Christian Dior. In early August, a 'Pardon of the Sea' melds religion with spectacle.Other attractions include a gallery of modern art and a wax museum.

☐ *4 Cours Jonville*

▶ *Leave Granville for Villedieu-les-Poêles on the D924.*

8 Villedieu-les-Poêles, Normandy

If every place-name tells a story, how to explain Villedieu-les-Poêles – 'God's Town of the Pots and Frying-pans'? The Knights of Malta (a military religious order) established here in the 16th century, called the place Villedieu, and it became a famous centre of craftsmen and metalworkers.

That great tradition continues. Here you can watch hand-beaten copper being worked at the Atelier du Cuivre and pewterware at the Maison de l'Étain. At the extremes of Villedieu's historic product range, the Fonderie des Cloches is a bell-foundry, and the Maison de la Poeslerie et de la Dentellerie displays the lace-work for which the women of the town were well known all over northern France.

☐ *Place des Costils*

▶ *Leave Villedieu-les-Poêles on the N175 as for St Hilaire. Go right on the D924 and D999, then left on the D33 and continue through Mortain. Turn left on the D907, go through Domfront-centre then follow 'Bagnoles-de-l'Orne' signs along the D908 and right on the D335.*

9 Bagnoles-de-l'Orne, Normandy

Retaining its old prominence as the most popular spa town in the west of France, Bagnoles, with the linked Tessé la Madeleine, lies among woodlands rising from the banks of the La Vée river. People come here for spa cures and to 'take the waters', but Bagnoles also offers excellent sporting facilities: golf, tennis, swimming, horse riding, fishing and archery.

Wooded walks extend through the parks of the spa buildings and the château at Tessé. One fine scenic path leads to the Roc du Chien (the Dog's Rock) above the narrow river valley where the spa itself is located.

Bagnoles' casino backs on to a very pleasant lake where pedaloes can be hired. Close to the lake there are several restaurants specialising in the substantial Normandy cuisine.

The château at Bagnoles-de-l'Orne adds to the attractions of this famous spa town

---

FOR CHILDREN

On the way from Villedieu-les-Poêles to Bagnoles-de-l'Orne, turn off the D33 for Le Village Enchanté, a beautiful estate where fairy-tale tableaux are laid out in the woodland.

SPECIAL TO...

At Bagnoles-de-l'Orne is the Musée des Sapeurs-Pompiers, which shows off France's finest collection of horse-drawn and hand-pumped fire engines. Look for La Distinguée, which operated as long ago as pre-Revolutionary times. Normandy is famous for its apples and pears. The region's rich tradition in apple- and pear-growing, and the making of cider, are all explained in the Maison de la Pomme et de la Poire. Reached by turning right after Barenton on the D335, it has indoor displays as well as a walk through an orchard specially planted with many varieties of apple and pear trees.

RECOMMENDED WALKS

Stop off on the way to Bagnoles and ask at the Mairie (town hall) in St-Pois on the D33 for the Circuits Pédestres leaflet. It describes a series of waymarked walks in the beautiful Normandy countryside. They explore the falls in the valley of the Glanon stream, granite quarries and the viewpoint ridge of Mont Buon.

[i] *Place du Marché*

▶ *Leave Bagnoles-de-l'Orne for St-Michel-des-Andaines on the D386. Go left and right on the D924 into Flers. Go right as for Caen along the D962, then take the D562 to Clécy and turn off for Clécy-centre.*

10 Clécy, Normandy
The River Orne at Clécy makes a dramatic curve below the densely wooded cliffs of La Suisse Normande (Norman Switzerland). Clécy is the main resort in this district whose name should not lead you to expect a Swiss-like landscape of lakes and mountains; but it is one of the most beautiful parts of inland Normandy nevertheless. In the pleasant town centre with its 18th-century houses, look for the Musée Hardy which displays the work of a local artist. An exhilarating walk climbs to the magnificent viewpoint of the Pain du Sucre (the Sugarloaf), high on the cliffs overlooking the Orne. The 16th-century Manoir de Placy houses the Musée des Antiquités Normandes, with a miniature railway and a train museum in the grounds.

FOR CHILDREN

In Clécy, 20-minute programmes at the Musée du Chemin de Fer Miniature show off more than 180 locomotives operating on the biggest model railway layout in Europe.

Bridge over the River Orne in the resort of Clécy

[i] *Place du Tripot*

▶ *Leave Clécy on the D133c, then go left as for St-Rémy. Just over the brow of a hill, go sharp right and follow Routes des Crêtes to St-Omer. Avoid St-Rémy itself. In St-Omer turn right as for Pont-d'Ouilly. Ignore the 'La Suisse Normande' turning. Go left at a stop sign to Bretteville and follow the D23. In Bretteville turn left on the D132, left at a give way sign, then return to Caen on the D562.*

SCENIC ROUTES

While many places on this tour offer beautiful coastal views, the inland roads generally beat the ones near the coast for scenery. The D33, after Villedieu-les-Poêles, runs through gorgeous Normandy countryside.
High above Clécy in the valley of the Orne, the Route des Crêtes sums up, without reaching any Alpine levels, the appeal of the Suisse Normande.

Green &
Pleasant Normandy

West of the cross-Channel port and fishing town of Dieppe, the white cliffs and deep valleys which slice into them are hidden from the main roads, but this tour twists along the coast to some very attractive holiday resorts whose sweeping curves border the Forêt de Brotonne and the Marais Vernier.

3 DAYS • 434KM • 270 MILES

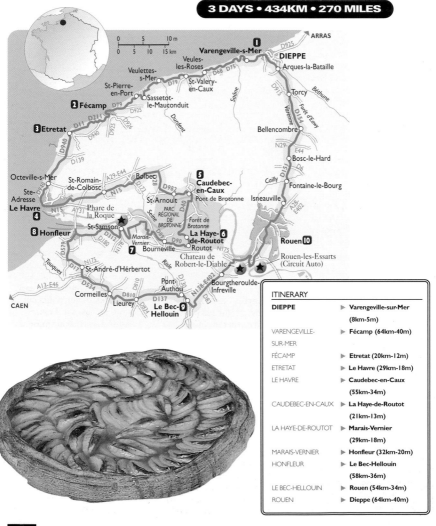

ITINERARY	
DIEPPE	▶ **Varengeville-sur-Mer** (8km-5m)
VARENGEVILLE-SUR-MER	▶ **Fécamp (64km-40m)**
FÉCAMP	▶ **Etretat (20km-12m)**
ETRETAT	▶ **Le Havre (29km-18m)**
LE HAVRE	▶ **Caudebec-en-Caux** (55km-34m)
CAUDEBEC-EN-CAUX	▶ **La Haye-de-Routot** (21km-13m)
LA HAYE-DE-ROUTOT	▶ **Marais-Vernier** (29km-18m)
MARAIS-VERNIER	▶ **Honfleur (32km-20m)**
HONFLEUR	▶ **Le Bec-Helllouin** (58km-36m)
LE BEC-HELLOUIN	▶ **Rouen (54km-34m)**
ROUEN	▶ **Dieppe (64km-40m)**

i | *Pont Jehan Ango, Dieppe*

FOR HISTORY BUFFS

On Dieppe seafront, look for the memorial to the disastrous raid of August 1942, by a force of mostly Canadian and Scottish troops.
The bitter lessons learned from its failure were put into practice on D-Day.
Appropriately, Canadians liberated Dieppe in 1944.

▶ *Leave Dieppe on the* **D75** *to Varengeville-sur-Mer.*

❶ Varengeville-sur-Mer, Normandy

You might be deep in the heart of an English county here, with villas and cottages in discreetly private grounds, wooded and grass-banked lanes, and half-timbered farms fitted like jigsaw pieces in between. There is a wonderful English-style landscape garden at the Parc Floral des Moutiers, the garden of the house called Bois des Moutiers created by the architect Sir Edwin Lutyens and landscape gardener Gertrude Jekyll. Up on the farmland plateau, the Manoir d'Ango is a Renaissance manor house with a beautiful dovecote.

At the foot of the Petit Ailly gorge you can wander along the stony shore under the towering cliffs. The artist Georges Braque, a founder of Cubism, is buried beside Varengeville's parish church, for which he designed one of the stained-glass windows.

RECOMMENDED WALKS

At Varengeville, three very attractive colour-coded walks follow pleasant country lanes and footpaths behind the great chalk cliffs of the coast. They all meet up close to the Parc Floral des Moutiers.

▶ *Continue on the* **D75**, *then go into St-Aubin and follow signs to St-Valery-en-Caux, leaving it on the* **D925**. *Turn right to Veulettes-sur-Mer on the* **D79** *then follow the signs to Fécamp.*

❷ Fécamp, Normandy

A fishing, freight and pleasure port at a dip in the cliffs, Fécamp has a shingle-bank beach and some remarkable places to visit. The Palais Bénédictine is the home of the liqueur of the same name, a distillation first carried out by monks of the Benedictine order, of 27 aromatic plants and spices whose precise recipe is a very closely guarded secret. There is a museum in the palace – a glorious 19th-century architectural confection of Gothic and Renaissance styles – which traces the history of Benedictine and also displays items of reli-

The painter Georges Braque (1882–1963) is buried in the churchyard at Varengeville-sur-Mer

gious art, furnishings and, in the Gothic hall, a magnificent oak and chestnut ceiling built by Fécamp shipwrights. The early Gothic abbey church, has one of the longest naves in France.

As well as a fine art museum, the town also has the Musée des Terre-Neuves et de la Pêche. While its displays go back to the Vikings, who colonised this coast, it concentrates on the years when the local fishing fleet used to spend months among the great cod banks of Newfoundland.

i | *113 rue Alexandre le Grand*

▶ *Leave Fécamp on the* **D940** *as for Etretat, then go right on the* **D211** *through Yport and follow the* **D11** *to Etretat.*

Renoir, Pissarro, Sisley and Dufy among others. The Musée de l'Ancien Havre illustrates the history of the town. Perhaps the best view of Le Havre is from the high-set fort at Ste-Adresse, a suburb to the northwest, which housed the Belgian government in exile during World War I.

i Place de l'Hôtel de Ville

FOR HISTORY BUFFS

In June 1940, while most of the British troops in France were being evacuated from Dunkirque, the 51st Highland Division was ordered to pull back to Le Havre. In this sacrificial manoeuvre, which helped to divert 10 German divisions, the Highlanders fought until their ammunition was exhausted, and thousands had to surrender at St-Valéry-en-Caux. A granite memorial on a hillside at St-Valéry commemorates the event, and the town is twinned with Inverness, the Highland capital.

▶ *Leave Le Havre on the N15 as for Rouen. Turn right for Trouville on the D40, then go straight on along the D29 and D28. Follow the D28 left as for Anquetierville, but bear right to avoid the village. Turn left at the T-junction for Caudebec-en-Caux.*

5 Caudebec-en-Caux, Normandy

Just downstream from the Pont de Brotonne suspension bridge which soars over the Seine, Caudebec is ideally situated to show off the commercial life of the river, to and from the container port at Rouen. The Musée de la Marine de Seine covers the history of river boats and river traffic.

Look for the remarkable Church of Notre Dame in 15th- and 16th-century Flamboyant Gothic style. It has a lovely fretted roof and a west frontage like lacework in stone, with 300 now

3 Etretat, Normandy

Etretat lies behind a beach at the foot of a wooded valley. To north and south rise tall white cliffs with weathered natural arches and a great isolated needle rock a little way off shore.

Paths climb to the cliffs called Falaise d'Amont north of the town and the Falaise d'Aval to the south. Amont probably has the finer overall view, as well as a seafarers' chapel with fish carved in the stonework, and a museum to the aviators Nungesser and Coli, whose plane was last seen over Etretat before disappearing during the first attempt in 1927 to fly the Atlantic from east to west.

i 9 place Maurice-Guillard

▶ *Leave Etretat on the D940 to Le Havre.*

4 Le Havre, Normandy

Parts of Le Havre look curiously all of a piece with their postwar

Guy de Maupassant compared the Falaise d'Aval to 'a carved elephant dipping its trunk in the sea'

FOR CHILDREN

Children can dress up in Viking costumes and engage in role-play at the Viking village at Gruchet le Valasse Abbey; in the evenings 2,000 years of Norman history is brought to life in a spectacular show with 700 actors and lots of special effects.

reinforced concrete buildings. The explanation for this is that the town was reduced to rubble in 1944, and had to be largely rebuilt after World War II.

Now it is once again a major freight and ferry port – the second busiest in France, occupying the harbour and miles of riverside along the Seine. You can take a harbour cruise.

A splendid fine arts museum, Musée des Beaux-Arts André-Malraux, shows works by heavily weathered figures of saints, prophets, musicians and gentlefolk of the town.

A stunning memorial beside the main road commemorates the Caudebec-built Latham seaplane which was lost in 1928 during a rescue mission in the Arctic. Roald Amundsen, discoverer of the South Pole, was one of the crew.

i Quai Guilbaud

▶ Leave Caudebec-en-Caux on the **D982** then turn left to cross the Pont de Brotonne. Go right on the **D65**, left on the **D40**, then bear left to La Haye-de-Routot.

6 La Haye-de-Routot,
Normandy
This fascinating village lies in farmland on the edge of the Fôret de Brotonne. La Haye's Four à Pain is a restored 19th-century brick-built bakehouse, run as a working museum. The Musée du Sabotier is a work-shop museum devoted to clogs (*sabots*). In early summer, look for the 15m (50-foot) pyramid of wood which, on the morning of 16 July, is set alight to create the Feu de St Clair, an old pagan ritual taken over by the Christian church. Opposite the

Four à Pain, a half-timbered cottage features a wall-niche model of the Feu de St Clair.

From the Café des Ifs (Yew-tree Café), marked walking routes radiate through the village and the forest.

▶ Leave La Haye for Routot. Go left, then right, at stops signs, then continue through Bourneville as for Quillebeuf-sur-Seine. Go left on the **D95** to Ste-Opportune and straight on at crossroads following the 'Réserve de Faune' sign. Hairpin right at the T-junction. Turn left at the 3.5t sign, then left at the T-junction. Follow Honfleur signs uphill to the view indicator.

7 Marais-Vernier,
Normandy
Bounded by an amphitheatre of wooded hills, this area was once marshland flooded by the Seine (*marais* means marsh). After vague earlier reclamation efforts, it was at the beginning of the 17th century that Dutch workers dug channels to drain the southern part of the marsh. They are still recalled in the name of the Digue des Hollandais (the Dutchmen's Dyke) alongside the D103. North of that road, the work

was tackled only in 1947.

Now the Marais-Vernier is mostly lush grazing land for Camargue horses and Highland cattle. Some pockets of boggy ground can still be found, and there are central scrubby wood-lands. In spring, pink and white blossom embellishes the surrounding farmland. La Grande Mare is the lake to which most of the drainage water flows on its way eventu-ally to the Seine.

BACK TO NATURE

Where the main route turns sharp right after Ste-Opportune, bear left and after about 0.8km (½-mile) watch for the 'Reserve de Faune' car park. A steeply stepped viewing tower overlooks the nature reserve around the Grande Mare. You will often see mallards, coots, grebes, teal, pochard and tufted duck on the lake itself or in the reed beds and drainage channels round it. Grey herons and Cetti's warblers are present, but more secretive.

Fifteenth-century Notre-Dame Church at Caudebec-en-Caux

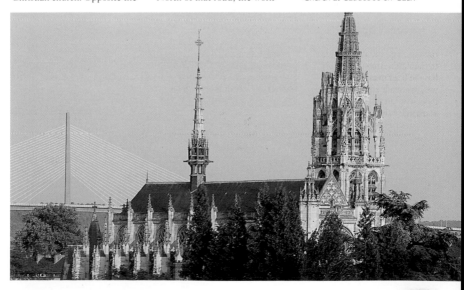

SPECIAL TO...

Upper Normandy is famed for apples and cider. Where the route goes straight on at Ste-Opportune, turn left for the Maison de la Pomme ('house of the apple') at Bourneville. Displays and a video presentation illustrate the cultivation of the apple and its use in cider and the famous Calvados brandy.

RECOMMENDED WALKS

Two walks, waymarked in green and red, head out from the centre of St-Samson along the wooded ridgetop overlooking the Marais-Vernier. For a different view, make for the Phare de la Roque, where an old river lighthouse provides a splendid viewpoint over the Seine.

▶ *After the view indicator, go right on the* **D100** *to St-Samson then left past the church on the* **D39**. *Bear right to the give-way sign then left at the T-junction on the* **N178**. *Go first right and follow the signs to Honfleur.*

8 **Honfleur,** Normandy

To all its other attractions, Honfleur adds the lovely old slate-roofed houses overlooking the sheltered harbour of the Vieux Bassin and, near by, some splendid survivals like the Grenier à Sel (salt stores) in the Rue de la Ville.

Erik Satie, the composer, was born in this fishing town. So was the artist Eugène Boudin, still admired for his skyscapes and his ability to 'paint the wind'. His work is featured in the museum which bears his name. Another museum has 12 rooms richly furnished in traditional Norman style and offers visits to the old town prison. The Musée de la Marine is lavishly stocked with ship models and other memorabilia of the sea.

Honfleur commemorates Samuel de Champlain. It was from here, on eight great voyages between 1603 and 1620, that he explored Canada, claimed it for France and founded the city of Quebec.

i **Place Boudin**

▶ *Leave Honfleur by the Rue de la République as for Pont-l'Evêque, then go left as for Tancarville on the* **D17**. *Turn right on to the* **N175** *then left on the* **D534** *to Cormeilles. Leave Cormeilles on the* **D810**, *continue into Lieurey and follow the* **D137** *to Pont-Authou. Go right on the* **D130** *then left on the* **D39** *to Le Bec-Hellouin.*

9 **Le Bec-Hellouin,** Normandy

This is a lovely hillside village, massed with flowers, including rosebeds by the timbered houses on the square. Many old buildings survive here, from the tiny red-tiled wash-house by a fast-flowing stream to the stalwart ruins of what was once a powerful abbey dating back to 1040. It has a great reputation as a centre of theological learning, and three of its 'sons' went on to become archbishops of Canterbury – Lanfranc in 1070, Anselm in 1093 and Theobald in 1138.

The village also has a fascinating museum of mechanical

The calm of Honfleur harbour belies the town's turbulent past music, with a variety of self-playing instruments, both large and small.

SPECIAL TO...

Roadside barriers along the D132 and N238, a grandstand and a starting grid are part of the Rouen-les-Essarts motor racing circuit. Fangio was the French Grand Prix winner here in 1957, while the American Dan Gurney won in 1962 and 1964.

16th centuries – contributed to the appearance of the cathedral in its doorways, towers, tombs, side chapels and stained-glass windows. From a distance, though, the most remarkable feature of the building is the tall, slim, tapering steeple added in the 19th century. Built entirely of fretted cast iron, it arrows towards the sky. There are museums here devoted to wrought ironwork (Musée Le-Seq-des-Tournelles), and the novelist Gustave Flaubert (in the suburb of Croisset). And

FOR CHILDREN

After leaving the N138 for the D3 on the way to Rouen, turn right uphill to the Château de Robert-le-Diable. There was no such person as Robert the Devil, but this is a genuine old stronghold of the Dukes of Normandy. In a curious mixture, as well as a Viking waxworks display, the castle also features mini-golf and children's games.

▶ *Continue on the **D39** then go left on the **N138**. At the stop sign, go straight ahead on the **D3** as for Rouen, through Moulineaux. Turn right at traffic lights as for Elbeuf, and right over the level crossing. Go sharp left on the **N238** and follow the signs to Rouen.*

🔟 **Rouen,** Normandy
The glory of the historic capital of Normandy is the magnificent Gothic Cathedral of Notre-Dame in the midst of a splendid 'old town' carefully restored after the devastation of World War II. Rouen's tourist office, for instance, occupies a very attractive Renaissance building, once the headquarters of the tax collector.

Architects and artists of many different eras – mainly 13th to

there is also a wax museum devoted to Jeanne d'Arc (Joan of Arc). After Rouen was lost to the English in the Hundred Years' War, it was here than Joan was brought as a prisoner and subjected to a shameful trial. Its aftermath was even more despicable when, her life having been previously spared, she was burned at the stake in the old marketplace. She was canonised in 1920. The Musée des Beaux-Arts has a good collection of 17th- to 20th-century French paintings.

ⓘ *Place de la Cathédrale*

▶ *Leave Rouen on the **N28** then go left on the **D928**, left on the **D151** to Bellencombre and left again on the **D154** to Dieppe.*

Richard the Lionheart's tomb in Rouen Cathedral

SCENIC ROUTES

From Dieppe westwards, the route runs along the rich farmland plateau then darts down breaks in the chalk cliffs to villages and harbours by the sea. Soon after Ste-Opportune, a magnificent view opens up of the farms, thatched cottages and waterways of the Marais-Vernier. You can look back on it from a viewpoint on the ridge. After Bellencombre, between Rouen and Dieppe, the D154 runs through a classic French rural landscape with rustic buildings in a valley floor, fishponds and cattle grazing.

The Emerald
Country

Starting from Rennes, the capital of Brittany, this tour is drawn briefly into Normandy to visit Mont-St-Michel on its fortified tidal island. Along the Brittany coastline there are headlands offering magnificent views, then it's inland to historic towns such as Vitré, Fougères and Dinan, and St-Malo, on the coast.

3 DAYS • 392KM • 243 MILES

ITINERARY

RENNES	▶ Vitré (43km–27m)
VITRÉ	▶ Fougères (27km–17m)
FOUGÈRES	▶ Le Mont-St-Michel (53km–33m)
LE MONT-ST-MICHEL	▶ Mont-Dol (31km–19m)
MONT-DOL	▶ St-Malo (44km–27m)
ST-MALO	▶ Dinard (13km–8m)
DINARD	▶ Cap Fréhel (44km–27m)
CAP FRÉHEL	▶ Erquy (20km–12m)
ERQUY	▶ Dinan (52km–32m)
DINAN	▶ Tinténiac (28km–18m)
TINTÉNIAC	▶ Rennes (37km–23m)

[i] *11 rue St-Yves, Rennes*

▶ *Leave Rennes as for Fougères on the N12. Go right on the D528 to Liffré and in the town centre turn right for Vitré via La Bouëxière. Enter Vitré on the D857.*

FOR HISTORY BUFFS

The Musée Automobile de Bretagne on the N12 after Rennes, tells the story of the French motor industry through such fine exhibits as a 1904 Renault with a basketwork canister for the passengers' canes and parasols. Veteran posters and accessories are also on display.

❶ Vitré, Brittany
In the days when Brittany was separate from France, Vitré was a frontier fortress. Its triangular-plan castle, high above the River Vilaine, houses the town museum in three of its towers. A fourth provides an all-encompassing viewpoint. Many medieval and Renaissance buildings are still in use. The

Centre Social, for instance, occupies a splendid 16th-century mansion with elaborate windows, doors and rooflines. Beautifully restored, the Rue de la Beaudrairie was the leather-workers' quarter.

Walks lead down into the pleasant valley of the Vilaine. On the southern outskirts, in the unlikely setting of an industrial estate, look for the Musée de l'Abeille Vivante (Museum of the Living Bee). Here you can see not only displays on all aspects of bee-keeping but also five colonies working in glass-sided hives.

[i] *Place St Yves*

▶ *Leave Vitré for 'Fougères par Taillis' on the D179.*

❷ Fougères, Brittany
The most important feature of this second medieval fortress town is the huge and superb castle on a peninsula site all but encircled by the Nançon river. But delay going to the castle itself until you have looked at it from the attractive Jardin Public in the high town. Its situation and layout are seen to best

effect from the garden (despite the background scar of a modern quarry). Below the castle, the low town retains many fine buildings, such as the Flamboyant Gothic Church of St-Sulpice and the 17th-century houses round the Place du Marchaix. In the high town, one 16th-century house is now the Musée Emmanuel de la Villéon, devoted to the locally-born artist who was one of the last Impressionists.

[i] *1 place Aristide-Briand*

RECOMMENDED WALKS

Ask at the tourist office at Rennes or Fougères for the leaflet showing the footpaths in the Forêt de Fougères. One, which crosses the route at the Carrefour du Père Tacot, wanders through the beechwoods, passes a line of druids' stones and follows the shore of a recreational lake.

Traditional-style half-timbered houses in Rennes

wizardry at Museographie tells the history of the bay, and a garden outside has a splendid view of the real thing.

i *Corps de Garde des Bourgeois*

▶ *Return to Beauvoir. Turn right for Les Polders, over the bridge and immediately left. Turn left at the first stop sign and right at the second stop sign. Go right on the D797 through St-Broladre, left on the D82 then right on the V5 to the village of Mont-Dol. Watch for a right turn before the Hôtel du Tertre up a steep and narrow road to Sommet du Mont-Dol.*

FOR CHILDREN

On the way back from Le Mont-St-Michel, call in at the Reptilarium in Beauvoir and let the children see the crocodiles, iguanas, lizards, pythons and boa-constrictors.

▶ *Leave Fougères as for St-Hilaire on the D177. Immediately after leaving Fougères bear right along a 'route forestière'. Go left at Carrefour du Père Tacot then straight on across the main road. At Carrefour des Serfilières bear left, taking the fourth exit. Turn right at the stop sign (this is the D108) to Parigné. Leave Parigné on the D108 as for Mellé. At the crossroads go straight on, avoiding the right turn to Mellé. Go right at the stop sign along the D798. Turn left on the D15 through Coglès, left briefly on the D296 then right on the D15 again. In Antrain, turn right at the stop sign to Pontorson and continue via Beauvoir to Le Mont-St-Michel.*

❸ Le Mont-St-Michel,
Normandy
From whatever angle, a first sight of this isolated tidal rock is a stunning experience. It rises from rampart walls and a clus-

Fougères Castle – a fine example of medieval military architecture

tered village to a magnificent abbey whose highest steeple spears the sky. Reached by a causeway, Mont-St-Michel lies among the mazy channels of a vast bay. The lowest towers and medieval sea-wall protect a village of lanes and stairways, where the Musée Grevin tells the story of the abbey and the island community in a series of tableaux, and the Archéoscope elaborates it with sound and lighting effects. More prosaically, the Musée de la Mer places the island in its marine and tidal context.

Crowning the summit, the abbey dedicated to the Archangel Michael is a triumph of Romanesque and Gothic design. Finest of all the architecture are the 13th-century buildings which include the refectory and cloisters.

On the mainland, the latest audio-visual and simulation

❹ Mont-Dol, Brittany
From this hilltop with its marvellous 360-degree view, note the great area of rich, reclaimed marshland of the 'polders' that you crossed after Beauvoir. Beyond them, across the bay, lies Mont-St-Michel.

A good display map shows the features of Mont-Dol itself – which include the scenes of the legendary struggle between St Michael and the Devil. There is also a chapel, an old seaward signalling tower, two 19th-century windmills and walks among the pines, gorse and rock outcrops.

▶ *Return from the summit. Go right to pass the Hôtel du Tertre. Leave Mont-Dol village on the D123. Turn right on the D155 and follow the signs towards Cancale on the D76. Go right on the VC15 signed 'Cancale le Port'. Leave Cancale following 'St-Malo par la Côte' and 'Pointe du Grouin' signs along the*

*D201. Go straight on along the **C6** to Pointe du Grouin then return to the **D201** for St-Malo.*

SPECIAL TO...

Cancale, to the east of St-Malo, is famous all over France for the high-quality oysters cultivated extensively in the bay.
They taste nowhere better than in the town's own seafood restaurants. Watch out for the Oyster Museum.

RECOMMENDED WALKS

One of the most glorious coastal walks in Brittany is the GR34 north of Cancale on the way between Mont-Dol and St-Malo. It takes a clifftop route with high-level views to offshore islands and faraway Mont-St-Michel, on the way to the magnificent bay at Port Briac.

BACK TO NATURE

On the breezy headland of Pointe du Grouin, telescopes are aimed at the rugged nature reserve of the Ile des Landes. It houses Brittany's biggest colony of cormorants.

⑤ St-Malo, Brittany
An extensive area of sheltered harbours continues the long maritime tradition of a town which was the historic base for privateers, explorers and the 16th-century Newfoundland fishing fleets. The heart of St-Malo is the granite-built district known as Intra Muros, inside the coastal rampart walls. It is almost entirely a reconstruction from the rubble of World War II. Look here for the historical Musée de la Ville in the 15th-century castle whose great keep and towers command impressive views of the harbour. Quic-en-Groigne is a waxwork museum recalling famous St-Malo characters and events. There is a well-stocked aquar-

ium as well as a museum of dolls and old-time toys.
 Ferries sail to destinations along the coast, and there is a hydrofoil service to Jersey. But the Château de Solidor recalls much grander voyages: it houses displays on the Cape Horners.

ⓘ *Esplanade St-Vincent*

▶ *Leave St-Malo as for Dinard. Go right on the **D114** and right on the **D266** into Dinard.*

SPECIAL TO...

After St-Malo, on the main road across the estuary of the Rance is an innovative hydro-electric generating station which uses tidal power in both directions – at the ebb and at the flow. The main road across the estuary runs along the dam, and you can take a guided tour of this splendid pollution-free scheme.

St-Malo was named after a Welsh monk called Maclow

6 Dinard, Brittany

To a beautiful seafront of bays, promontories, sandy beaches and offshore rocky islets, Dinard adds hotels, restaurants, a casino, a golf club, an equestrian centre and other sporting facilities to maintain its reputation as the premier resort of Brittany's Emerald Coast. The weather is mild, some of the vegetation Mediterranean along the footpaths which wander by the coast.

Fine villas stand in lovely wooded grounds, many of them dating from the turn of the century when British high society favoured Dinard – Edward VII and George V are remembered in street names today.

Dinard attracts many musical, film and artistic events. Every summer evening at dusk there is a *son et lumière* presentation on the seafront Promenade du Clair de Lune.

ⓘ 2 boulevard Féart

▶ Leave Dinard on the **D786** through St-Briac-sur-Mer and continue as for St-Brieuc. After Port-à-la-Duc turn right to Cap Fréhel on the **D16**.

7 Cap Fréhel, Brittany

In the 1920s a company tried to sell off building plots on this dramatic cliff-ringed headland. Fortunately, the misbegotten scheme failed. From the approach road, you may think that the cape ends at the lighthouse – completed in 1847, immense care having been paid to the design and the masonry work (visits can be arranged most afternoons) – and the 18th-century fortification known as the Tour Vauban. In fact, Fréhel extends much further out to sea.

A stroll around the cape, whose majestic rock stacks are a nature reserve, opens up views into precipitous wave-lashed inlets as well as southeastwards to the spectacularly located Fort la Latte, a medieval fortress situated on a headland some 4km (2½ miles) away.

ⓘ *Tour Vauban*

BACK TO NATURE

Cap Fréhel and its offshore rock stacks are busy with gulls, fulmars, cormorants and guillemots, for whom this is France's premier nesting area. In summer the approach to the cape is purple with heather and gold with the flowers of gorse and bird's-foot trefoil.

FOR CHILDREN

Sables-d'Or-les-Pins, after Cap Fréhel, caters well for children, with sandy beaches, pony rides, 'bouncy castles' and pedal cars for hire. Look for the little battery-powered electric cars. Kids love to drive these 'grown-up' vehicles on their own.

▶ Return from Cap Fréhel and turn right on the **D34a** as for St-Brieuc. Rejoin the **D786** for Erquy.

8 Erquy, Brittany

Built round a west-facing bay well sheltered from the northerly wind, Erquy is a pleasant and unpretentious little resort with no trace of obtrusive modern building. The bay is busy with courses in canoeing and windsurfing, and there is a local shellfish fleet.

Take the road to the Cap d'Erquy and you will climb to an exhilarating headland where the heath and low-lying scrub are criss-crossed by wandering footpaths. There are cliff edges to be carefully explored, views to the broken water over dangerous offshore reefs, and a splendid if unexpected east-

The medieval town of Dinan on the River Rance, where boats depart for St-Malo and Dinard facing beach. There are also ditches and other signs of prehistoric fortifications, some as old as 4,500 years.

i *Boulevard de la Mer*

▶ *Leave Erquy on the **D786** as for St-Brieuc, then go left for Dinan via Plancoët. Enter Dinan on the **N176**.*

9 Dinan, Brittany
Since its appearance in the Bayeux Tapestry, in the 11th century, Dinan has had a clear line of history, each era marked by its own architectural styles in ramparts, towers, gateways and attractive houses. Streets in the old town bear the names of medieval trade guilds. The castle is a fortress of mellow stonework whose unusual 14th-century oval keep houses the local museum. You can admire Dinan from the upper viewing gallery of the 15th-century belfry, the Tour de l'Horloge

(Clock Tower). Another good viewpoint, although disappointing as an actual garden, is the Jardin Anglais (English Garden). It overlooks the valley of the Rance, in which enticing footpaths lead under the stately viaduct over which you approached the town, towards the downstream quays.

In the Church of St Saveur is buried the heart of Bertrand du Guesclin, who fought in single combat in the Place du Champ Clos in 1359 to free his brother from his English captors.

i *6 rue de l'Horloge*

▶ *Leave Dinan from Lanvallay and turn right through Évran on the **D2**, which becomes the **D68** as for Bécherel. In La Barre turn left for Tinténiac on the **D20**.*

10 Tinténiac, Brittany
The church here, with its cupolas and sturdy but ornate

stonework, looks slightly puzzling. In fact it is a complete turn-of-the-century rebuilding of an old ecclesiastical site, and well worth a visit.

Tinténiac lies on the Canal d'Ille et Rance. At the Quai de la Donac, a redundant grain store is now the Musée de l'Outil et des Métiers (Museum of Tools and Trades), displaying tools and machinery from half-forgotten rural trades.

East of Tinténiac, the Musée International de la Faune is a spacious zoo park which also features a scented rose garden and a well-equipped children's playground.

FOR HISTORY BUFFS

Before Tinténiac, turn right in La Barre, through Bécherel to the Parc de Caradeuc and its château. The 18th-century lawyer Caradeuc de la Chalotais was devoted to the independence of the Breton parliament. Louis XV imprisoned him without trial. A message he smuggled out of jail, written with a toothpick in ink made from soot, vinegar and sugar, caused a sensation.

▶ *Continue on the **D20** to Dingé. Watch for a right turn on the **D82** before the Confiserie/Épicerie shop. Return to Rennes.*

SCENIC ROUTES

Approaching Vitré, the D22 runs through a pleasant rural landscape, which continues along the D179 to Fougères, with long eastern views. Even at times of hectic traffic, the approach to stately Mont-St-Michel has a magic all its own.
The coastal stretch of the D155 looks over salt marshes and oyster beds to the rocky islets off Cancale. A succession of cliffs and sandy bays follows the D34a after Cap Fréhel.

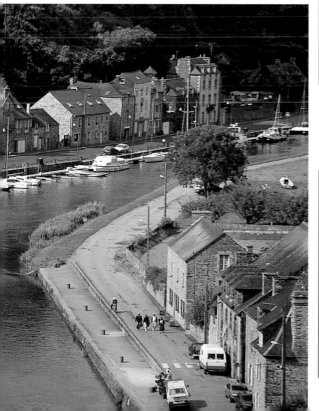

The Celtic
Connection

Quimper is the capital of old Cornouaille. This is Celtic country, as you will see from the place-names. The Breton language is still spoken by more than half a million people, giving western Brittany the position in France which Wales occupies in the UK.

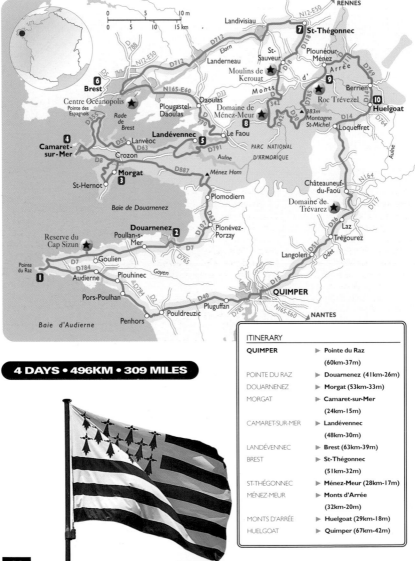

4 DAYS • 496KM • 309 MILES

ITINERARY

QUIMPER	▶	**Pointe du Raz**
		(60km-37m)
POINTE DU RAZ	▶	**Douarnenez (41km-26m)**
DOUARNENEZ	▶	**Morgat (53km-33m)**
MORGAT	▶	**Camaret-sur-Mer**
		(24km-15m)
CAMARET-SUR-MER	▶	**Landévennec**
		(48km-30m)
LANDÉVENNEC	▶	**Brest (63km-39m)**
BREST	▶	**St-Thégonnec**
		(51km-32m)
ST-THÉGONNEC	▶	**Ménez-Meur (28km-17m)**
MÉNEZ-MEUR	▶	**Monts d'Arrée**
		(32km-20m)
MONTS D'ARRÉE	▶	**Huelgoat (29km-18m)**
HUELGOAT	▶	**Quimper (67km-42m)**

Pointe du Raz, Cap Sizun – a sanctuary for seabirds

[i] *7 rue Déesse, Quimper*

▶ *Leave Quimper on the D785 as for Pont l'Abbé, then through Pluguffan and follow the D40 through Pouldreuzic to Penhors. Bear right as for Plozévet, then left, and follow signs to Pors-Poulhan. Climb from the harbour, then turn sharp left following 'Allée Couverte' sign. Turn left at two stop signs. In Audierne, look for 'Pointe du Raz' signs and take the D784 to Pointe du Raz.*

❶ Pointe du Raz, Brittany
One of Brittany's classic headlands plays host to a commercial square of souvenir shops and cafés. A wasteland of bare, trodden earth and rock leads beyond the coastguard station to the actual point, and then the atmosphere changes. No careless exploitation can damage the magnificent seaward views. Pointe du Raz looks over a savage strait where jagged rocks, the last topped with a lighthouse, march towards the weird outline of the Île-de-Sein – reminiscent of a Pacific atoll moved to the

windswept Atlantic edge. Guides escort parties of visitors round the cliff paths, and with or without them it is easy to appreciate why the statue near the point is to *Notre-Dame des Naufragés* – Our Lady of the Shipwrecked. Knowing that Sein was once the mainland coast makes the legend of the drowned city of Ys, out in the Bay of Douarnenez, something to ponder.

FOR HISTORY BUFFS

The Alée Couverte, at Pors-Poulhan, is a reconstructed burial chamber. Great rock slabs form the walls and others are laid across them as the roof.

▶ *Return from Pointe du Raz and turn left for Douarnenez par le CD7 on the V8 and D7. On the approach to Douarnenez, follow 'Autres Directions' and 'Toutes Directions' signs at roundabouts, then turn left on the D765 and left to Centre-Ville.*

BACK TO NATURE

Turn left off the D7 for the Réserve Ornithologique on the seabird cliffs of Cap Sizun. This was the first bird reserve in France with a definite educational programme. The movements and associations of whole gull colonies are followed by computer.

❷ Douarnenez, Brittany
Douarnenez is the fifth busiest fishing port in France. The narrow river inlet of Port-Rhu slices deep into Douarnenez, but the main harbour of Rosmeur is on the east side of the peninsula which it helps to form. There are early morning fish auctions here, and cruise boats visit the cliffs, inlets and grottoes of the bay. Town beaches are scattered in some unexpected locations, and a good coastal walk leads from Rosmeur along the Sentier des Plomarc'hs. Le Port-Musée is located here. A tidal wall has

been built to dam a basin 2km long at Port Rhu. Visitors can explore dozens of boats and admire craftsmen rebuilding a 19th-century clipper. This floating museum is unique in France.

☐ *1 rue du Docteur Mével*

▶ *Leave Douarnenez as for Brest on the **D7**, then turn left*

South of Morgat, just before the village of St-Hernot, the interesting Maison des Minéraux houses a fascinating array of crystals, fossils and semi-precious stones such as agates and amethysts from all over Brittany, in their natural state as well as cut and polished. Make sure you see the fluorescent cabinet where many of them gleam in exotic colours.

Vauban, the great 17th-century military architect, fortified Camaret. The local history museum in the Tour Vauban recalls events such as the British and Dutch landing of 1694, which was furiously and famously repulsed.

The prehistoric standing stones of Lagatjar retain their strict straight-line alignment and, to the south, the Pointe de

on the **D107** to Plonévez-Porzay. Watch for the left turn on to the **D63**, then take the **D47** through Plomodiern and left to Ste-Marie. Turn left on the **D887**, right to the Ménez-Hom summit and return to the **D887**. Follow 'Morgat' signs through Crozon, watching for an unexpected left turn. In Morgat, follow 'Maison des Minéraux' signs towards St-Hernot.

8 **Morgat**, Brittany
This resort on the sheltered side of Douarnenez Bay is well equipped for watersports and enjoys good, extensive beaches with coastal promenades. There are daily summer cruises to the marine caverns of La Chambre du Diable (the Devil's Chamber), La Cheminée des Cormorans (the Cormorants' Chimney) and the loveliest, l'Autel (Altar Grotto).

☐ *Boulevard de la Plage*

▶ *After the Maison des Minéraux, bear right as for Kerdreux then almost immediately right at crossroads. Go straight on at the stop sign, follow 'Crozon' signs, then turn right at a T-junction (**D308**) into Crozon. At the round-about, take the third exit along the **D8** to Camaret-sur-Mer.*

4 **Camaret-sur-Mer**, Brittany
Set on a stunning peninsula, Camaret is a resort surrounded by beaches facing in different directions. A substantial crayfish fleet is based here, and some discarded fishing boats are beached as rotting hulks. Lobster is also fished locally, so the seafood restaurants, naturally, are well and freshly stocked.

Camaret-sur-Mer's beach is strewn with shipwrecks

Penhir is a majestic clifftop viewpoint with dramatic natural rock formations.

☐ *Quai Kléber*

> ### BACK TO NATURE
>
> Well out of reach of any road approach, the dramatic rock stacks of the Tas des Pois – the Pile of Peas – can be visited on the *Sirène IV*, which sails from Camaret. Their cliffs teem with gulls, fulmars, cormorants, guillemots and storm petrels.

▶ *Leave Camaret-sur-Mer on the **D355** to Pointe des Espagnols and through Roscanvel. At a roundabout take the **D55** to Lanvéoc,* *then the **D63** as for Brest. At the brow of a hill at Maison Blanche, watch for a left turn at crossroads. Turn right at the crossroads at a stop sign. At the give-way sign, turn left on the **D60** to Landévennec.*

5 Landévennec, Brittany
Occupying an attractive peninsula where the estuaries of the Aulne and the Faou combine, Landévennec is a village in which a glance down almost any lane offers a view of the water. Brittany's oldest abbey was founded here in 485 by the Welsh missionary St Gwennolé. It crumbled away after the Revolution. The ruins of the final Romanesque buildings are approached by a palm-tree avenue. Exhibitions explain the history of the abbey itself, and also how Brittany rose from the wreckage of the Roman Empire, colonised in Gwennolé's time by Celts driven from Britain by the Anglo-Saxon invasions.

▶ *Return along the **D60** to the **D791** and turn left. In Le Faou go left as for Hanvec, over a bridge and left – at first along the riverside through Lanvoy. Turn left at a T-junction and through Daoulas on the **D770**. Follow signs for Brest on the **N165**.*

6 Brest, Brittany
For almost 2,000 years, the sea has been Brest's delight and its despair. From Roman times its great roadstead – perhaps the most beautiful in Europe, with its bays, peninsulas and feeder rivers – has been a naval base. Such places are vulnerable in time of conflict. Brest came out of World War II shattered by bombing raids. Even the street plan was redrawn at the time of rebuilding. This remains the home of many capital ships. Only French citizens, though, may visit the base itself, but foreigners are more than welcome at the Musée de la Marine, repository of Brest's tumultuous history, housed in

the medieval castle, is open to all. Excellent parks include the Vallon du Stangalard, with its lawns, lakes, tree-shaded walks and Conservatoire Botanique, preserving hundreds of endangered plant species.
Océanopolis is a fascinating complex of aquariums (the largest in Europe with 500,000 litres [125,000 gallons] total capacity), marine exhibitions and pictures beamed from weather satellites in space.

Only the ruins of the Abbey of St Gwennolé testify to Landévennec's monastic beginnings

ℹ *Place de la Liberté*

FOR CHILDREN

Children are always delighted by a boat trip, and across the bay at Rade de Brest, gleaming white pleasure cruisers are waiting to whisk you around the harbour, with views of the warships, merchant ships and pleasure craft on the waters. The duration of the trips vary between half an hour for the straight crossing and three hours for the restaurant cruise.

SPECIAL TO...

Breton is a Celtic language, related to Cornish and Welsh, which has survived consistent attempts to crush it by French governments of the past. The late 20th century saw a growing movement to preserve and promote its use, and secondary schools now offer Breton courses to thousands of pupils.

▶ *Leave Brest for Landerneau on the **D712**. Follow the 'Centre Ville' sign at a roundabout in Landerneau. Continue to Landivisiau, still on the **D712**, then as for Morlaix on to the **N12**. Take the exit for St-Thégonnec.*

7 St-Thégonnec, Brittany
In the past, Breton villages would vie for glory with their neighbours, particularly in the splendour of their churches. Consequently, at St-Thégonnec, the 16th- to 18th-century masonry work of the church is far more elaborate than is justified by the status of the little place. The churchyard gateway and the funeral chapel are similarly ornate, and the calvary of 1610, its clustered figures telling the story of the Passion, was one of the last in the exuberant Breton style. Inside the church, look for the intricately carved pulpit of 1683.

RECOMMENDED WALKS

The Pont Hir walk at St-Thégonnec follows a waymarked route across rural landscapes to an eerie tunnel taking the River Coatoulsac'h through a railway embankment. Another feature of the walk is a wood where quiet walkers may sight roe deer.

SPECIAL TO...

At the stop sign after Croas-Cabellec, turn left for the restored hamlet of Les Moulins-de-Kerouat, with its two antique watermills. Lessons are sometimes given on how to bake your own country-style bread. There is also the miller's home with its traditional furniture and an exhibition relating the history of the village through the lives of five generations of millers.

▶ Leave St-Thégonnec as for Sizun on the **D118**, then the **D18**. After St-Sauveur, carry straight on at the crossroads at Croas-Cabellec, following '5 Sizun' sign. After a double-bend sign, take the first left, then go straight on at the stop sign as for Goas ar Vern. Follow the 'Barrage du Drennec' sign, then continue to St-Cadou. Turn right on the

The numerous statuettes on St-Thégonnec's elegant 1610 calvary depict the Passion

D30, left on the *D130* as for St-Eloy, and watch for a left turn to Ménez-Meur.

8 Ménez-Meur, Brittany
The wooded surroundings of this estate conceal a series of open grazing areas where you can admire red, Sika and fallow deer, wild boars, several breeds of horses, and other domesticated specialities such as the long-haired Highland cattle and Swaledale sheep.

Ménez-Meur is approached along a beautiful avenue, where interlocking trees arch over from mossy walls. There are three waymarked trails within the estate, which have animal, forest and general countryside themes, and the estate is famous for its displays, fairs and festivals celebrating the sturdy Breton horse.

▶ Continue to St-Rivoal on the *D30*, then turn left on the *D785*.

9 Monts d'Arrée, Brittany
The D785 runs along the upper reaches of the Monts d'Arrée, where the Parc National

d'Armorique opens out in a world of moorland summits. Mont St-Michel is one of the highest points, at 383m (1,256 feet). From it, a superb all-round view gives a slightly perplexing impression of a completely circular horizon. Roc Trévezel, further along the road, is a granite tor which offers another fine viewpoint.

RECOMMENDED WALKS

Off the D785 is an access point to the footpaths shown in the Yeun Elez leaflet published by the Parc d'Armorique. One of them climbs the open moorland to Mont-St-Michel and circles back by the lovely countryside around St-Rivoal.

▶ *Continue on the D785 to Plounéour-Ménez. Turn right on the D111, right on the D769 and follow signs to Huelgoat, turning right on the D14 in Berrien.*

10 Huelgoat, Brittany
Built beside a peaceful lake, this is an inland resort with two contrasting characters. The town is bright and open, with lakeside walks, pedalo hire and fishing. Go to the bridge over the lake's outflow, and you look immediately into a more dramatic world. From a chaos of jumbled rocks, footpaths wander through the most beautiful forest in Brittany. Beech, oak and conifers clothe a landscape of leafy glades, tumbling streams and mysterious Celtic stones, where the legends of King Arthur, Merlin and the Druids survive.

SPECIAL TO...

The Moulin du Chaos, in Huelgoat, is an old mill housing exhibits of archaeology, geology, flora and fauna.

Great moss-covered boulders litter the streams and tumbled hills in Huelgoat Forest

i *Place Aristide-Briand*

FOR HISTORY BUFFS

On the return route to Quimper, the Maison des Pilhaouerien in Loqueffret recalls the 'rag and bone' families who, until the 1950s, toured the district with their donkey carts. After Châteauneuf-du-Faou, the rose castle in the beautiful park of Trévarez was one of the last built in France. During World War II it was a rest centre for the German Navy, until gutted in an RAF bombing raid. History, art and floral exhibitions are held here.

▶ *Leave Huelgoat for Loqueffret on the D14. Turn sharp left on the D36 through Châteauneuf-du-Faou. Follow 'Domaine de Trévarez' signs, then continue on the D36 to Trégourez. Turn right on the D51 and return to Quimper.*

SCENIC ROUTES

The Ménez-Hom road, the D83, climbs to one of the finest viewpoints in Brittany. After Camaret, the D355 rounds a peninsula with a beautiful outlook over the roadstead of Brest. Later, look for the view from the suspension bridge that takes the D791 over the River Aulne. Around St-Rivoal, the D342 is a lane set in wooded combes.

THE LOIRE & CENTRAL FRANCE

As it sweeps from the mountain country of the Central, by the Valley of the Loire and the Cognac vineyards, to the coastline and islands around La Rochelle, this area illustrates the great variety of landscape in France.

Not far from the industrial city of Clermont-Ferrand you drive through a country of ancient volcanoes, with high cattle pastures closed till the clearance of winter snows. In the valleys of the Loire and its principal tributaries you will encounter many of France's most magnificent castles. The 'conspicuous consumption' they represented was one of the elements which brought about the French Revolution. Fortunately, the major castles such as Chenonceau and Blois survive.

At high levels you will find windy, upland pastures and conifer plantings, and there is a chance of snow flurries even in late spring. Lower down lies a pastoral area of arable farms, but the finest ground, especially near Tours and along the valley of the River Charente, is reserved for vineyards. This is the country of Pays Nantais, Vouvray, Rosé d'Anjou, Cognac and Côtes d'Auvergne wines.

The two islands of Ré and Oléron are microcosmic worlds of their own. Rimmed by beautiful beaches and holiday resorts, with fine climates tempered by the Atlantic breezes, they have a strong off-season life. Farms, vines and oyster beds all play their part, and the little towns enjoy intriguing histories. Ré, for instance, was the last place on metropolitan French soil seen by criminals shipped to Devil's Island.

As in most of France, the road network is extensive. In some places, for instance approaching Angoulême on the La Rochelle tour in the attractive valley of the Charente, you should keep a close watch on the route instructions.

Recently, ferries to the major islands have been replaced. The drive to Ré is notable for the splendidly proportioned toll bridge from the mainland. This is how an island should be approached, on a dramatic, high-level curve.

Clermont-Ferrand

A great industrial centre in the heart of France, Clermont-Ferrand is the world headquarters of the Michelin tyre company. The city is dominated by its Gothic cathedral, but not far from it there stands another church of equal if not greater architectural merit, Notre-Dame-du-Port. The Musée des Beaux-Arts is housed in a wonderful old restored building. The Musée Bargoin recalls the victory of Vercingetorix and the Gauls over the legions of Julius Caesar, on the plateau of Gergovia near by.

Limoges

Limoges is the city of porcelain. Its Musée National Adrien-Dubouché shows porcelain in all its colour, elegance and stages of preparation. Enamelware is one of the specialities of the Musée Municipal. As in Clermont-Ferrand, there are attractive individual houses, churches and public buildings in Limoges, as well as gardens around the old Roman arena and overlooking the River Vézère.

La Rochelle

La Rochelle carefully guards its waterfront. Le Gabut is an engaging modern harbourside development whose colour-washed wooden buildings, with stairs and gangways, have a maritime air. The older houses have an agreeably regular appearance, forced on the builders by strict town-planning laws.

Museums here include one of mechanical toys, another of model ships, planes and railways, a third devoted to yacht racing. The maritime collection occupies a sturdy harbour-entrance tower, and there is a weathership museum and a major modern aquarium.

Nantes

Very much a river city, Nantes includes two channels of the Loire, three of its tributaries and, for good measure, a canal. The city centre has undergone a major face-lift and has an efficient modern tram network. Look for the moated castle of the dukes of Brittany, the cathedral, begun in 1434, the old quarters and the half-dozen parks, includ-

ing a riverside Japanese garden. A planetarium complements the nearby museum devoted to the life and works of the science fiction pioneer Jules Verne.

Tours

If you want to hear perfect spoken French, go to Tours. The capital of Touraine is spacious and unhurried, with elegant public buildings and a beautiful cathedral. There are promenades on rivers – the Loire and the Cher. The Château-Royal houses historical museums. The Musée des Beaux-Arts is in an archbishops' old palace. Archaeology, and Renaissance and medieval art are found in the Musée Archéologique in the superb 16th-century mansion called the Hôtel Gouin. Other museums and studios cover the wines of Touraine, dolls, gemstones and enamelwork, military transport, the story of journeymen-craftsmen and the handloom weaving of silk.

Opposite: Fontenay-le-Comte, an old market town on the Vendée
Below: Tours has managed to preserve (with much restoration) its historic heart

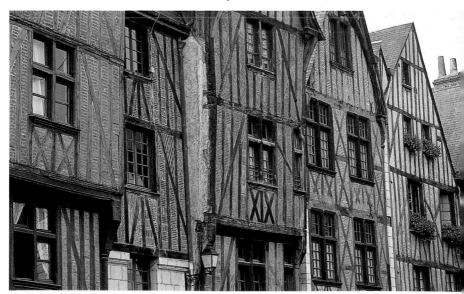

Land of Quiet
Volcanoes

Clermont-Ferrand has the advantage of backing immediately on to hill country, and these are no ordinary hills. They are the relics of huge volcanic convulsions thousands of years ago. Now green and wooded, they provide space in the valleys for holiday resorts, including spas whose thermal waters were famous in Roman times. The area's 20 mineral springs supply the nation with bottled water.

3 DAYS • 334KM • 210 MILES

ITINERARY

CLERMONT-FERRAND	▶ Royat (18km-11m)
ROYAT	▶ **Puy de Dôme** (11km-7m)
PUY DE DÔME	▶ **Col de Guéry** (30km-19m)
COL DE GUÉRY	▶ **La Bourboule** (28km-19m)
LA BOURBOULE	▶ **Le Mont-Dore** (13km-8m)
LE MONT-DORE	▶ **Besse** (26km-16m)
BESSE	▶ **St-Nectaire** (17km-11m)
ST-NECTAIRE	▶ **Ambert** (83km-52m)
AMBERT	▶ **Moulin Richard-de-Bas** (5km-3m)
MOULIN RICHARD-DE-BAS	▶ **Thiers** (57km-35m)
THIERS	▶ **Clermont-Ferrand** (46km-29m)

i *Place de la Victoire Gergovia,
Clermont Ferrand*

► *Leave Clermont-Ferrand on
the **N89** as for Tulle. Go right
on the **D767** then right on
the **D941c** to Royat.*

❶ **Royat,** Auvergne
Royat is a perfect example of a
French spa which has moved
with the times. Since Roman
times, people have drunk the
mineral waters and relaxed in
thermal baths here, but its
development as a fashionable
spa dates from the 19th
century. Today everything is up
to date, with attractive modern
buildings.

Its central area is crammed
into a narrow river valley where
there is still room for parks and
open spaces as well as for the
Etablissement Thermal and the
inevitable casino. Among the
alleyways of the upper town,
look for the Maison du Passé
(House of the Past), the
museum of old Royat, and for
the Taillerie, where crystals and
gemstones are cut and polished.

i *Avenue August Rouzaud, Place
Allard*

Imposing Puy de Dôme, the
highest peak (1,416m/4,645 feet)
in an extinct volcanic chain

SPECIAL TO...

Stilll under construction at the
time of going to print, but well
worth seeking out if it is open,
is Vulcania, the European
Volcano Centre. The building is
mostly underground, and its
exhibition galleries simulate the
rocky depths, complete with
fissures showing glowing red
imitation lava. On to screens of
rock, dramatic images of
volcanic action are projected.
Outside the centre has some of
the most spectacular views in
the whole of Europe.

► *Leave Royat on the **D68**. Go
left on the **D941a** and immediately right on the **D68**. Go
straight on to join the toll road
to the summit of Puy de
Dôme. Check for 'ouvert' sign.*

❷ **Puy de Dôme,** Auvergne
The toll road to this volcanic
summit spirals upwards at an
average gradient of 12 per cent
(1 in 8.3). It reaches a high-level
world apart – Puy de Dôme is a
glorious viewpoint, a spectacular
hang-gliders' launch area, the
site of a Roman temple, dedicated to Mercury and an exhilarating walkers' hill. You may be
lucky enough to see colourful
hot-air balloons wafting across
the lovely Auvergne countryside. The modern world, in the
form of an observatory, television mast and souvenir shop,
is also present on top. The story
of access to the Puy de Dôme is
a fascinating one and many old
illustrations are displayed
locally. The first car reached the
summit in 1913, but in those
days the usual way up was by a
steam train. The toll road
opened only in 1926. On the

summit look for the statue of
Eugène Renaux. In 1911 his
biplane landed safely on the
plateau at the end of a prize-
winning flight from Paris. The
elegant lava and wood buildings
covered with copper roofs house
a reception and information
centre.

SPECIAL TO...

Just before the junction with
the D941a, the Village
Auvergnat is a shopping centre
where many of the specialities
of the region are on sale,
including honey, jams, liqueurs,
the well-known local cheese
and Côtes d'Auvergne wines.

35

FOR CHILDREN

Before the Puy de Dôme toll
road, the Zoo des Dômes
includes an imaginative
children's playground. The
'mini-plane' roundabout introduces youngsters to the thrills
of hang-gliding without actually
launching them into the air.

BACK TO NATURE

At 1,465m (4,085 feet) the Puy
de Dôme is the highest of 80
extinct volcanoes in the
district. It dominates a characteristic volcanic landscape.
Some hills retain their hollow
crater shapes; others are the
old volcanic cores. Flowers and
butterflies are abundant, and
look for red kites and honey
buzzards in the skies above.

▶ *Return to the **D941a** and
turn right. Go straight ahead
on the **D216** then on the
D27 and on the **D983**. Stop
at a major car park immediately before the junction with
the **D80**.*

3 **Col de Guéry,** Auvergne
This is one of the most dramatic
viewpoints in the Auvergne,
looking down the precipitous
valley between La Roche
Tuilière and La Roche
Sanadoire.

These two huge rock towers
rise from a wooded crater and
are the remains of a volcanic
eruption which occurred something like two millions years
ago. Like the Puy de Dôme,
they are included in the biggest
regional nature park in France,
the Parc des Volcans
d'Auvergne (Regional Nature
Park of Auvergne Volcanoes).

Tuilière, as you will see close
up later from the D80, was the
vent of the volcano, whose lava
spewed out from the earth's
molten core and cooled into the
tall, brittle columns exposed
today. Sanadoire was part of the
cone. But the landscape was
shaped by more than just
volcanic activity: the valley
between the rock towers was
ground out by a retreating Ice-
Age glacier.

▶ *Turn right on the **D80** to
Rochefort-Montagne, then
turn left and follow the **N89**
and **D922** to La Bourboule.*

4 **La Bourboule,** Auvergne
Two thermal establishments
continue the spa traditions of
this little valley town where
tree-lined streets follow the
banks of the upper Dordogne.
The mineral waters here
contain arsenic – in medicinal,
not murderous proportions. La
Bourboule is very well supplied
with sports facilities, and its
Musée de Geologie Botanique
organises a variety of themed
geological outings of discovery
into the surrounding area.

The Parc Fenestre is a pleasant wooded area with pathways,
a lake and a narrow-gauge railway. It also houses the town
station for the cable-car system
to the Plateau de Charlannes. At
1,250m (4,100 feet), Charlannes
is a place of wide-ranging views,
and a ski resort in winter. For a
more intimate view of La
Bourboule itself, walk up to the
granite boulder called Le
Rocher des Fées (the Fairies'
Rock) which rises some 50m
(165 feet) over the town to the
northwest.

⚬ *Place de la République*

The pretty spa of La Bourboule
is also a thriving winter resort

RECOMMENDED WALKS

Many people visit Orcival, to the north of La Bourboule, for its beautiful pilgrimage church. This village in the deep wooded valley of the Sioulet is also an excellent walking centre. Waymarked paths climb through forests, to the crater-lake of Servière, and to the dizzily-balanced Roche Branlante (the Rocking Stone).

but a forest clearing reached by a funicular railway (built in 1898 and now a historic monument) and then a final climb on foot. The superlative high-spot of Le Mont-Dore is up the D983 as it climbs a steeply wooded valley to the ski runs and chairlifts on the alpine meadows below the Puy de Sancy. Be ready for a drop in temperature. Take a cable-car and then walk to the summit at 1,885m (6,180 feet), to admire the colossal views from the highest point in the Auvergne.

BACK TO NATURE

On the Col de la Croix St-Robert look for the roadside wildflowers – violas, vetches, trefoils and many others. The sound of cowbells is a sign that these grassy uplands provide rich summer pasture.

6 Besse-en-Chandesse, Auvergne

This is an engaging little town which has preserved, in narrow

▶ Leave La Bourboule on the *D130 to Le Mont-Dore.*

5 Le Mont-Dore, Auvergne
Upstream from La Bourboule, here is another spa resort. Le Mont-Dore is well known for activities as diverse as fishing, mountaineering and amateur classical music. Instrumentalists and singers from all over France gather here to practise, rehearse and perform in concert. The Promenade des Artistes is a pleasant walk on the woodland ridge overlooking the town. There are higher attractions here, too: the Salon du Capuchin for instance, is not some elegant town-centre hall,

i Avenue de la Libération

FOR CHILDREN

At Le Mont-Dore, the Parc des Loisirs offers an exhilarating summer toboggan ride, and boats rush down a series of cascades. A carousel and an Apache fort add to the fun.

▶ Return on the **D983** from the Puy de Sancy, then right on the road signed 'Besse par Col-Croix St Robert'. Check 'ouvert' sign. Follow the **D36** to Besse-en-Chandesse.

The pleasant little village of Orcival nestles among the hills on the banks of the Sioulet

streets and tiny squares, many old houses from the 15th and 16th centuries. Some have connecting doors which allow the townspeople – walking through their neighbours' homes – to reach the church in winter while avoiding the chill open air. The Auvergne has snowy winters, and Besse has created a satellite ski resort called Super-Besse. One fascinating place to visit in the old town is a ski museum, the first in France. Here, Pierre-André Chauvet has assembled a remarkable collection of skiing memorabilia. There are skis and bindings ancient and modern, of many different styles, from France, Switzerland, Norway, Sweden and the Austro-Hungarian empire. Illustrations cover curiosities such as historic Russian army snowploughs, and early events of the pioneering ski club of Besse, founded in 1902.

i   *Place du Docteur-Pipet*

▶ *Leave Besse on the **D5** to Murol then go right on the **D996** to St-Nectaire.*

7 St-Nectaire, Auvergne

One of the most exuberant of the typical Romanesque churches of the Auvergne is the one in this village split into upper and lower parts in the winding and wooded valley of the Courançon. A hundred and more ornamented pillars surround the nave and the choir.

The Maison du St-Nectaire allows you the chance to sample the local cheese – St-Nectaire gave its name to a round, nutty-flavoured cheese made in many parts of the Auvergne – as well as the wines and bayberry liqueur special to the district.

St-Nectaire is another spa. There are modern thermal baths, but at the Cornadore grotto you can see the naturally warm water welling up. Try the mineral waters at a little pavilion in the parkland at Les Thermes.

i   *Les Grands Thermes*

▶ *Continue on the **D996** to Champeix. Follow signs to Coudes and Vic-le-Comte, then continue on the **D225** and **D996** (sometimes signed **N496**) to Ambert.*

FOR HISTORY BUFFS

A Scottish-Auvergne connection exists in the 16th-century Sainte-Chapelle at Vic-le-Comte, built for Jean (or John) Stuart, a descendant of the Scottish royal family and regent of Scotland during James V's minority. He was Duke of Albany and Comte d'Auvergne. The chapel features an unexpectedly light interior and a splendid balustraded gallery with statues of the Apostles. There are also remains of the castle of the Comtes d'Auvergne.

The Puy de Sancy, at 1,886m (6,185 feet), is the highest peak in the Massif Central

8 Ambert, Auvergne

Two notable buildings here are the granite church of St John and the curious town hall. Begun in 1471 in Flamboyant Gothic style, and decorated by a master mason obviously enjoying himself, St-Jean Church has later additions such as a frisky little Renaissance belfry. Look for the carved coat of arms of Ambert's old trade guilds – saddlers, shoemakers and the rest – and for the optical illusion which makes the interior seem longer than it really is.

The Hôtel de Ville (town hall) is entirely circular and arcaded all the way round. It was built in 1820 as the grain market. In the industrial area, a splendid museum of steam and traction engines, road rollers, tractors and mobile distillation plants is known, thanks to the French passion for acronyms, as AGRIVAP.

In the centre of town a museum of a different kind is devoted to the 'divine cheese' Fourme d'Ambert. Tasting sessions follow the guided tour.

i   *Place de l'Hôtel de Ville*

▶ *Leave Ambert on the D57 for Moulin Richard-de-Bas.*

9 Moulin Richard-de-Bas, Auvergne

Traditional papermaking is one of the most fascinating industrial processes. This restored 14th-century mill is in the valley of the River Laga, which still turns its waterwheel. It tells the story of papermaking, from ancient Egyptian papyrus via the strict rules of the craft laid down by the Chinese in about AD105, to the Arabs' discovery of its secrets from Chinese soldiers captured in the defence of Samarkand in 751, and on beyond the invention of mechanical printing.

All the traditional processes of crushing linen into the basic pulp, the smoothing, drying and pressing are displayed. There are early manuscripts on show, a gorgeous 18th-century atlas, a mid-19th-century printing press, parchments, vellums and thousands of watermarks.

Richard-de-Bas also produces papers of the highest quality. One speciality, made when the petals of cornflowers and marigolds from the mill's own gardens are mixed with the pulp, is flowered paper, where each sheet is individually patterned.

▶ *Return to Ambert and take the D906 then the N89 to Thiers.*

RECOMMENDED WALKS

Much of this tour is in the Livradois-Forez regional nature park.
There are dozens of official footpaths here, one starting from the Salle Polyvalente in Olliergues on the D906 between Ambert and Thiers. Taking about three hours, it explores the farmlands, woods, old village churches and rural lanes above the valley of the Dore.

10 Thiers, Auvergne

France's 'capital of cutlery' is an attractive town with its red roofs rising on a hillside from a bend on the River Durolle. Many fine medieval and later half-timbered houses survive along the steep streets of the old quarter.

The museum and workshop of La Musée Maison de Couteliers displays an astonishing variety of knives, scissors, table settings and hallmarks. There are workshops all over the town where modern craftsmen and designers keep up the ancient tradition. Down on the Durolle, several little waterfalls used to provide power for the cutlery factories. Look for the Creux d'Enfer, much less forbidding than its name – the 'Drop to Hell' – suggests.

☐ *Maison du Pirou*

A papermaker at work in Moulin Richard-de-Bas

▶ *Return from Thiers on the N89 and continue to Clermont-Ferrand.*

SCENIC ROUTES

The D27 is a high road through typical Auvergne countryside of cattle farms, woodlands, attractive villages and little valleys. Then the tour enters the magnificent volcanic landscapes around the Roche Sanadoire. The Col de la Croix St-Robert road, brightened by splashes of hillside broom, looks to deep valleys and wooded summits. Beyond St-Nectaire, the D996 goes through a narrow glen with thickly wooded sides and exposed rock faces. After Vic-le-Comte, it wanders past farms and broadleaved woodlands, conifer plantations and little river valleys, then swoops down to Ambert on the plain.

Heartland
of France

Porcelain from Limoges and tapestries from Aubusson are two of the main features of this tour, where historic towns are matched by fine recreational facilities, especially on and around two beautiful wooded reservoirs. Limoges, the starting point, has been an industrial centre for centuries and is still expanding.

3/4 DAYS • 411KM • 255 MILES

ITINERARY

LIMOGES	▶ **Ségur-le-Château** (58km-36m)
SÉGUR-LE-CHÂTEAU	▶ **Arnac-Pompadour** (10km-6m)
ARNAC-POMPADOUR	▶ **Uzerche (25km-15m)**
UZERCHE	▶ **Tulle (31km-19m)**
TULLE	▶ **Gimel-les-Cascades** (11km-7m)
GIMEL-LES-CASCADES	▶ **Les Monédières** (40km-25m)
LES MONÉDIÈRES	▶ **Treignac (20km-12m)**
TREIGNAC	▶ **Lac de Vassivière** (40km-25m)
LAC DE VASSIVIÈRE	▶ **Aubusson (49km-30m)**
AUBUSSON	▶ **Guéret (41km-26m)**
GUÉRET	▶ **Limoges (86km-54m)**

ℹ Boulevard Fleurus, Limoges

▶ Leave Limoges on the **D704** to St-Yrieix-la-Perche, then take the **D18**, which later becomes the **D6**, to Ségur-le-Château.

❶ Ségur-le-Château,
Limousin

Visitors to Ségur-le-Château may be mystified by the number of rivers here. In fact, there is only one – the Auvézère – which double loops through a narrow, winding valley. The tiny medieval town has long since lost its influential position, but once aristocratic mansions still fight off the years. Riverside mills remain in place, and the ruined 12th-century castle (not open to the public) broods absent-mindedly on its hilltop overlooking the town.

RECOMMENDED WALKS

Clearly waymarked from the D6 through Ségur-le-Château, four numbered pathways explore a beautiful countryside of modest hills and woodlands. The 'rivers and streams' walk wanders along the banks of the Auvézère, and there are fine views down to the river from the low ridges which follow its winding course.

SPECIAL TO...

Ségur-le-Château is noted for the craft of working with chestnut wood. By the riverside here look for the little hut with a display illustrating the work of the *feuillardiers* – the woodcutters who supplied the chestnut stakes for the plants in the Périgord vineyards. Dozens of craftsmen in the district still work with chestnut wood.

▶ Continue on the **D6**, then the **D7** to Arnac-Pompadour.

FOR HISTORY BUFFS

Turn right at the entrance to St-Yrieix on the way from Limoges to Ségur-le-Château, for the unobtrusive but well-stocked Musée de la Porcelaine at the Les Palloux china factory. Limoges, Meissen, Delft, Chinese and Japanese figures, vases and dinner services are all on display. It was the kaolin deposits of St-Yrieix which launched the porcelain industry at Limoges.

On the return route to Limoges, La Tour de Zizim in Bourganeuf was the home (or, in some versions of the story, the prison) of an exiled 15th-century Ottoman prince who equipped it with Turkish baths and even a harem. It is now a museum with less glamorous exhibits.

The tiny medieval town of Ségur-le-Château

❷ Arnac-Pompadour,
Limousin

In the 18th century this was the estate of the Marquise de Pompadour. Since 1872 it has been the home of the French National Stud Farm, devoted principally to the breeding of Anglo-Arab horses. The stallions are stabled in the Puy Marmont; La Jumenterie de la Rivière is the home of the mares and their foals. Flat and cross-country races, show-jumping and carriage-driving events are held regularly.

ℹ Château de Pompadour

▶ Leave Arnac-Pompadour on the **D901** to Lubersac, then follow the **D902** and turn right on the **N20** to Uzerche.

3 Uzerche, Limousin

Historic gateways and fine old houses with towers, turrets, carved lintels, ornamented windows and heraldic designs are all preserved here. Uzerche stands on a peninsula ridge bounded on three sides by the River Vézère, and there are attractive views from the high-set Esplanade de la Lunade. Behind the esplanade, the Romanesque Church of St-Pierre features an eerily impressive crypt built around 1030.

[i] *Place de la Libération*

▶ *Leave Uzerche on the* **N20***, then immediately take the* **N120** *to Tulle.*

4 Tulle, Limousin

You may find this a place of odd contrasts. The pleasant approach road swinging down wooded valleys arrives at a town whose modern parts are dull; but it has a fascinating old quarter crossed by lanes and stairways, and there is a bustle around its riverside quays. Tulle gave its name to a fine-woven silk, but one of its main

industries now is armaments.

There is some fine modern stained glass in the 12th-century cathedral, and the Musée de la Cloître, built round the arcades and gardens of a dignified old Benedictine monastery, illustrates local history in a quiet and peaceful setting. Paintings, sculptures, porcelain and archaeological finds share a building with historic firearms.

You will need a strong stomach to look over some of the illustrations in the Musée de la Résistance et de la Déportation, which recalls the grim days of World War II when many local men were deported, never to be heard of again.

[i] *2 place Emil Zola*

▶ *Leave Tulle as for Clermont-Ferrand. After a hairpin climb out of the built-up area, go straight on under a bridge, following the* **D9** *then the* **D53e** *to Gimel-les-Cascades.*

5 Gimel-les-Cascades, Limousin

On the approach to Gimel, try to catch a glimpse of the dash-

ing waterfalls of the Montane which gave the village its name. From Gimel itself there is a dramatic outlook down a steeply wooded ravine. Footpaths wander past the spray-soaked triple falls. Although nowadays it is off the main roads, a hint of Gimel's previous religious importance is given by the great treasure of its parish church – a 12th-century gold and bejewelled reliquary of St Stephen. The saint's stoning to death is one of the scenes picked out in fine enamel and precious stones.

▶ *Leave Gimel-les-Cascades following the 'Tulle 13' sign. Turn right following the 'Etang de Ruffaud' signs, then follow 'Gare de Corrèze' and 'vers RN 89' signs. Cross the* **N89** *and continue on the* **D26** *through Corrèze. Go right on the* **D32** *to Chaumeil, left on the* **D121***, right on the* **D128** *as for Lestards, then take a side road right to Les Monédières.*

Uzerche, the 'Pearl of Limousin', stands on a spur above the Vézère

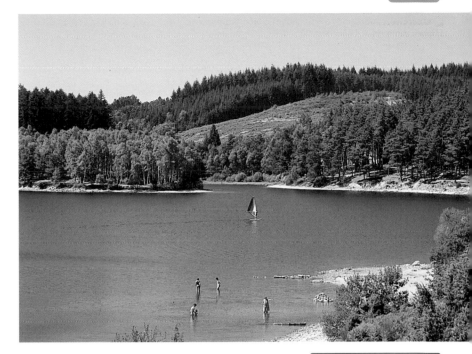

6 Les Monédières, Limousin
At about 911m (2,990 feet)
above sea-level, the summit
here is a magnificent all-round
viewpoint. Many of the faraway
hills are *puys* – the remains of
extinct volcanoes. The hilltop is
a favourite launching-place for
hang-gliders.

BACK TO NATURE

On the Monédières hills,
conifer plantations rise above
the lower deciduous
woodland. The original forest
was deliberately set on fire,
once by Julius Caesar and again
during the 16th-century
religious wars. *Myrtilles*, or
blueberries, grow in profusion
and are sold locally. Wild boar
are occasionally seen in
autumn and fungi grow in
profusion.

▶ *Return to the D128 and turn
right following 'Chaumeil' sign.
Go left on the D32 to
Lestards then left on the
D16 to Treignac.*

Lac de Vassivière offers many
facilities for sports

7 Treignac, Limousin
Roofs are slaty-grey colour here,
a sign that this is a different part
of the country from the warmer
villages visited before Les
Monédières. There is a fine
view of the town from a viewpoint tower in the centre. Closer
investigation reveals medieval
and Renaissance buildings
descending to the Vézère river,
which is crossed by a 15th-
century bridge. A museum
exhibits historic furnishings,
craft and farm tools, weaving
equipment and local ironwork.
The restored parish church
displays locally-worked stained
glass and there is a simple little
chapel, reached by a walk past
the Stations of the Cross, which
offers a good view westwards
through a woodland clearing.

i Place de la République

▶ *Leave Treignac on the D940
as for Eymoutiers. Turn right
on the D132e which
becomes the D69, signed 'Lac*

RECOMMENDED
WALKS

Treignac offers high- and low-
level paths, some to hilltop
viewpoints. Best of these is
the walk past the local
hospital, by wooded lanes and
an open hillside, to the poised
granite boulder called La
Pierre des Druides (the
Druids' Stone).

BACK TO NATURE

In the winding gorge of the
Vézère just below Treignac, the
Rocher des Folles is a series of
granite pillars on the edge of a
weathered cliff.

*de Vassivière'. Go right on the
D992 to La Villedieu, where
you should watch for a left
turn on the D34. Go straight
on avoiding a '19t' sign, left at
a Stop sign as for Beaumont,
then follow signs 'Ile de
Vassivière'.*

range from reproduction style Louis XIV to something suitable for TGV trains.

☐ *Rue Vieille*

▶ *Leave Aubusson on the **D942a** and turn left on to the **D942** to Guéret.*

10 Guéret, Limousin
You may be tempted to skip through Guéret, but its museums deserve a visit. Occupying an 18th-century mansion surrounded by pleasant formal gardens, the Musée de la Sematorerie has valuable collections of tapestries; ceramics from France, the Netherlands and Ming dynasty china; and some wonderful religious art, especially 12th-century enamelwork. The Musée de Presidial features natural history, agriculture, bygone trades and traditional costumes.

☐ *1 avenue Charles de Gaulle*

▶ *Leave Guéret on the **D940** then follow 'Limoges' signs through Pontarion and remain on the **D940**. Go through Bourganeuf and continue before turning right on the **D5** as for Ambazac then watch for a junction where you should bear left uphill on the **D29** at the 'Limoges 27' sign. Return to Limoges.*

8 Lac de Vassivière,
Limousin
The route here stops before a bridge across to the main island in an extensive and well-wooded reservoir. The lake offers sports and leisure activities along its 45km (28-mile) shoreline, and visitors can walk

Aubusson's museum proudly displays the town's heritage

to the island, where there are woodland paths, outdoor sculpture displays and a castle.

▶ *Retrace your route and turn right on the **D222** as for Peyrat-le-Château. Turn right at the stop sign to Royère. Go left on the **D3**, watch for a right turn signed 'Aubusson 24' and continue to Aubusson.*

9 Aubusson, Limousin
At heart Aubusson is a dignified old town with many discreetly restored buildings. Most of all, though, it is the capital of French tapestry, introduced here in the 14th century by Flemish weavers.
La Maison du Vieux Tapissier displays hundreds of tapestries, from classical works of the 17th century to dazzling modern abstracts. Several tapestry workshops and studios are open to visitors. Their designs

---

FOR CHILDREN

There are sandy beaches at the wooded Barrage de Treignac reservoir, formed by a dam on the Vézère. It is ideal for fishing, swimming and sunbathing parties. Swimming from the main beach, beside the D940, is supervised in summer.
Further on, the Lac de Vassivière offers tuition in sailing, windsurfing and horse and pony rides. This beautiful reservoir is a noted recreational area, and there are easy walks, suitable for children, in the forest which surrounds it.

SCENIC ROUTES

From St-Yrieix to Ségur-le-Château the D18 and D6 run through pleasant undulating country of low hills and little valleys, and woodlands interspersed with grazing land. The N120 sweeps down wooded valleys to Tulle, the D9 to Gimel is a fine winding road with views to the tumbling waterfalls, and after Gimel there are attractive roadside fishing lakes. West of Chameil, alpine-like country rises to conifer-clad summits.

Of Rivers
& Islands

The arms of La Rochelle feature a full-rigged ship with cannons at the ports. That mixture of war and sea dominates the history of the coast and islands here. Inland, this is the country of the Cognac vineyards, and in the gentle Marais Poitevin you will be tempted to explore the canals of what was once the Gulf of Poitou.

ITINERARY		
LA ROCHELLE	▶	**Île de Ré (11km-7m)**
ÎLE DE RÉ	▶	**Rochefort (109km-68m)**
ROCHEFORT	▶	**Brouage (19km-12m)**
BROUAGE	▶	**Île d'Oléron (15km-9m)**
ÎLE D'OLÉRON	▶	**Saintes (154km-96m)**
SAINTES	▶	**Angoulême (76km-47m)**
ANGOULÊME	▶	**Niort (113km-70m)**
NIORT	▶	**Coulon (20km-12m)**
COULON	▶	**Fontenay-le-Comte**
		(40km-25m)
FONTENAY-LE-COMTE	▶	**La Rochelle (50km-31m)**

4 DAYS • 607KM • 377 MILES

$\boxed{i}$ *Place de la Petite Sirène, La*
Rochelle

▶ *Leave La Rochelle over the*
toll bridge to Île de Ré. Take
the 'Itineraire Nord', visiting La
Flotte and St-Martin-de-Ré on
the way to Phare des
Baleines. Return by the D201
via Le Bois-Plage, then right
on the D735 back over the
toll bridge.

❶ Île de Ré, Poitou-Charente
Linked to the mainland by a
modern bridge, the island is
28km (17 miles) long and
3–5km (2–3 miles) wide, ringed
with holiday beaches. The old
fishing and trading port of La
Flotte once shipped salt and
brandy to America. St-Martin-
de-Ré, the principal town, has
unexpected rampart walls, a
town centre virtually on an
island, and the Musée Ernest

Cognac, which is named after a
native of St. Martin. There is
also a citadel where visitors can
admire the outer defences and
the old quay. The inner part is a
state prison. At the northern
point of the island you can visit
the Phare des Baleines, a lighthouse named after the whales
that used to be seen offshore.

$\boxed{i}$ *Quai de Sénac in La Flotte and*
5 bis, rue de la Blance, Le-Bois-
Plage-en-Ré

FOR CHILDREN

There is plenty for children at
L'Arche de Noé (Noah's Ark)
before the Phare des Baleines
on Île de Ré.

St-Martin-de-Ré, the principal
town of Île de Ré

FOR HISTORY BUFFS

Until 1938, prisoners shipped
to Devil's Island, the infamous
penal colony in French Guinea,
left from the citadel at St-
Martin-de-Ré. There is still a
prison here.

▶ *Follow the D735 as for La*
Rochelle, on to the dual-
carriageway numbered N237
then N137, and continue to
Rochefort.

❷ Rochefort, Poitou-
Charente
You may wonder, entering it
through unremarkable suburbs,
if Rochefort is worth a visit, but
this is a special town. In 1666
thousands of workers, under the
orders of Louis XIV's chief
minister Jean Baptiste Colbert,
built a huge arsenal and naval
shipyard here. There are guided
tours of the beautiful mansard-
roofed Corderie Royale, with its
372m (1,220-foot) hall where
the ropes were twisted.
Museums in Rochefort cover art
and history, and its background
as a military port. The unobtrusive but exotically furnished
Maison de Loti, house of Pierre
Loti (1850–1923), who mixed
two careers, as a marine officer
and a novelist of the sea, stands
in a quiet side street.

$\boxed{i}$ *Avenue Sadi Carnot*

▶ *Leave Rochefort on the D733*
as for Royan, then go right on
the D238e to Soubise and
left on the D3 signed 'Hiers-
Brouage'.

❸ Brouage, Poitou-Charente
Away from main roads, this fine
little fortified town is now also
away from the sea and today it
stands half deserted among the
salt marshes. The retreat of the
waters ruined its position as a
busy trading port. From the
ramparts, the French tricolour
and the maple leaf of Canada fly
side by side. Samuel de
Champlain, the founder of

Quebec, was born here in 1567. There is a comprehensive exhibition in the church on the founding of what was at first 'New France'.

i Porte Royale

▶ *Continue on the D3, turn right at the traffic lights over the toll bridge on to Île d'Oléron. Bear right on the D734 through Le Château-d'Oléron. Go right in Dolus on to the D126 through Les Allards and Boyardville, then via Foulerot, Port du Douhet, La Brée and St-Denis to the Phare de Chassiron. Return to St-Denis, then take the D734 to Dolus and follow 'Le Viaduc' signs back over the toll bridge.*

FOR HISTORY BUFFS

Reached by ferry from Boyardville on the Île-d'Oléron, the Napoleonic museum on the little island of Aix, Maison de l'Empereur, recalls how Napoleon spent his last night on French soil before surrendering to the British ship *Bellerophon*.

4 Île d'Oléron, Poitou-Charente
Larger than Ré (30km/18 miles long and 6km/3½ miles wide), this is another holiday island of villages, picturesque harbours, vineyards, woodlands and fine sandy beaches.

Look for the grassy site of the 12th-century fortress which gave the island's main town of Le Château-d'Oléron its name, the river resort of Boyardville with its pinewood dunes and beach, and the lighthouse tower of the Phare de Chassiron, where the waves are seen breaking over offshore reefs and shallows.

RECOMMENDED WALKS

Go north through Boyardville on the Île d'Oléron to the Forêt des Saumonards, where you can follow any number of pinewood paths behind the sand dunes. In the channel between Oléron and Aix, look for the isolated rock prison of Fort Boyard, for a time in the 19th century a French equivalent of Alcatraz.

The fortified town of Brouage was once an important port

i Place de la République, Château-d'Oléron

BACK TO NATURE

On the Île d'Oléron, turn left in Les Allards for the extensive nature reserve of pools, canals and woodland at the Marais des Oiseaux. Wildfowl, waders, storks and birds of prey are all featured.

FOR CHILDREN

Before you leave Île d'Oléron, turn right for St-Trojan-les-Bains and the narrow-gauge railway which potters for 6km (3½ miles) through pinewoods.

▶ *Follow the D26 off the island then turn right at the 'La Tremblade' sign. Go right opposite Camping les Pins, and right at the T-junction over another toll bridge. Go right on the D25 to Royan, then take the N150 to Saintes.*

L'Arc de Germanicus, Saintes' Roman triumphal arch

▶ Leave Angoulême on the **D939** to Matha. In the town centre, turn right to Aulnay, following the **D121**. After Aulnay, go right on the **D950** left on the **D109** and join the **D1** through Chizé. Turn right on the **N150** to Niort.

RECOMMENDED WALKS

Turn right off the D939 on the way between Angoulême and Niort, at St-Cybardeaux, for the informal paths which penetrate a hilltop woodland and reveal the unexpected sight of a Gallo-Roman theatre with tiers of stone-blocked seats facing what was once the stage.

5 Saintes, Poitou-Charente

Back from the resorts and islands of the coast, this is a handsome district capital. There is a good regional museum here, others concentrating on fine arts, folklore and archaeology. Roman remains include a triumphal arch. Saintes lies astride the River Charente, and cruise-boats sail from its garden-backed quays.

ℹ️ 62 cours National

SPECIAL TO...

At Cognac and Jarnac, are such world-famous cognac houses as Hennessy, Martell, Rémy Martin and Courvoisier and Hine. Saintes has a cognac museum.

▶ Leave Saintes on the **D24**, which becomes the **D83**. Go right on the **N141** and right on the **D83** to Cognac. Take the **N141** through Jarnac, then turn right on the **D22**. After Vibrac watch for a left turn – away from Châteauneuf-sur-Charente – to St-Simieux. Go right through Sireuil, left on the **D53**, right on the **D84**, left on the **D41** and right on the **D72** to Angoulême.

6 Angoulême, Poitou-Charente

This is a busy industrial town, but its old upper town is worth a visit. Of special note are its imposing hilltop location, the views from the wooded paths round its ramparts, and the glorious façade of its cathedral (much restored in the 19th century). There are museums, exuberant Renaissance buildings, and rare active survivors of the papermills which once made Angoulême's fortune.

ℹ️ 7 bis rue du Chat, Place des Halles

7 Niort, Poitou-Charente

Niort, on the River Sèvres, is a working town with various industries. The riverside has walks and footbridges, gardens and vestiges of old mill streams. Past and present town halls are richly ornamented, and there is much fine Renaissance design. Customers bustle around the glass-and-wrought-ironwork market hall. The multi-towered castle or donjon may have been built by the 12th-century English Kings Henry II and Richard the Lionheart.

ℹ️ Place de la Poste

▶ Leave Niort on the **N11**. Turn right on the **D3**, then right on the **D1** to Coulon.

8 Coulon, Poitou-Charente

In the heart of one of the most appealing landscapes in France – the farms, market gardens, woodlands and waterway maze of the long-drained Marais Poitevin – Coulon is an attractive village where punts are available for hire, and escorted cruises also start, on some of the 40,000km (25,000 miles) of water channels. Not all, of course, are navigable, but they are an enchanting haven. Some picnic sites, accessible by water, are remote from any road. Coulon's museum tells the story of the marshes, and the aquarium displays all the fish species of this 'Green Venice'.

ⓘ Place de l'Eglise

BACK TO NATURE

Turn left off D1 after Chizé for Zoorama, a park and study centre concentrating on European animals such as wildcat, lynx, bison, deer and tortoise.

▶ Leave Coulon on the **D123** as for Le Vanneau, then go right on the **D102**, which becomes the **D104** through Damvix. Go straight on at the give way sign, then right on the **D15** through Maillezais. Go left on the **N148** to Fontenay-le-Comte.

🅓 **Fontenay-le-Comte,**
Loire Valley West
There are no fishing-smacks now, sailing under the Pont des Sardines (Sardine Bridge) at Fontenay, but the riverside is a pleasant recreational area with footpaths and little gardens. Fontenay preserves its historic buildings – even the tourist office was once a toll-house for the port. The Église Notre-Dame is an impressive Gothic church with a beautiful walnut pulpit and, high on an outer wall, a gilded Madonna. Beside it there is a regional museum. The Château de Terre-Neuve is a splendid 16th-century castle whose richly ornamented fireplaces feature alchemists' symbols and griffins.

During the Renaissance, the town became the home of poets and writers, including Rabelais, who was educated in a convent here.

ⓘ Quay Poëy d'Avant

SPECIAL TO...

At Ré and Oléron are the oysterbeds which cover great areas and are a vital part of the local economy. You can join a tour of the beds from La Flotte on Ré, and there is an oyster museum at St-Trojan on Oléron.

▶ Leave Fontenay on the **D938ter** for La Rochelle.

SCENIC ROUTES

Once off Oléron, the route follows a minor road towards the next toll bridge, with attractive views of the strait between the island and the mainland. Then the D25 to Royan runs through the undulating pine-clad sand dunes of the Forêt de la Coubre. From Saintes to Cognac, the D24 follows the River Charente through a pleasant countryside of farms, vineyards and woodlands. Beyond Jarnac, still in the Charente valley, there is a succession of quiet villages off the usual tourist trail.
The Marais Poitevin is an understated landscape, but it is particularly attractive where the route winds alongside the Sèvre Niortaise west of Coulon, and again on the approach to Damvix.

The charming canalside village of Coulon is typical of the marsh villages of the Marais Poitevin

The Western
Loire Valley

Starting in Nantes, this tour soon leaves all Breton influences behind as it heads for the valleys of the Loire and the Sarthe. You will find some of France's finest *son et lumière* presentations here, one of the world's most famous motor-racing circuits, and the Pays Nantais and Anjou are packed with vineyards.

5 DAYS • 512KM • 319 MILES

ITINERARY	
NANTES	▶ **Clisson (27km-17m)**
CLISSON	▶ **Cholet (36km-22.5m)**
CHOLET	▶ **Doué-la-Fontaine**
	(58km-36m)
DOUÉ-LA-FONTAINE	▶ **St-Hilaire (29km-18m)**
ST-HILAIRE	▶ **Saumur (4km-2.5m)**
SAUMUR	▶ **Baugé (44km-27m)**
BAUGÉ	▶ **Le Lude (24km-15m)**
LE LUDE	▶ **Le Mans (circuit auto)**
	(75km-47m)
LE MANS (CIRCUIT	▶ **Le Mans (10km-6m)**
AUTO)	
LE MANS	▶ **Angers (106km-66m)**
ANGERS	▶ **Nantes (99km-62m)**

[i] 7 rue Valmy, Nantes

▶ Leave Nantes for Clisson on the **D59** through St-Fiacre. In Gorges go left of the **D113** then take the **D59** again into Clisson.

❶ Clisson, Loire Valley West
The Vendée Wars and the savage reprisals of the Revolutionary government army all but obliterated this little town. Then it was completely rebuilt, but not as it had been before. Present-day Clisson is mostly a tribute to Palladian Italy, with colonnades, loggias and belltowers of a style seen nowhere else in western France.

Look for the stabilised but unfurnished ruin of the 13th- to 15th-century castle, the 15th-century market hall, the two medieval bridges contrasting with the soaring 19th-century road viaduct, and Italianate creations such as the Temple d'Amitié and the Church of Notre-Dame.

There are beautiful walks in the valleys of the Sèvre Nantaise and the Moine. Local wines may be tasted. But Clisson itself is the great attrac-tion, especially its Italianate skyline and leafy riverside view.

[i] Place du Minage

▶ Leave Clisson on the **N149**. Turn left as for Beaupréau on the **D762** then go along the **N249** and follow signs to Cholet.

❷ Cholet, Loire Valley West
Only 20 buildings were left standing in the brutal aftermath of the Vendée Wars of 1793–96. A section of the Musée d'Artes et de l'Histoire explains how the Vendée rising against the Revolutionary government's policies of mass conscription and the overthrow of all previous loyalties, was at first successful, then viciously crushed.

Other exhibitions are at the Musée Paysan with its old-style dairy and country house interiors in the leisure park by the Ribou lake.

This is a famous textile town with a Musée du Textile illustrating the industry. Its trademark is the red-and-white handkerchief – the *mouchoir de Cholet* – whose design is rooted

Clisson's impressive ruined 13th-to 15th-century castle sits atop a rocky outcrop

in another incident of the Vendée Wars. The town also has a shoe museum and at nearby Maulévrier there is a fine Oriental Garden which mirrors the Buddhist stages of human existence.

[i] Place de Rougé

▶ Leave Cholet on the **D20** as for Poitiers. In Maulévrier turn left and right as for Vihiers, then left on the **D196** through Chanteloup to Coron. Go right on the **D960** to Doué-la-Fontaine.

SPECIAL TO...

Puy du Fou is a historical theme park with costumed actors and superb re-creations, including a medieval city, Renaissance castle and 18th-century village. The *Cinéscénie* spectacular, staged on certain nights, uses over 80 actors, special effects and fireworks.

FOR HISTORY BUFFS

In a forest clearing beside the D196 after Maulévrier (on the way from Cholet to Doué-la-Fontaine), the chapel at the Cimetière des Martyrs commemorates victims of the Revolutionary fury in the Vendée Wars. Virtually alone in France, the Vendée region saw little to celebrate at the bicentennary of the Revolution in 1989.

❸ **Doué-la-Fontaine,** Loire Valley West

If you arrived in the middle of Doué without paying attention to its outskirts, you might shrug it off as an ordinary little town. It is far from that. The zoo, adapted from the cliffs, caverns and ditches of a disused limestone quarry, houses lions, tigers, lemurs, birds of prey, deer, emus, rarities such as snow panthers, and 15 separate monkey enclosures. Its Naturoscope has displays relating to the problems of threatened species and the destruction of their habitats.

The Musée des Commerces Anciens features seven old-style shops and a rose-water distillery, in partly-restored 18th-century stables.

Nobody is certain about the origins of Doué's arena, which is Roman in style but of a much later date. However, there is no doubt about the Moulin Cartier. Built in 1910, it was the last windmill raised in the region of Anjou.

BACK TO NATURE

Doué-la-Fontaine is France's great rose-growing centre. The Jardin des Roses displays dozens of different varieties, coloured crimson, scarlet and yellow – *Caroline de Monaco, Sarabande* and *Moulin Rouge* among them. Every July, an exhibition of 100,000 roses is held in the arena.

ℹ *Place du Champ de Foire*

▶ *Leave Doué on the D69 to Gennes. Go right as for Saumur on the D751 through La Mimerolle and into St-Hilaire.*

FOR HISTORY BUFFS

After Doué-la-Fontaine, turn left off the D69 for Rochemenier and its strange troglodyte village. You can visit furnished underground dwelling houses – with their cowsheds, barns, wine-cellars and even a chapel – still inhabited early this century.

❹ **St-Hilaire,** Loire Valley West

Just before this village suburb of Saumur, the Musée du Champignon, in a cave system cut into the roadside cliffs, is more than simply an exhibition about mushrooms and how they are grown. The underground galleries were dug in medieval times, part of a network of more than 480km (300 miles) throughout the district, which produces 75 per cent of France's cultivated mushrooms. Turn right in St-Hilaire for the École National d'Équitation. This is France's national riding academy, excellently housed and staffed. In the practice arena, in front of high wall mirrors, you may see members of the acadamy's Cadre Noire put their horses through the intricate, disciplined and stylish movements for which they are famous all over Europe. They also perform summer season shows.

▶ *Continue on the D751 into Saumur.*

❺ **Saumur,** Loire Valley West

Straddling the Loire, this very appealing town is passionate about horses and the cavalry, wines, museums and exuberant outdoor displays. The Château de Saumur, overlooking the river, houses three separate collections. The Musée des Arts

Décoratifs concentrates on the decorative arts – ceramics, enamelware, carvings in wood and alabaster. Another, Musée du Cheval, celebrates centuries of horsemanship; the third, Musée de la Figurine-Jouet has more than 20,000 models and figurines.

The cavalry has two separate exhibitions, one recalling its mounted days, the other taking the story to more recent times with a comprehensive display of tanks and armoured cars.

Second only to Champagne, Saumur is famous for its sparkling wines. Several firms welcome visitors to their cellars. Notre-Dame de Nantilly, dating from the 12th-century, houses a valuable collection of medieval and Renaissance tapestries. And the old quarter of Saumur with its restored 17th-century houses adds to the attractions of a justifiably self-confident town.

[i] *Place de la Bilange*

▶ *Leave Saumur on the N147 as for Le Mans. At the round*

······· SPECIAL TO... ·······

In Saumur, numerous wine cellars offer tastings of the region's wines.

about take the second exit to Vernantes on the D767. In Vernantes, turn sharp left at the traffic lights as for Baugé, then right on the D58 as for Baugé through Mouliherne. In Le Guédéniau go right in the D186 as for Lasse. Turn left following 'Les Caves de Chanzelles' sign. At the round-about in the forest take the fifth exit for Baugé. Rejoin the D58 and continue to Baugé.

❻ Baugé, Loire Valley West
Plenty of space has been left around Baugé's 15th-century castle, originally a hunting lodge of Good King René, Duke of Anjou. Holding displays of weapons, coins and ceramics,

The château at Saumur has been dubbed 'the castle of love'

it stands beside public gardens dipping to an attractive riverside. The Convent of La Girouardière houses a venerated relic – a jewelled cross believed to contain a piece of the True Cross brought to France by a crusader knight. Its unusual design was adopted as the Cross of Lorraine. Look also for Baugé's charming 17th-century Hospice-St-Joseph (not open to the public).

Sometimes an unfamiliar language may be seen or spoken here, describing Baugé, for instance, as 'bela kaj malmova urbeto': the Château de Grésillon, on your exit route from 'this fine old town', is an international Esperanto centre (not open to the public).

[i] *au Château*

········ BACK TO NATURE ········

Before Baugé, pause in the Forêt de Chandelais. Three-quarters of its trees are oak, most of the rest beech. Roe deer, wild boars and foxes live in the forest, and the beechwoods are alive with birdsong, including the liquid, fluty song of the golden oriole.

▶ *Leave Baugé on the D817, which becomes the D305, then go right on the D306 to Le Lude.*

❼ Le Lude, Loire Valley West
Pride of this little town is the richly furnished château, rebuilt in Renaissance style after an English garrison was driven out – with heavy damage to the fabric – in 1427. Its situation is most attractive, above balustraded gardens rising from the River Loir, whose waters eventually feed the larger Loire. One of France's most dramatic *son et lumière* presentations takes place here. It recalls five centuries of events and personalities, from the English occupation to the Second Empire. This outstanding show is enhanced

by fountains and a lively firework display reflected in the river. Cultural life in Le Lude includes a number of special events and festivals featuring horticulture, theatre, music, and children's events.

i Place Nicolay

▶ Leave Le Lude on the D307 to Pontvallain. Go right on the D13 through Mayet and across the N138 to Le Grand-Lucé. Turn left at the give way sign and left on the D304 as for Le Mans. Go under the bridge, then left following the 'Angers' sign, under another bridge and follow the 'Tours' signs along the N138. Go right at the roundabout on the D140 as for Arnage, then right on the D139 to the grandstands of the racing circuit.

RECOMMENDED WALKS

At the first right-hand bend after crossing the N138 between Le Lude and Le Grand-Lucé, bear left and follow signs to the Fontaine de la Coubre. A map opposite shows the waymarked footpaths in the Forêt de Bercé. They explore the beautiful deciduous woodland crossed by streams in the unexploited part of the forest, and the conifer plantations beyond. As the Foyer Rural Musée in Jupilles shows, this was once a great centre for ships' timbers and, later, wooden clogs. When you continue from Fontaine de la Coubre, turn right at the first crossroads then left to rejoin the D13 through Jupilles.

at speeds of over 320kph (200mph).

There is a smaller but linked Bugatti Circuit. The two tracks play host to five major car and motor-cycle events, plus a 24-hour truck race! You can watch test sessions from the main grandstands, which are informally open on non-competition days.

An excellent motor museum also recalls that this was where Wilbur Wright, over from the United States, made the first powered flight in Europe in 1908.

▶ Continue on the D139 into Le Mans.

9 Le Mans, Loire Valley West
Many first-time visitors to Le Mans will notice a familiarity – if, that is, they saw the film, *Cyrano de Bergerac*, which was

FOR CHILDREN

Le Lude has a number of attractions for children, including a swimming pool with a 43m (140ft) slide, canoe and pedalo hire, mini-golf, horse riding and a roller-skating track.

8 Le Mans Circuit, Loire Valley West
Prosaically, they may be the N138, D140 and D139, but these roads are also part of the great motor-racing circuit where the Le Mans 24-Hour Race is held every June.

The N138 is the Mulsanne Straight, along which Jaguars, Porsches and Mercedes howl

Fascinating exhibits in Le Mans' automobile museum

filmed in the shadow of the magnificent cathedral. It lies at the heart of a warren of cobbled medieval streets, lined with half-timbered buildings and Renaissance mansions. One of the lovliest of these houses the Musée de la Reine Bérengère, a celebration of Sarthe history. Queen Bérengère was Richard the Lionheart's widow, and she built the Cistercian abbey outside the town. Art lovers should make for the Musée de Tessé, which has a superb collection of paintings. In early July, a lively street festival takes over the town.

i Rue de l'Étoile

▶ Leave Le Mans on the **D309** as for Sablé. In Parcé cross the river then go first right at the crossroads, left to Solesmes then continue to Sablé-sur-Sarthe. Go straight across the **D306** for Centre-Ville. At the roundabout take the last exit, then a side road right for Pincé. This is the **D159**. Bear right on the **C15** for 'Pincé par la Forêt'. Rejoin the **D159** then follow the **D18** and **D52** through Morannes. Continue through Etriché and Tiercé. Go straight on along the **N160** then right on the **N23** to Angers.

10 Angers, Loire Valley West
Here in the heart of Anjou lies a university town of parks, gardens and colourful floral decorations, with a grand Plantagenet castle rising in towers of banded stonework. The Cathédrale Saint Maurice, is best approached by the Montée St-Maurice, a stairway climbing from the River Maine.

The longest tapestry in France, *La Tenture de l'Apocalypse*, completed in the late 14th century to show the Apocalypse, is on display in the castle. Angers is a tapestry town. Many others, ancient and modern, are on show in the castle itself and in individual museums and galleries.

Fine Renaissance buildings survive, both around the cathedral and elsewhere. River cruises follow the Maine, and for the adventurous there are hot-air balloon flights to waft you high above the castles, vineyards and villages of Anjou.

i 1 place du Président Kennedy

▶ Leave Angers through Les-Ponts-de-Cé on the **N160**. In Mûrs-Érigné, turn right to go through Chalonnes-sur-Loire and Champtoceaux on the **D751** and return on the **N249** to Nantes.

Detail of Catédrale St-Maurice's tympanum above the 12th-century west front door in Angers

FOR CHILDREN

On the return route to Nantes, turn left instead of right in Mûrs-Érigné to visit the Aquarium Tropical. It shows a brilliantly coloured collection of exotic fish from Asia, Africa and America swimming in tanks which have unexpected décors, such as the Grand Canyon or craters of the moon.

SCENIC ROUTES

From Nantes to Clisson the route runs through the attractive Muscadet vineyards. Around the D13, the Forêt de Bercé is one of the most beautiful areas in the district. The D751 after Angers runs along the lovely Corniche Angevine above the Loire. The Layon vineyards are impressive, but the route is at its best near the 'panorama' viewpoint at La Haie Longue ('the long hedge'). A roadside memorial commemorates the pioneer aviator René Gasnier, whose first flights were from the level fields across the river.

SPECIAL TO...

Angers is the home of Cointreau, which has been produced here since 1849. Guided one-hour tours of the distillery (La Distillerie Cointreau) show off the processes, production methods and famous advertising posters of this much-exported liqueur, but the recipe remains a secret.

Through
Château Country

Some of the most elegant castles in Europe are within easy
reach of Tours, in and around the valley of the Loire. Vineyards
abound in Touraine, 'the garden of France'. Although this route
starts and finishes beside the Loire, it also goes into the lonely
area of pools, farms and woodlands known as the Sologne.

3/4 DAYS • 428KM • 267 MILES

ITINERARY	
TOURS	▶ **Amboise (24km-15m)**
AMBOISE	▶ **Chenonceau**
	(13km-8m)
CHENONCEAU	▶ **Valençay (51km-32m)**
VALENÇAY	▶ **Romorantin-Lanthenay**
	(29km-18m)
ROMORANTIN-	▶ **La Sologne (18km-11m)**
LANTHENAY	
LA SOLOGNE	▶ **Gien (74km-46m)**
GIEN	▶ **Orléans (89km-55m)**
ORLÉANS	▶ **Chambord (54km-34m)**
CHAMBORD	▶ **Blois (17km-11m)**
BLOIS	▶ **Vouvray (50km-31m)**
VOUVRAY	▶ **Tours (9km-6m)**

i 78 rue Bernard-Palissy

▶ Leave Tours on the **D751** to Amboise.

❶ **Amboise,** Loire Valley Central

You will enter Amboise along a classic plane-tree avenue, with the Loire out of sight beyond the riverside embankment. The château's massive walls tower over the town centre streets. This impressive building is only a fifth of the size it was during its 16th-century heyday. A *son et lumière* presentation brings to life François I's glittering court of those days. In the Musée de la Poste, model coaches, postilions' liveries, records, engravings and other relics tell the story of the mail service by land, sea and air.

On the climb out of Amboise, pause at the exotic 18th-century pagoda of Chanteloup (all that remains of a château there). The topmost gallery of this 44m (144-foot) hillside tower is a splendid viewpoint over the Loire.

i 233 quai Général de Gaulle

SPECIAL TO...

In Amboise, be sure to visit the brick and stone house called Le Clos Lucé, home till his death, in 1519, of Leonardo da Vinci. The great artist and engineer was installed here by his patron François I, King of France, who was to buy the *Mona Lisa* and *Virgin on the Rocks* after Leonardo's death. Here Leonardo worked on astonishing engineering drawings. Forty of these, featuring machines resembling an aeroplane, a helicopter and an army tank, have been turned into an amazing display of three-dimensional models such as Leonardo himself never saw in his lifetime.

▶ After the pagoda turn left then right as for Chenonceaux on the **D81**. Go left on the

---

D40, then right to Château de Chenonceau.

❷ **Chenonceau,** Loire Valley Central

Lacking the final 'x' of the similarly named little town near by, with its ivied houses and old coaching inns, this 16th-century riverside castle was one of the most striking architectural exercises of its day. The bridge which linked it to the south bank of the Cher was adapted as a gallery of two storeys and attic-level rooms, with the River Cher flowing through the arches underneath. Extending for almost 61m (200 feet) across the river, this is still the most noteworthy feature of a richly furnished castle. Chenonceau stands surrounded by water channels. The woodland grounds include formal riverside gardens, and a waxworks museum recalls the personalities involved in its lively story. There are excellent *son et lumière* shows.

▶ Continue on the **D40**. In Chisseaux, go straight on the **D80** to Francueil, take the **D81** to Céré-la-Ronde, then the **C5** and **D90** to St-Aignan. Go left on the **D675**, right on the **D17**, right for Valençay on the **D33**, left on the **D37** in Villentrois and right on the **D956** into Valençay.

❸ **Valençay,** Loire Valley Central

The great 16th-century castle here was owned by several famous financiers. A half-inter-

Basilique St Martin's Tour Charlemagne, in Tours

est in the vast 19,000-hectare (47,000-acre) estate was briefly held by the Scotsman John Law, who introduced the system of credit. In 1719–20 he dominated the French banking system, until his enterprises collapsed in insolvencies and rancour.

Later, Valençay became the residence of Talleyrand, Napoleon's foreign minister, whose diplomats and dignitaries were extravagantly entertained. From 1808 to 1813 Ferdinand VII of Spain was held in virtual house arrest here, which is why the town's Hôtel d'Espagne is so named. A *son et lumière* show brings these varied characters back to life.

The castle is still lavishly furnished. Fallow deer graze in a sunken park, and you will hear peacocks' screams echoing through the grounds. Do not be put off by the ramshackle

---

FOR CHILDREN

On the way to Valençay turn right on the D657 in St-Aignan to the Zoo Parc de Beauval. Originally a bird garden, Beauval has expanded to house a splendid collection of lions and tigers, panthers, pumas and jaguars.

---

appearance of the separate motor museum, whose exhibits include a spidery Bedelia cycle-car of 1914, a lovely little 1930 Amilcar sports model and an Alpine-Renault of 1971.

[i] *2 avenue de la Résistance*

▶ *Leave Valençay on the D4 through Chabris, then continue straight ahead on the D128. Cross the N76 and follow the signs to Romorantin-Lanthenay.*

❹ Romorantin-Lanthenay, Loire Valley Central

In this 'capital' of the Sologne district, the River Sauldre splits into several channels. From the main-road bridge there is a most beautiful view downstream to the ivy-covered walls and colourful flower boxes of the restored watermills.

The town centre includes several attractive buildings, notably the ancient-timbered Carroir d'Orée which houses an archaeological museum. The Musée de la Sologne, housed in an old mill, is devoted to local rural life and traditions, with domestic, hunting and historical art displays of the Sologne.

Matra, the aerospace company, has a factory here. The town's L'Espace Matra Automobile, under develop-

Valançay château is a fine example of classic Renaissance architecture

ment at the time of writing, houses historic Matra competition cars, such as a Le Mans 24-Hour Race winner and Jackie Stewart's Formula One Matra-Ford V8.

[i] *Place de la Paix*

▶ *Leave Romorantin-Lanthenay for Loreux on the D49 and continue to Marcilly-en-Gault. Turn left at the T-junction there and first right for St-Viâtre, still on the D49.*

❺ La Sologne, Loire Valley Central

At St-Viâtre you are well into the Sologne, a huge tract of more than half a million hectares (nearly 2,000 square miles). It is an all but level countryside of heath and woodland, widely separated arable and livestock farms, red-tiled brick houses and hundreds of lonely pools. In this slightly mysterious landscape, whose people are regarded in other parts of France as clannish and self-contained, only the trees create any kind of horizon.

The Sologne is also a land of hunters, wild-fowlers and fishermen. Until the second half of the 19th century much of it was unhealthily covered by even greater areas of stagnant water. Extensive drainage schemes and tree-planting created the landscape of today.

▶ Leave St-Viâtre on the **D49**, then avoid the left turn for Lamotte-Beuvron and go straight ahead on the **D93** to Nouan-le-Fuzelier. Go left as for Orléans, then right as for Chaon on the **D122** and left on the **D44**. Go right on the **D923** as for Aubigny to Clémont. Turn left at the crossroads on the **D7**, then follow signs to Étang du Puits. Continue to the **D948**, turn right for Argent-sur-Sauldre then left on the **D940** to Gien.

cation to St Joan is appropriate. It was here in 1429 that she first made contact with the Dauphin's army and began her mission to liberate France.

ⅰ *Centre Anne de Beaujeu, Place Jean-Jaures*

▶ Leave Gien for Lorris on the **D44**. Continue as for Bellegarde. Immediately after the 'La Chaussée' sign take the first left. Go right on the **V3** into Coudroy. Turn left at the stop sign, through Vieilles-Maisons-sur-Joudry and left on the **D88**. Bend right then left, and watch for a right turn at the crossroads along a gravel forest road, passing the '3t' sign. Bear left at a junction

of forest roads, left after a 50m warning sign for give way ahead, and turn right along the tarred road (this is the **D961**). Turn right on the **D952** and follow the **N60** and the **N152** to Orléans.

FOR CHILDREN

The kids will have plenty of opportunity to work off some energy at the Étang du Puits, before you reach Gien. This wooded recreational lake offers sandy beaches, rowing boat and pedalo hire, pony rides and a little children's playground. Sailing dinghies and windsurfers skim the water.

6 Gien, Loire Valley Central
From a leafy promenade by the Loire, the hillside in this town, famous for its faïenceware, rises to a little plateau shared by the 15th-century castle and the modern church, both of brick rather than stone. The castle houses the Musée International de la Chasse, with displays on every aspect of hunting.

Replacing a building wrecked in World War II, the church shows inside and out, what decorative effects can be achieved in brickwork. Its dedi-

Gien has been meticulously restored since World War II

RECOMMENDED WALKS

Pause for a few minutes at Coudroy, after leaving Gien. Here, there is a short footpath which follows the bank of the Orléans Canal. Only fishermen now come to this 300-year-old waterway, long since closed to navigation.

FOR HISTORY BUFFS

In Lorris, after leaving Gien, turn left on the D961 to find the Musée de la Résistance et de la Déportation. Set in well-tended gardens, it tells the story of the Resistance movement in World War II through displays of documents, photographs, maps and weapons, and newspapers of the clandestine press.

i   *Place Albert 1er*

▶ *Leave Orléans on the N152
as for Blois, avoiding the
autoroute. Continue through
Meung-sur-Loire to
Beaugency. Go left on the
D925 as for Limoges, crossing
the river bridge. Continue
straight over the D951 and
on to La Ferté-St-Cyr. Go right
on the D103 to Crouy, left on
the D33 and continue
through the Parc de
Chambord to Chambord.*

SPECIAL TO...

At Beaugency, between Orléans
and Chambord, follow signs to
the Musée Dunois. In a 15th-
century castle, the arts and traditions of the district round
Orléans are preserved. Each of
its rooms has a special theme
such as furniture, toys or
costumes.

FOR HISTORY BUFFS

On the way from Orléans to
Chambord, turn left in Meung-
sur-Loire for the château and
its grim medieval dungeons.
They feature a torture
chamber and a hideous underground oubliette where prisoners generally died in an agony
of starvation or disease. One
famous prisoner in the 15th
century was the vagabond poet
François Villon.

7 Orléans, Loire Valley
Central
Every spring, Orléans organises
a festival celebrating Joan of
Arc's intervention – not at all
appreciated by the French official army commanders – which
raised the English siege of the
city in 1429. Visit the Maison
Jeanne d'Arc for the whole
dramatic story. Her equestrian
statue stands in the Place du
Martroi.

The Musée des Beaux-Arts
houses a valuable collection of
French and Italian paintings.
Now used for civic receptions,
the luxuriously furnished 16th-
century Hôtel Groslot is open to
visitors. The Musée Historique
et Archéologique (local history
and archaeology) is housed in
the Renaissance surroundings of
the Hôtel Cabu.

Cathédrale Sainte-Croix
dominates the townscape above

Orléans' splendid neo-Gothic
Cathédrale Sainte-Croix

the Loire. Look inside for its
stained-glass windows telling
the story of Joan of Arc, its
beautifully carved choir stalls
and its 32 18th-century medal-
lions illustrating the life of
Christ.

BACK TO NATURE

In Orléans, the magnificent
floral park called La Source
takes it name from a curious
natural feature. Officially, the
River Loiret rises here. In fact,
its waters are diverted from
the Loire almost 30km (19
miles) upstream. They disappear
underground for all that
distance before welling up again
in the park.

8 Chambord, Loire Valley
Central
The Renaissance château of
Chambord is the biggest of all
the castles of the Loire. Begun
as the favourite hunting lodge of
François I, it has no fewer than
440 rooms, and stands in the
midst of a 5,443-hectare
(13,450-acre) estate circled by a
32km (20-mile) wall.

Most of the forested estate is
a hunting reserve, but parts of it
are open to visitors. Chambord
is beautifully furnished, with

fine paintings and tapestries. It houses an exhibition on hunting, and another on its own history. A viewing terrace stands high among the intricate rooftop decorations.

BACK TO NATURE

Turn left off the **D33** in the Parc de Chambord for a high-level 'hide', from which you can watch a herd of red deer in a grazing enclosure in the forest.

▶ Continue on the **D33**. After Nanteuil go under the bridge through St-Gervais-la-Forêt and right on the **D956** to Blois.

9 **Blois,** Loire Valley Central
A gorgeous open-air staircase built for François I (and possibly designed by Leonardo da Vinci) is only one of the architectural delights of the hilltop castle here. The same king commissioned the decorated façade which overlooks the lovely little garden in the Place Victor-Hugo.
    Archaeological and fine arts museums are housed in the castle and there is a gallery

devoted to Robert Houdin, the great 19th-century conjuror from whom the escapologist Houdini took his stage name. In the town, a street, a stairway and a statue commemorate Denis Papin, an early steam-engine pioneer. There is also an excellent museum on the natural history of the area, situated in the ancient cloisters of Les Jacobins.
    Attractive old buildings include the half-timbered Maison des Acrobates, with its carvings of jugglers and tumblers. Bicycles can be hired from the railway station and several shops in town.

ℹ️ 3 avenue du Dr-Jean-Laigret

RECOMMENDED WALKS

Ask at one of the tourist offices about walks around the Val de Cisse. Monteaux, between Blois and Vouvray, is a good centre for them. Using minor road and field tracks, you can wander through farms, woods and vineyards on a fresh, airy plateau above the valley of the Loire.

▶ Leave Blois on the **N152** as for Tours. In Veuves, turn right on the **D65** to Monteaux. Bear left for Cangey along the **D58** which becomes the **D1**. Continue through Limeray. Keep left in Pocé-sur-Cisse as for Amboise then go right following the 'Vouvray' sign. Turn left on the **D46** and continue to Vouvray.

10 **Vouvray,** Loire Valley Central
There hardly seem to be enough vineyards around Vouvray to justify its reputation as a white wine village, but most are on the upland plateau hidden by lime stone cliffs. You can buy wine at several caves, some of them dug into the limestone. The Écomusée explains the cultivation of vines, shows old-style crafts including the sewing of the local embroidered bonnets, and describes the impact on the countryside of the TGV superexpress railway lines.

ℹ️ Rue Gambetta

▶ Leave Vouvray on the **N152** and return to Tours.

Royal Blois: a former capital of France and famous for its château

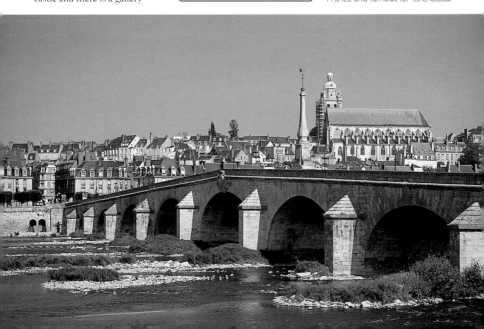

THE DORDOGNE & SOUTHWEST FRANCE

Here is another region which shows the remarkable variety of France. On the coast there are uninterrupted expanses of surf-washed beaches. Behind them stretch vast areas planted with pines. The Pyrenean foothills offer bracing spa resorts where walks by mountain streams and wildflower meadows are the order of the day. In the valleys of the Dordogne and the Vézère you will find the greatest cluster of prehistoric sites in Europe, many of them troglodytic dwellings quarried thousands of years ago.

Lourdes attracts millions of pilgrims and visitors every year. Smaller numbers make the journey to the glorious hilltop church in St-Bertrand-de-Comminges. You can visit weird underground caverns, one group bizarrely reached, not by going deep into the bowels of the earth, but by heading uphill in a cable car, and you can find out about traditional rural crafts and ways of life in display areas large and small.

Oysters are a major crop where the Bordeaux route reaches the coast. Inland, connoisseurs of wine and brandy can lose themselves among the vineyards of Armagnac, Bergerac, Barsac, Graves and Sauternes.

West and south of Bordeaux there are few natural obstacles to divert the roads from long, flat straights through the forests. Winding river valleys are the norm for Périgueux. The Pau tour, as it climbs into the Pyrenees, is for pass-stormers.

Some of France's most glorious towns and villages are here. Rocamadour is one of the most stunningly located places in Europe, but there are also Domme and Sarlat and Labastide-d'Armagnac to cherish.

Wildlife parks include bird reserves, zoos for endangered species and an atmospheric place devoted to the ancient worship of the bear. You can find out in museums and exhibitions about tobacco, seaplanes, prehistoric art, clockwork figures and hussars.

Bordeaux

Bordeaux is the capital of Aquitaine and of wine, the heart of a region of world-renowned vineyards. It was one of the first cities in France to pedestrianise its shopping streets, and a pioneer in computerised traffic management. Among its elegant public buildings, look for the river façade of the 18th-century Place de la Bourse and the sumptuous Grand-Théâtre of the same era. There are bustling covered markets, craft shops and studios of every kind. Museums and galleries take in painting and decorative arts, the history of the region of Aquitaine, vintage printing presses, natural history collections with magnificent crystal displays, the customs service, military history and the Resistance movement. Cruise boats sail down the Garonne and their joint estuary, the Gironde. A particularly exciting touring opportunity is a helicopter jaunt over your own selection of Bordeaux vineyards.

Périgueux

Périgueux is a handsome town whose beautiful old quarter, where the merchants and craftsmen used to live, includes many fine Renaissance and medieval buildings. The perhaps over-restored cathedral, Saint-Front, is a fascinating sight, all domes and cupolas, giving Périgueux an almost Ottoman-Empire skyline.

The Musée du Périgord in Cours Tourny has expanded well beyond its original brief to exhibit the results of excavated Roman sites. The Musée Militaire shows uniforms and weapons from several centuries, and tells the story of the district's war-ravaged past. There are pleasant gardens, and squares with pollarded trees. You can stroll along the rue des Gladiateurs to the site of the Roman arena. This is a cool place in summer, planted with shrubs and trees, its fragmentary Roman archways within sight and sound of a modern mosaic-tiled fountain.

Pau

In the 19th century, the British invaded Pau, but not with any martial intent. Three Scots laid out a golf course for the British colony. At the turn of the century and through the 1920s, Pau was one of the great British resorts of Europe. There was American influence, too. Orville and Wilbur Wright set up the world's first aviation school here. The town has lovely parks and gardens. Find the boulevard des

Opposite: vineyard in Bordeaux
Above: the opulent, fertile valley of the Dordogne at Périgueux

Pyrénées and you will see not only a fine promenade, but also a glorious southern mountain horizon. A rebuilt funicular railway climbs from a lower avenue.

Some of the finest state rooms in France are in the majestic, much restored, château, which houses a rich collection of tapestries. On one weekend in June, Pau echoes to the scream of high-pitched engines. There is a famous racing circuit here, including public roads and driveways to the leafy Parc Beaumont.

Coast, Dunes
& Forests

South of Bordeaux, the flatness of the Landes region is disguised by two notable features. Along the coast there are long fine-sand beaches backed by substantial dunes, while inland lies a huge forest area with carefully watered croplands in extensive clearings.

4 DAYS • 486KM • 301 MILES

ITINERARY		
BORDEAUX	▶	**Gujan-Mestras** (47km-29m)
GUJAN-MESTRAS	▶	**Arcachon** (13km-8m)
ARCACHON	▶	**Biscarrosse** (42km-26m)
BISCARROSSE	▶	**Mimizan** (38km-24m)
MIMIZAN	▶	**Sabres** (47km-29m)
SABRES	▶	**Mont-de-Marsan** (81km-50m)
MONT-DE-MARSAN	▶	**Labastide-d'Armagnac** (29km-18m)
LABASTIDE-D'ARMAGNAC	▶	**Barbotan-les-Thermes** (16km-10m)
BARBOTAN-LES-THERMES	▶	**Nérac** (42km-26m)
NÉRAC	▶	Sauternes (82km-51m)
SAUTERNES	▶	Bordeaux (49km-30m)

[i] 12 cours du XXX Juillet,
Bordeaux

▶ Leave Bordeaux on the
N250. Go straight ahead on
the **D650** through Le Teich to
Gujan-Mestras.

BACK TO NATURE

Turn right in Le Teich, on the
way to Gujan-Mestras, at the
'Parc Ornitholigique' sign. The
bird reserve herein the scrubland delta by the Bassin
d'Arcachon is especially strong
in wildfowl, but you should also
look for whiskered terns, black-
winged stilts, herons, storks and
little egrets, as well as
numerousdragonflies.

---

❶ Gujan-Mestras, Aquitaine
The two parts of this strung-out
cluster of villages on the southern side of the great Bassin
d'Arcachon could hardly be
more oddly matched. Take any
of the streets with 'port' signs,
to the right of the main road,
and you enter the almost timeless world of the oyster farmer.
The ports are seven rectangular
inlets of the bay, lined by identi-
cal wooden workshop cabins.

Outside lies the paraphernalia
of oyster cultivation – boat
tackle, mounds of emptied
shells and sharpened wooden
stakes to be driven into the sea
bed where the oysters grow.

Elsewhere, Gujan-Mestras is
a modern holiday resort. Turn
left for the 'Parc Aquatique'
(water park) called Aqualand.
The pools, slides, wave
machine and water chutes of
Aqualand share the large leisure
area at La Hume with the
Village Médiéval d'Artisans
d'Art, where serious craftworkers settle every summer. There
is also a well-stocked museum
of ship models and ship design.

[i] 19 avenue du mal de Lattre
de Tassigny

FOR CHILDREN

Street signs in Gujan-Mestras
are decorated with ladybirds –
coccinelles – the emblem of the
town La Coccinelle animal park
at La Hume continues the
theme. Here, children can walk
among domestic and farm
animals, with pony rides,
trampolines, swings and
toboggans as a bonus.

Arcachon's modern yacht marina
provides a safe haven

▶ Continue on the **D650** to
Arcachon.

❷ Arcachon, Aquitaine
Although the oysters of the
Bassin d'Arcachon have been
celebrated since the 16th
century, the town itself is a
resort created in the railway age.
Arcachon has a well-equipped
yacht haven and fishing port. A
high-set figure of Christ blesses
the harbour. Walk to the end of
the breakwater and you will see
not only the far-out oyster beds
but also a stone anchor sailors'
memorial. The aquarium and
museum specialise in the crea-
tures of the bay and the open
sea. You can sail to the oyster
beds, to the Île aux Oiseaux
(Bird's Island) in the bay, and
across the mouth of the bay to
the peninsula resort of Cap
Ferret. Back from the waterfront the town has lively shopping and café areas, and it is
generously supplied with woods
and parkland. Arcachon's status
as the most stylish resort on the
Côte d'Argent ('silver coast') is
well deserved.

[i] Esplanade Georges Pompidou

BACK TO NATURE

South of Arcachon, the Dune du Pilat is the greatest sand dune in Europe, more than 106m (350 feet) high and extending for nearly 3km (1¾ miles). You will not be able to see its imperceptible wind-driven inland movement, but take the long stairway to the summit for a beautiful view of pine forests and the sea. Heathland in the area supports Dartford warblers, red-backed shrikes and wrynecks, as well as plenty of insect life.

RECOMMENDED WALKS

After the Dune du Pilat south of Arcachon, the D218 runs through the pinewoods, scrub and sandhills of the Forêt de la Teste. Park here, and you will find many informal footpaths off to the right, leading to beaches lapped by the Atlantic breakers.

▶ *Leave Arcachon on the D218 to Pyla-sur-Mer and past the Dune du Pilat to Biscarrosse.*

8 Biscarrosse, Aquitaine
A pinewood resort with bunga-lows, hotels and a few colour-washed apartment blocks, Biscarrossé-Plage has a not-yet-finished air, added to by the fact that sand blows around its streets. But there is a splendid beach here, backed by dunes, with white-topped breakers creaming in. The older part of the settlement, Biscarrosse-Bourg or Biscarrosse-Ville, is separated from the beach resort by a full 9.6km (6 miles) of open road. This is a handsome place. Its church stands among bright and well-watered gardens dotted with birch trees.

On the southwestern edge of town lies an attractive lake rimmed by low wooded hills. This is a good sailing and angling centre, and it was briefly, between the wars, the French base of a flying-boat service from New York. The Musée de l'Hydraviation, on the road to the lake, recalls those flying-boat days, and there is a Musée de la Nature.

☐ *439 avenue de la Plage*

▶ *Leave Biscarrosse on the D652 through Parentis-en-Born to St-Eulalie, then take the D87 to Mimizan.*

FOR HISTORY BUFFS

Parentis-en-Born, on the way from Biscarrosse to Mimizan, is a place with a rustic appearance and a pleasant lakeside. Incongruously, since 1954, oil has been pumped from the lake bed and from offshore deposits. The Musée du Pétrole tells the story of this local industry.

4 Mimizan, Aquitaine
This is another split-personality town, approached along the shore of the Étang d'Aureilhan, where Winston Churchill was often a guest of the Duke of Westminster on an estate there. He left several paintings of local scenes. Mimizan divides at the Papeteries de Gascogne, a huge papermill which wafts an unmistakable smell along the prevailing wind. The holiday resort is very modern, with fine beaches ideal for surfing. You can explore the forest to the south, on foot or along the cycle tracks.

The inland part of Mimizan is built round a largely derelict

Mimizan's fine sandy beach lies to the west of the town

11th-century Benedictine abbey. The little town museum faces it. In summer the riverside bull-ring promotes *courses landaises*, acrobatic affairs, similar to the Provençal form of bull-fighting in which the bulls are unharmed. Stilt-walking is another speciality.

i 39 avenue Maurice Martin

▶ Leave Mimizan on the **D44** to Sabres.

FOR HISTORY BUFFS

On the D44 before Sabres, the village of Solférino recalls a battlefield in Italy. The estate here, owned by Napoleon III, was given the name after his successful part in the battle against Austria in 1859. A museum holds mementoes of his Second Empire.

---

5 Sabres, Aquitaine
A pleasant if unremarkable road-junction village, with its half-timbered houses and old church, Sabres still has a station on the railway built in 1890 to link it with Mimizan. The line is now used to take visitors to the remotely located Écomusée at Marquèze, 5km (3 miles) to the northwest.

This splendid place is part of the Parc Régional des Landes de Gascogne. Displays make it clear how the great forests used to support little local industries such as iron and glass works, brick and tile kilns. Then, in the second half of the 19th century, the government decided to manage the pine forests on a virtually industrial scale.

Marquèze, based on a large forest clearing, shows you both how the timber resources have been exploited and what kinds of activity were discarded – charcoal-burning, water-mills, sheep-farming and the cultivation of fruit trees. Traditional buildings, many of them raised on stilts, have been painstakingly reconstructed here.

▶ Leave Sabres on the **N134** as for Bordeaux. In Trensacq turn right on the **D45**. Turn right on the **D651** through Luxey, then continue to Mont-de-Marsan.

FOR CHILDREN

On the way to Mont-de-Marsan, to keep the children occupied on the drive across the flat forest and farmland after Trensacq, ask them to count how many bends there are in the 18km (11 miles) of the D45.

SPECIAL TO...

On the way to Mont-de-Marsan, turn left in Luxey following the 'Écomusée' sign, and park beside the church. The nearby museum deals with the uses of resin from the vast pine forests of the Landes.

The Écomusée at Marquèze is an open-air museum documenting the life of the Landes region

6 Mont-de-Marsan,
Aquitaine
You will not be long in Mont de-Marsan before realising that this is a place of some consequence. Its elegant 19th-century public buildings, immaculately kept, stand among modern equivalents, which are imaginative in design, but do not clash. In fact, Mont-de-Marsan is an important government centre.

It stands where the Rivers Midou and Douze merge into the waggishly named Midouze. The Parc Jean Rameau is an attractive woodland area, with many flowering shrubs, overlooking the Douze.

Musée Despiau Wlérick, the only museum in France devoted exclusively to 20th-century sculpture, is named after two local sculptors. Its terrace offers a superb view over the town and river. The town also has a modern art gallery, with varied collections. The Church of Ste Madeleine is worth visiting for its marble-work and elegant ornamented ceiling.

Like Mimizan, Mont-de-Marsan is a centre for *courses landaises*, but the great sporting enthusiasm is for horse-racing. The impressive race-course plays host to a dozen meetings every year.

[i] *6 place du Général Leclerc*

cursory mention, but go to the flowery Place Royale and you will find an architectural gem.

Away from the square, a 17th-century chapel houses an exhibition of the *bastides*, the historic fortified villages.

Beyond Labastide, turn right on the C1 for Château Garreau. At the end of a dusty gravel road between its ridgetop vineyards, the estate's Musée du Vigneron has exhibits on old distillery techniques and equipment, and on local rural life.

[i] *Place Royal*

SPECIAL TO...

About 2.4km (1½ miles) beyond Labastide-d'Armagnac, look for the isolated 11th-century church called Notre-Dame des Cyclistes. Since 1959 this historic building has been a cyclists' sanctuary, with old machines and the jerseys of famous race-winners on display.

Cool, shady arches in the Place Royale, Labastide-d'Armagnac

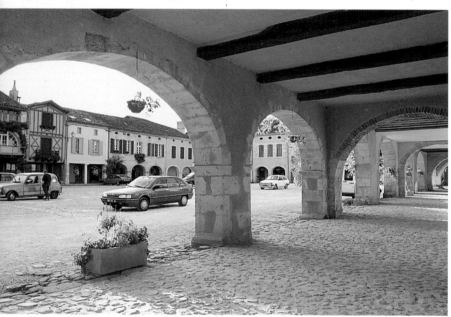

▶ *Leave Mont-de-Marsan on the **D932** as for Roquefort. Bear right on the **D933** to St-Justin, then right on the **D626** to Labastide-d'Armagnac.*

7 Labastide-d'Armagnac,
Aquitaine
Almost miraculously, the arcaded square here, Place Royale, has survived with little alteration since 1291. Three sides are still taken up by arches and cool, covered walk-ways. The fourth features the 15th-century church. Some guidebooks give Labastide a

RECOMMENDED WALKS

Ask at the tourist office in Labastide-d'Armagnac for the map of the waymarked walks southwest of the little town. They climb gently into a lush landscape of woodlands, farms and Armagnac vineyards.

▶ *Continue on the **D626** to Cazaubon and turn left on the **D656** to Barbotanles-Thermes.*

8 Barbotan-les-Thermes,
Aquitaine
Unlike the spa towns of some other countries, those in France have not mouldered away. Barbotan, whose thermal baths were probably known to the Romans, has been completely refurbished. Brightly decorated hotels, shops, cafés and restau-rants line the busy and effec-tively pedestrianised main street. Sparkling new buildings house the baths which attract an increasing number of *curistes* (cure-seekers) – more than 20,000 of them every year.

There are attractive gardens, pleasant walks and an opportunity to admire relics of the past, such as the 12th-century church whose clocktower is built above one of the medieval town gateways.

Just outside Barbotan is the Lac de l'Uby. This well-equipped leisure area offers sailing, tennis and mini-golf facilities as well as a sandy beach, pony rides, pedalo hire and a children's play park.

[i] *Maison du Curiste*

▶ *Continue on the D656 through Gabarret to Nérac.*

9 Nérac, Aquitaine
Only one wing remains, high above the River Baïse, of Nérac's lovely Renaissance château. Climb the stairs to the elegant, open, first-floor gallery, and you will find a museum of archaeology and history. Close by, the Church of St Nicholas has a severe frontage but some good 18th-century stained glass. There are grand views across the river to Petit Nérac, a hillside quarter of fine old buildings with dark red roofs. Its church spire soars in glorious silhouette against the sky.

River boats run cruises on the Baïse. Upstream, the Promenade de la Garenne offers you a stroll through a pleasant woodland park with fountains and an open-air theatre.

▶ *Leave Nérac on the D930 to Lavardac, then go left to Casteljaloux and follow signs to Bazas. Continue to Villandraut Turn right on the D8 through Nouillan and Brouquet, then left on the D125 to Sauternes.*

10 Sauternes, Aquitaine
Arriving at Sauternes, the centre of one of the most famous white wine districts, you will come to the Place de l'Église, which would be the heart of the village if there were a village for it to be the heart of. Only a handful of

buildings surround the square, one of them where the local wine producers offer their wares. There is also a map locating the eight vineyards which regularly welcome visitors.

Not included in this display is the aristocratic 16th- and 17th-century Château Yquem. Its Château Yquem wine, with the superlative classification of *Premier Grand Cru Classé*, was the first to be produced from grapes affected with the 'noble rot' provoked by the misty mornings and warm afternoons of autumn.

[i] *11 rue Principale*

▶ *Continue on the D125 as for Budos, then go right on the D114. Follow this road over the autoroute to the N113. Turn left there through Barsac and return to Bordeaux, avoiding the autoroute.*

The Church of St Nicholas in the town of Nérac

SCENIC ROUTES

Heading south for Biscarrosse-Plage, the D218 runs through the attractive pine and sandhill country of the Forêt de la Teste.
Later, the D146 continues in similar country over a low winding pass among the pinewood dunes.
Around Luxey, the D651 leads across a lovely quiet countryside of forests and farms, with characteristic timber-framed houses and attractive villages drowsing in the summer sun.
Immediately after Sauternes, the D125 opens up a delicious little landscape of undulating vineyards in the valley of the River Ciron.

Journey into
Prehistory

Although there are remains of old Roman buildings in the heart of
Périgueux, this tour, featuring two of France's loveliest rivers, the
Dordogne and the Vézère, takes you much further back into the
history of man. Here, limestone provides the huge cliffs, the amazing caves and underground rivers, and the golden building stone of
beautiful towns like Sarlat and Domme.

4 DAYS • 383KM • 238 MILES

ITINERARY

PÉRIGUEUX	►	Grotte du Grand Roc (44km-27m)
GROTTE DU GRAND ROC	►	Les Eyzies (3km-2m)
LES EYZIES	►	Lascaux II (30km-19m)
LASCAUX II	►	Sarlat-la-Canéda (27km-17m)
SARLAT-LA-CANÉDA	►	Souillac (34km-21m)
SOUILLAC	►	Gouffre de Padirac (38km-24m)
GOUFFRE DE PADIRAC	►	Rocamadour (29km-18m)
ROCAMADOUR	►	Domme (52km-32m)
DOMME	►	Les Milandes (15km-9m)
LES MILANDES	►	Bergerac (62km-39m)
BERGERAC	►	Périgueux (49km-30m)

[i] *26 place Francheville, Périgueux*

▶ *Leave Périgueux on the*
N2089 as for Brive. Go right
on the D710, left on the D45
then right on the D47 to
Grotte du Grand Roc.

SCENIC ROUTES

The approach to the Grotto du
Grand Roc on the D47
introduces the stunning
limestone cliffs which
characterise this tour.

---

❶ Grotte du Grand Roc,
Aquitaine
The great natural limestone
wall here, facing the Vézère,
with its overhangs forming the
pitched roof lines of some
bizarrely located houses, is
honeycombed with ancient
dwellings and caverns. In the
Grotte du Grand Roc you will
find an underground wonder-
land whose cave floors and
hanging gardens of fretted limestone look like a spiky coral reef
(wire grills protect some of the
formations). In the same
magnificent cliff, the prehistoric
rock shelters of Laugerie Haute

and Laugerie Basse, which
yielded countless objects left
behind by their Ice-Age inhabi-
tants, are open to visitors.

Less forbidding than its
name, the Gorge d'Enfer
(Gorge of Hell) is set in a little
wooded, grassy side valley
whose caves display 25,000-
year-old wall carvings. There is
also a fishing lake and a picnic
site. Further on, the Musée de
Spéléologie, entered by a stairway up a colossal overhanging
cliff, illustrates the daring work
of the modern cave explorers.

▶ *Continue on the D47 into*
Les Eyzies.

❷ Les Eyzies, Aquitaine
If the Vézère is the 'valley of
mankind', the village of Les
Eyzies, spectacularly located
between a northern limestone
cliff and the river, is at the heart
of the greatest concentration of
prehistoric sites. The Musée
National de la Préhistoire, built
into the cliff face, is devoted in
particular to the palaeolithic era,
starting perhaps 2½–3 million
years ago with the first traces of
primitive man. Near by, the
Abri Pataud is a cliff shelter
dating back to more than 20,000

years ago, and Abri de Cap
Blanc has prehistoric sculptures
of bison and horses. A new
museum and research centre is
due to open in 2000.

[i] *Place de la Mairie*

▶ *Leave Les Eyzies on the*
D706 to Montignac. Turn right
on the D704, then right again
for Lascaux II.

❸ Lascaux II, Aquitaine
The caves at Lascaux were
discovered in 1940 by some
boys, out on a rabbiting expedi-
tion. They are decorated with
the most celebrated prehistoric
paintings in the world – lively
representations of bulls, deer
and horses created nearly 18,000
years ago by Cro-Magnon man.
The caves have had to be closed
to the public to prevent deterio-
ration of the original paintings,
but painstakingly exact replicas
are on display at the neighbouring site called Lascaux II. A
visit here cures visitors of any
notion that our ancestors of 800
generations ago were nothing
more than primitive louts.

Périgueux has a rich historical
mixture of architectural styles

Replicas of Lascaux' original cave paintings on show at Lascaux II

Much older than Lascaux, the nearby cave site of Régourdou is open to visitors. The brown bears in its park match displays in its museum about the pre-historic cult of the bear.

ⓘ *Place Léo-Magne, Montignac*

▶ *Return to Montignac and turn right on the **D704** to Sarlat-la-Canéda.*

FOR HISTORY BUFFS

Off the **D706**, after Les Eyzies, several sites illustrate the everyday life of our very remote ancestors. La Roque-St-Christophe is an amazing troglodytic fortress town, lived in from prehistoric days to the 18th century, with five great terraces overlooking the River Vézère. At Le Thot, a modern museum and gallery explain the environment and art of prehistoric times. In the parkland, present-day animals such as red and fallow deer, bison, tarpan and Przewalski's horses can be compared with life-size replicas of mammoths and aurochs (an extinct type of ox).

---

❹ Sarlat-la-Canéda, Aquitaine

The golden stone of Sarlat and the effortless grace of its Gothic and Renaissance buildings make this one of the loveliest towns in the Dordogne region. Even the tourist information office is housed in a 15th-century mansion near the handsome cathedral of the 16th and 17th centuries. Shaded alleys and courtyards in the old town are busy with a craftsmen's market and shops, many selling *foie gras*. There is an imaginative Aquarium concentrating on the 30 or more species of fish found in the River Dordogne. On a wooded hillside above the square, pleasant public gardens can be found.

ⓘ *Place de la Liberté*

▶ *Leave Sarlat-la-Canéda on the **D46** for Vitrac. In Vitrac-Port watch for a left turn on to the **D703** to Carsac and Souillac. Turn left on to the **N20** in Souillac.*

SCENIC ROUTES

The first ridge-top road on the tour is the **D704** to Sarlat, giving wide-ranging views over rolling wooded hills.

---

❺ Souillac, Midi-Pyrénées

The glory of this busy centre in the Dordogne valley is the restored 12th-century Romanesque church called Abbatiale Sainte Marie, whose red-and-white tiled roofs culminate in a series of cupolas, as in the cathedral at Périgueux. The carvings in the church are particularly fine. Behind the church you may hear the incongruous music of a 1920s jazz band. This is just one of the lifelike exhibits in the Musée de l'Automate. Tableaux of moving life-size figures also include a glamorous lady snake-charmer, a clown and a splendid 19th-century Passion Play.

ⓘ *Boulevard Louis-Jean Malvy*

FOR CHILDREN

The prehistoric dwellings of Les Eyzies are as fascinating to children as they are to adults, but Prehisto-Parc wraps it all up for them in theme park style. It features outdoor tableaux of Neanderthal and Cro-Magnon (a type of 'modern' man), hunting expeditions and household scenes of 15,000 years ago.

► Leave Souillac on the **D703** to Martel. Turn right on the **N140**, then left on the **D70** and then right on the **D11** to Miers and left on the **D91**. Go left on the **D60**, right at the Y-junction at the stone cross, then finally right at the T-junction to Gouffre de Padirac.

SCENIC ROUTES

After Montvalent, on the way from Souillac to Padirac, there is a landscape change as the D70 and D11 run through the parcels of sheep-grazed land on the limestone plateau known as the *causse*.

6 Gouffre de Padirac, Midi-Pyrénées

Open since the late 19th century when it was discovered, the Padirac chasm is one of the greatest underground sights in Europe. Lifts and stairways descend to the otherworldly cavern of a subterranean river where, by boat and pathway, you can visit glorious floodlit limestone chambers like the Great Dome Gallery, walls of stalagmites and a petrified waterfall. Cafés and restaurants, a picnic area and a small zoo are clustered above ground.

► Continue on the **D90** to Padirac, turn left and follow signs to Gramat. Leave Gramat on the **N140** northwards, then turn left on the **D36**. Turn left on the **D32** into Rocamadour.

7 Rocamadour, Midi-Pyrénées

Words and pictures rarely do justice to the reality of Rocamadour, the magnificent fortified pilgrimage town whose historic houses, sanctuary churches, bishops' palace, museums and – at the highest level – skyline castle cascade down a terraced limestone cliff. It became a place of pilgrimage

in the 12th century, visited by the great and the good of Christendom. Lifts and staircases, including the long and tiring pilgrims' Holy Way, are threaded through the town. Once you have turned on to the D32 you should pause to admire the stunning situation of the place, from the viewpoint beside the Hotel Belvedere. In

RECOMMENDED WALKS

At busy times, you may appreciate leaving the narrow streets of Rocamadour for a walk, steep in places, based on old sheep tracks in the Alzou Valley. It starts from the bridge on the D32 below the town and heads up-river.

Rocamadour itself, the finest view is from the castle ramparts. The D32 road avoids the town centre often crammed with visitors. There are parking places in the valley.

FOR CHILDREN

Just after the Jardin des Papillons on the D36 before Rocamadour, La Féerie du Rail (The Enchanted Railway) is a huge model layout with 60 trains hauling coaches and freight wagons past mountain villages, farms, a castle, a fairground and a windmill, and over a viaduct menaced by the ice cliffs of a glacier.

The ancient town of Rocamadour, situated above the Gorge of Alzou

BACK TO NATURE

Turn left in Gramat, then take the D677 and the D14 to the Parc Animalier. This zoo houses more than 300 species from around the world as well as those that are native to the area. They include bear, chamoix. lynx, yak and moufflon. There are also birds of prey, and various French breeds of farm animals, which are considered to be 'in peril of extinction', such as Limousin, Gascon and Normandy pigs. On the D36 approaching Rocamadour there is an impressive Forêt des Singes (Monkey Forest), where macaques (similar to the Barbary apes that inhabit the Rock of Gibraltar) roam freely. The Rocher des Aigles in Rocamadour is home to a large variety of birds of prey, not just eagles, but also hawks and falcons. Demonstrations of birds in flight are a regular feature of the park, weather permitting.

SCENIC ROUTES

After Rocamadour, the D32 climbs above a deep canyon with tiers of limestone cliffs. The riverside road from Castelnaud beyond Fayrac opens up a tremendous view to the castle of Beynac, and the D29 runs past rapids and wooded islets in the Dordogne on the way to Lalinde.

▶ *Continue on the D32 to Couzou, go right on the D39 through St Projet, right on the D1 then join the D673 to Gourdon. Turn left as for Sarlat then left as for Salviac, leaving Gourdon on the D763. Go right on the D6, which becomes the D46 to Cénac. Go right on the D49 to Domme.*

8 Domme, Aquitaine
This lovely, mellow hilltop town, founded with defensive ramparts and gateways around 1280, provides one of the finest viewpoints in France. The River Dordogne curves below the town, giving way to fields, farmhouses and lines of poplars on the riverside plain.

Limestone cliffs, woods and hill villages march to the horizon. In Domme itself there are beautiful townscape views round every corner. A good museum illustrates local domestic life in the past. Shops sell local honey, jams, truffles and *foie gras*. In the central square, an old covered market hall is now the entrance to a marvellous series of underground caverns with mirror lakes and floodlit limestone columns.

[i] *Place de la Halle*

RECOMMENDED WALKS

A leaflet you can collect at Domme shows three waymarked walks, starting from the walled gateway of the Porte des Tours. They descend by shady paths to the River Dordogne and wander through higher farmland.

▶ *Return to Cénac and go straight on along the D50, through St-Cybranet, then continue as for Siorac-en-Périgord. In Pont-de-Cause bear right for Castelnaud. In Castelnaud, go straight ahead for Fayrac and Les Milandes. Turn left on the D53 as for Siorac then after a 'virages' sign watch for a sharp right uphill signed 'Château des Milandes'.*

9 Les Milandes, Aquitaine
Perched on a terrace giving spreading views over the Dordogne valley, the restored 15th-century castle in the attractive and tucked-away hamlet of Les Milandes was owned from

Domme's spectacular hilltop position has made it a coveted prize throughout France's turbulent history

1949 to 1969 by the American singer Josephine Baker, star of the Paris cabarets between the wars. It was here that she founded a philanthropic foundation to look after children from all over the world.

Beyond the castle, the white courtyard of the farm which was also part of Josephine Baker's estate houses a rural museum explaining the improvements in agricultural techniques through the years.

FOR HISTORY BUFFS

On the way from Domme to Les Milandes, on a glorious viewpoint site above the village of the same name, Castelnaud is a restored medieval castle which houses displays on artillery and siege warfare. During much of the Hundred Years' War, the castle was held by the English.

▶ *Continue from the farm museum and bear left as for Veyrines-de-Vergt. Turn right on the* **D53** *then take the* **D50** *to Siorac and the* **D25** *to le Buisson-de-Cadouin. Follow signs to Lalinde, then Bergerac.*

🔟 **Bergerac,** Aquitaine

A cobbled car park which slopes down towards the River Dordogne is a convenient base for a stroll round the restored old town at the heart of present-day Bergerac. There are narrow lanes of part-timbered houses, and tiny squares, one of them shaded by chestnut trees where a statue of Rostand's hero Cyrano de Bergerac, the 17th-century nobleman and soldier famous for his large nose, stands, nobly cloaked.

The impressive Musée du Tabac in the town hall (Maison Peyrarède) illustrates the discovery of tobacco, its sources, and the local tobacco trade, as well as displaying beautifully worked pipes, cigarette holders, snuffboxes and tobacco jars. Its

Medieval houses grace the revived old town in Bergerac

curious second-floor exit leads back down to street level through the town museum (history and regional ethnography).

Near by, the Musée du Vin de la Batellerie et de la Tonnellerie combines several long-standing Bergerac interests – wine, barrel-making and river traffic. The old monastery is the home of the wine council on which all the Bergerac growers are represented.

ℹ️ *97 rue Neuve d'Argenson*

▶ *Leave Bergerac on the* **N21** *and return to Périgueux.*

SPECIAL TO...

Two great gourmet specialities of the Dordogne are truffles and foie gras. Truffles are rare edible fungi which grow underground, often in oak woods, and are dug out by truffle-hunting dogs – and even pigs. These trained animals are weaned on truffles and are trusted not to eat the precious quarry. The production of pâté de foie gras – goose or sometimes duck-liver pâté – involves grotesque force-feeding of the birds with huge quantities of maize. The pâté is preserved, often with a minute portion of truffle included, and sold at a luxury price.

Through the
High Pyrenees

This is primarily a summer tour, exploring some of the highest roads in the Pyrenees mountains. The Col du Tourmalet usually opens only after the snows clear in June. The mountain roads are exhilarating in fine weather, hair-pinning to great summit view-points. There are pleasant resorts in the foothills.

ITINERARY	
PAU	▶ Tarbes (38km-24m)
TARBES	▶ **Bagnères-de-Bigorre** (20km-12m)
BAGNÈRES-DE-BIGORRE	▶ **St-Bertrand-de-Comminges** (65km-40m)
ST-BERTRAND-DE-COMMINGES	▶ **Bagnères-de-Luchon** (35km-22m)
BAGNÈRES-DE-LUCHON	▶ **Col du Tourmalet** (87km-54m)
COL DU TOURMALET	▶ **Gavarnie** (37km-23m)
GAVARNIE	▶ **Cauterets** (40km-25m)
CAUTERETS	▶ **Lourdes** (29km-18m)
LOURDES	▶ **Grottes de Bétharram** (13km-8m)
GROTTES DE BÉTHARRAM	▶ **Pau** (28km-17m)

4 DAYS • 392KM • 243 MILES

i	*Havas Voyages, place Clemenceau, Pau*

▶ *Leave Pau on the **N117** to Tarbes, avoiding the autoroute.*

1 Tarbes, Midi-Pyrénées
With centuries of history as a regional capital behind it, Tarbes is a busy, prosperous and confident city. There is a strong summer programme of musical, theatrical, artistic, floral and sporting events.

Just off the town centre, the Jardin Massey is an attractive woodland park with pools, statues, a bandstand, an open-air theatre and peacocks' outlandish cries echoing over the lawns. Be prepared to give way to families of mallards waddling between the ponds and streams. In the heart of the park, the Musée Massey is an elegant 19th-century mansion with a fine collection of French, Flemish and Italian paintings, and a superb display on the hussars, the élite cavalry corps not only of France, but also of countries all over the world.

Although the present-day hussars stationed at Tarbes are mechanised units, the national stud of Anglo-Arab horses founded in 1806 continues to flourish. The stables are regularly open to visitors, and Tarbes hosts several show-jumping and dressage events during the year.

i *3 cours Gambetta*

> ### FOR HISTORY BUFFS
>
> In Tarbes, the boyhood home of the great World War I commander Marshal Foch is a museum with films and photographs, uniforms and honours, and the moving text of his final order of the day in 1918.

▶ *Leaves Tarbes on the **D935** to Bagnères-de-Bigorre.*

2 Bagnères-de-Bigorre, Midi-Pyrénées
Offering thermal baths, a casino, sports facilities and healthy walks, with industry kept discreetly in the outskirts, Bagnères is a typical southern spa nestling in the forested foothills of the Pyrenees. Occupied in prehistoric times, it was taken over by the Romans, who were the first to build bathhouses over its warm-water springs. Its reputation as a spa increased through the years and came to a peak in the 19th century, as the architecture of the thermal establishments shows. The Musée Bigourdan has local displays, while the Musée Salies is given over mostly to paintings.

Bagnères is well known for its authentic folk-singing concerts. Tennis and the hiring of horses, ponies or all-terrain bicycles can be arranged. As well as fishing, often for rainbow trout, the River Adour running through the town is used for lively white-water canoeing.

View from the Pic du Midi de Bigorre

i *3 allées Tournefort*

> ### RECOMMENDED WALKS
>
> On the south side of Bagnères, make for the wooded Parc Thermal de Salut. Pathways zigzag to the crest of a beautiful forested ridge, with views down over the spa town in the valley floor.

▶ *Leave Bagnères-de-Bigorre on the D938 as for Toulouse. Turn right on the D26, then right on the D929 through Hèches. Watch for a left turn, just as you see the 'Rebouc' sign, down over a level crossing and immediately left, following the D26 again. In St-Bertrand-de-Comminges, go right at the crossroads, uphill on the D26.*

❸ St-Bertrand-de-Comminges, Midi-Pyrénées

Here is a most attractively located village whose red-roofed houses climb a modest ridge between the farmlands of the plain and the wooded Pyrenean foothills.

The village and its unexpectedly majestic cathedral both take their name from a 12th-century bishop buried here. Pilgrims have been coming in great numbers since the Middle Ages. In the 16th century the cathedral interior was remodelled with stunning carved-wood screens around the choir. The splendid organ also dates from that time, and is played at many recitals. Outside, the beautiful arcaded cloisters look incongruously across to the wooded hillsides, which were a refuge for Resistance fighters in World War II.

The village preserves several fine old buildings, such as the 15th-century Maison Bridaut with its stone tower and timber-framed upper storeys. The tourist office gives access to a museum of sculptures and local archaeological finds.

Below the village stands an

St-Bertrand-de-Comminges can trace its history back to 72BC

isolated 12th-century basilica in Italianate surroundings with tall cypress trees. Much of its masonry was taken from the ruins of a Roman settlement.

ⓘ Les Olivetains

▶ *Return downhill then go straight ahead on the D26 through Valcabrère. Turn right on the N125 and follow signs to Bagnères-de-Luchon.*

❹ Bagnères-de-Luchon, Midi-Pyrénées

Most elegant and luxurious of the Pyrenean spas, Luchon (as it is generally known) is centred on a lively tree-lined avenue, with pavement cafés leading to the gardens of the thermal establishment. There is a stylish atmosphere both about the town itself and about the way it conducts its business. Walking, rock-climbing, fishing, clay-pigeon shooting, canoeing and rafting, tennis, hang-gliding and horse-riding, archery and golf are all catered for here. Many visitors come to the spa (the largest and most fashionable Pyrenean spa) not because they are unwell, but because they want a 'toning-up'.

The history of the town and district is well illustrated in the Musée du Pays de Luchon. This 18th-century mansion has a dozen exhibition rooms also devoted to the wildlife of the Pyrenees, the development of mountaineering and 2,000 years of *curistes* from the time of notable Romans such as Pompey and Tiberius, who sojourned at the even-then handsomely equipped resort they knew as *Ilixion*.

> **SPECIAL TO...**
>
> You can see the great Basque game *pelota* being played at Luchon. It is a fast and exciting contest, something like squash, with the racket replaced by a curved wickerwork scoop called a *chistera*.

ⓘ *Allées d'Étigny*

FOR CHILDREN

The Col de Peyresourde near Luchon is an area where the children can play place-name games. Ask them to find the villages with no consonants in their names, and the one which sounds singularly unhealthy.

RECOMMENDED WALKS

After Luchon, turn left on the D76 towards the Lac d'Oô. From a car park in this green steep-sided Pyrenean glen, it is a straightforward walk up to the lake, fed by a 275m (900-foot) cascade from Lac d'Espigno higher still.

SPECIAL TO...

The passes of Aspin and Tourmalet are classic stretches of the famous Tour de France cycle race. If you are here on the day of the Tour, forget about driving. Park among the thousands of spectators and watch the battle for the coveted 'King of the Mountains' title.

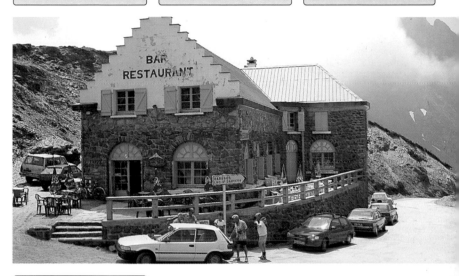

BACK TO NATURE

In summer, the foothills of the Pyrenees are carpeted with wildflowers – aconites, asphodel, Pyrenean lilies and many more. The Office de la Montagne in Luchon organises guided visits to some of the best botanical areas. For ornithologists, the area might afford sightings of Alpine choughs, snow finches, golden eagles and griffon vultures.

▶ *Leave Luchon on the **D618** over the Col de Peyresourde. In Arreau go right on the **D929** then, opposite the Esso station, not before, bear left uphill over the Col d'Aspin on the **D918**. Turn left in Ste-Marie-de-Campan to follow the **D918** to Col du Tourmalet.*

The ski resort of Col du Tourmalet, virtually deserted in summer, livens up in the winter

🛈 Col du Tourmalet, Midi-Pyrénées

At an altitude of 2,114m (6,936 feet), this is the highest through-road summit in the French Pyrenees. The road climbs relentlessly under five avalanche shelters to the ski resort – almost a ghost village at the height of summer – of La Mongie. Hairpin bends then take it up the final stretch, overlooked by colossal granite peaks and pinnacles, to the Col. From the top, the view ahead is magnificent, over peaks and ridges ranged to the horizon.

At a neck-craning angle to the north you will see the still higher observatory buildings and soaring television mast on the 2,865m (9,400-foot) summit

of the Pic du Midi. A right turn just after the actual Col leads along the steep and twisting toll road – to be driven cautiously – which climbs towards the summit and its astounding viewpoint.

BACK TO NATURE

From July till September, when the toll road is open, visitors are welcome to find out about extra-terrestrial affairs at the dramatically located Observatoire et Institut de Physique du Globe on the Pic du Midi. It has carried out pioneering work on cosmic rays and the huge, arching solar protuberances, and produced some of the finest-quality photographs ever taken from Earth.

▶ *Immediately after the summit of the Col du Tourmalet, bear left through Barèges to Luz-St-Sauveur. Turn left on to the D921 to Gavarnie.*

6 Gavarnie, Midi-Pyrénées
The narrow road to Gavarnie can be a trial in summer, because it is the busy dead-end approach to one of the most dramatic landscapes in Europe. South of the village lies the sublime Cirque de Gavarnie, a mountain amphitheatre piled with snow, whose rim at over 3,000m (10,000 feet) marks the boundary between France and Spain. Of its many waterfalls, the Grande Cascade, one of Europe's biggest, drops 442m (1,450 feet). You can only get really close to the Cirque on foot or on horseback. A less energetic alternative is to drive the spectacular winding road that climbs through wild country from Gavarnie to finish at a border col further to the west.
    Gavarnie itself lies in a fine location with a river crashing through. It has an information centre for the Parc National des Pyrénées (Pyrenees National Park) and, in the heart of a famous climbing area, several monuments to the pioneering mountaineers. Try to be here in

the evening after the press of day visitors has eased. In the mountains, dusk brings a special magic.

[i] *Maison du Parc National*

▶ *Return to Luz-St-Sauveur and take the D921 as for Lourdes. Immediately after leaving Soulom, turn left on to the D920 to Cauterets.*

7 Cauterets, Midi-Pyrénées
Situated in a narrow river valley, Cauterets is the remotest of the Pyrenean spas. In medieval times it was believed the waters cured sterility. It has sulphur waters, thermal baths, a casino, unexpectedly handsome town houses and hotels, and well developed winter sports facilities. Victor Hugo and George Sand were among the famous literary figures who came this way and helped to spread its reputation.
    There is another information centre here for the Pyrenees National Park, which you can enter by various roads and footpaths. There is also a small museum with seasonal film shows. Waterfalls tumble down near by, especially alongside the road to the Pont d'Espagne.
    One of the most engaging

A variety of excursions into the Pyrenean valleys are possible from Cauterets

features of Cauterets is that, although the railway which used to serve it has long since gone, the glorious rustic station, all varnished ornamental woodwork, has been lovingly preserved. Looking at it, you are not quite literally transported back to the 19th century, but the atmosphere remains.

▶ *Return to the D921. Turn left and continue to Lourdes.*

8 Lourdes, Midi-Pyrénées
In 1858, a 14-year-old girl called Bernadette Soubirous, walking by the rocky banks of the river at Lourdes, experienced the first of a long series of visions of the Virgin Mary. During her lifetime, pilgrims in increasing numbers, having heard of these wonders, journeyed to Lourdes. Two splendid basilicas were built beside the original grotto. In 1958, a third underground basilica was opened.
    The beautiful riverside parkland where this complex is located attracts millions of visitors every year, many of them seeking cures for ailments or disabilities. The Pavilion

Notre-Dame tells the story of St Bernadette and the pilgrimages (Musée Bernadette) and there is also a museum of sacred art (Musée d'Art Sacré du Gemmail). Climbing through woodland, the Chemin du Calvaire passes the 14 Stations of the Cross.

Lourdes itself is often crammed with people and their cars. Overlooking the town from a rocky bluff, the medieval château-fort houses the Musée Pyrénéen, a museum of the arts and traditions of the folk of the foothills. One-tenth scale models show off typical Pyrenean architecture.

Take the funicular railway to the Pic du Jer. It opens up elevated views of the town, the valleys and the mountains.

i Place Beyramalu

FOR CHILDREN

Young visitors to Lourdes will be enchanted by 'The Animated Crib'. Recreated biblical scenes tell the story of Jesus' childhood, and there is a 100 square metre layout of a Pyrenean village on Christmas Eve, all with animated models, sound and light.

FOR HISTORY BUFFS

Away from the sanctuary area, Lourdes has two museums devoted to showing how it looked in 1858, the year of Bernadette's first vision. The Musée de Lourdes features shops and street scenes, while the Musée du Petit Lourdes is a miniature stonework reproduction of the original simple village, towered over by its château-fort.

▶ *Leave Lourdes on the D937, following 'Bétharram' signs. Go through St-Pé-de-Bigorre, then turn left off the D937 and left*

again to the Grottes de Bétharram.

9 Grottes de Bétharram,
Midi-Pyrénées

These underground caverns are explored by remarkably varied forms of transport – cable cars, boats and a little 'train' of towed wagons. There are five different levels of caves and stalagmites, stalactites and curious limestone formations such as the Sphinx Window. You are shown old river levels, and taken for a cruise on a subterranean lake in a cavern 50m (165 feet) high. The fourth and fifth levels are linked by the present river dashing over a series of 80m (260-foot) falls.

▶ *Return to the D937, turn left and continue to Pau.*

SCENIC ROUTES

After Bagnères-de-Luchon, the D26 is a constantly twisting road round the wooded foothills ending in lovely farming country near St-Bertrand-de-Comminges.
The approach to Luchon takes you through an ever-narrowing wedge of valley towards the Pyrenean mountain wall. While the lower Col d'Aspin has more varied views, the Tourmalet is a classic of granite mountain landscape. From Luz-St-Sauveur, the D921 threads its way through a spectacular gorge to Gavarnie.

The grandeur and opulence of Lourdes' enormous basilica

THE SOUTH OF FRANCE

There is no single theme along the littoral of the south of France, nor even a single name for it. West of Marseille lie the flamingo lagoons, the pools, the rice fields and the summer pastures of the Camargue. East of the city stretches a sublime coast of capes and rocky inlets – the beautiful *calanques*. Beyond the great roadstead of Toulon are the islands off Hyères, including, at Port Cros, an entire island nature reserve.

St-Tropez is ... quintessentially St-Tropez, and you can have a great deal of fun simply people-watching. On a grander scale are the great resorts of the Côte d'Azur – Cannes, Nice, the immensely wealthy and independent principality of Monaco, and Menton.

Behind Nice and Monaco is the *arrière-pays*, the 'back country', the mountain country. Europe's answer to the Grand Canyon lies there.

Back from the Camargue lie Avignon and the haunting remains of the troubadours' court at Les Baux; Arles and St Rémy with their memories of the artist Vincent van Gogh; and the landscapes made famous in the mocking tales of Alphonse Daudet.

On the Cannes and Nice routes, be ready for hairpinned mountain roads, although most have been improved for tourist traffic.

On the coast, try the seafood restaurants serving Mediterranean mullet, bass and cod, and the great bouillabaisse. Be ready for lots of garlic and olive oil. In Nice, the cuisine reflects the Italian past. Vines were planted here by Greek colonists 2,500 years ago. Most of the modern wines are classified as Côtes de Provence, and the most attractive vineyard country is perhaps around Gassin and Ramatuelle on the St-Tropez peninsula. There is also intense cultivation behind the little resort of Cassis.

Should the coast become too crowded and stylish for you, half an hour inland you will find yourself in a dramatically different world of hills and mountains, forests and river valleys, where time slows down in delightful hilltop villages drowsing beneath a dazzling southern sky.

Marseille

Marseille is the greatest port in France, extending west to the faraway oil refineries of the Golfe de Fos. The yacht harbour, right in the heart of the city, makes a pleasant area for a stroll. The story of Marseille from the days of the Ligurians, Greeks and Romans, by way of the Revolution and the patriotic song which came to be called *La Marseillaise*, is told in four separate museums. Other museums cover art, pottery, furniture, tapestries, marine life etc.

There are many substantial churches, parks, gardens and, at La Canebière, a renowned avenue of shops, hotels, restaurants and pavement cafés. A magnificent view opens up from the hilltop Church of Notre-Dame-de-la-Garde. Offshore lies the sea-bound rock of the Château d'If. You can sail here and recall the story of Dumas' Count of Monte Cristo.

Cannes

In Cannes, the great boulevard de la Croisette stretches eastwards from the casino and the Palais des Festivals.

Every May, during the world-famous Cannes Film Festival, the Palais steps are staked out by twitchy television crews. The finest viewpoint is the observatory at Super-Cannes, at 325m (1,065 feet) above sea-level and 2km (1 mile) to the northeast, from which the town is seen in its wider landscape context between the Alps and the sea. Sail to the Îles des Lérins: St-Honorat is a monastery island and on Ste-Marguerite, which offers scented forest walks, was the prison of the real-life Man in the Iron Mask.

Nice

Nice is the capital of the Côte d'Azur. Its Promenade des Anglais recalls the 19th-century British visitors who made its name. The Russian royal family also favoured Nice, and you will see the green and gilded towers of the Orthodox cathedral where they and their court, which transferred here en masse every year, used to worship. There are fine shops, markets (notably the flower market), squares and gardens. Corsica ferries leave from the port. Eastwards, by the Cap de Nice, expensive villas hide above flowery balustrades. In addition to churches, palaces, museums and galleries, there is the Parc des Miniatures, enjoyed by children, which tells the story of Nice itself. The Musée Terra Amata is an imaginative exhibition based on a prehistoric site, whose story starts 400,000 years ago.

Nîmes

Nîmes found favour with the Romans. Their arena, with space for 21,000 spectators, plays host to concerts and bullfights today. The Maison Carrée is a pillared 1st-century BC temple (one of the best preserved in existence) housing a little museum. Archaeology, history, the planets, fine arts and the story of Nîmes are topics covered in other exhibitions. Below a hillside park lies the grand if somewhat faded Jardin de la Fontaine. Its 18th-century masonry and water channels were built on the site of the Roman baths, providing a cool retreat from the harshness of the Provençal summer sun.

Opposite: the view west from Les Baux-de-Provence
Below: Marseille's harbour

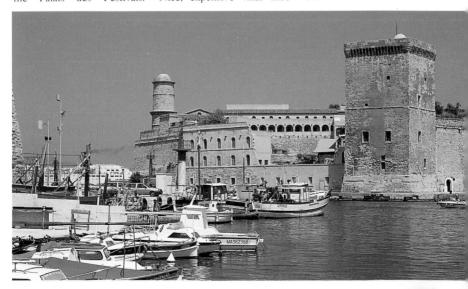

East From
Marseille

Starting from Marseille, France's second biggest city, this tour visits fishing villages which now have their own substantial holiday clientele, and larger resorts as different in style as Hyères and St-Tropez. All these places have grown up over the centuries, but Port-Grimaud is a modern development. Inland, the tour follows the high wooded ridges of the Massif des Maures as well as visiting an awesomely remote monastic house and the country of a film-maker who captured the soul of Provence.

4 DAYS • 352KM • 221 MILES

ITINERARY	
MARSEILLE	▶ Cassis (23km-14m)
CASSIS	▶ Cap Canaille (7km-4m)
CAP CANAILLE	▶ Bandol (25km-16.5m)
BANDOL	▶ Toulon (35km-22m)
TOULON	▶ Hyères (25km-16.5m)
HYÈRES	▶ Gassin (69km-43m)
GASSIN	▶ St-Tropez (18km-11m)
ST-TROPEZ	▶ Port-Grimaud (8km-5m)
PORT-GRIMAUD	▶ Grimaud (6km-4m)
GRIMAUD	▶ Chartreuse de la Verne (24km-15m)
CHARTREUSE DE LA VERNE	▶ Aubagne (93km-58m)
AUBAGNE	▶ Marseille (19km-12m)

| *i* | 4 La Canebière, Marseille

▶ *Leave Marseille on the **D559** to Cassis.*

❶ Cassis, Provence-Alpes
With cream and ochre-washed buildings overlooking the harbour, bars, cafés and seafood restaurants, and convenient beaches, Cassis has the obvious look of a holiday resort. But it is a fishing port too, and boats take visitors to the beautiful *calanques*, the rocky inlets in the roadless coastline to the west.

Cassis has a life and history independent of the summer tourist crush. A ruined castle (not accessible to the public) on a cypress-clad hill watches over it. A modest but informative local museum shows how the settlement dates back to Roman times and before. The town hall is also worth a visit; illustrations show how it was rebuilt from a shambolic ruin in the 1980s.

| *i* | Place Baragnon

▶ *Head out of Cassis on the **D559** then right following 'Route des Crêtes' signs on to the **D41a** and the **D141** to Cap Canaille.*

FOR CHILDREN

In Cassis, a pleasant little park by the post office includes a pond with goldfish, mallards and terrapins. There is a scrambling frame which takes the shape of jocular-looking fish with gaping mouths.

SPECIAL TO...

Cassis is noted for the highly regarded white wines which the sheltered climate and fine soil of the hillsides behind the town allow more than a dozen vineyards to produce. The vines here were wiped out by disease in the 19th century, but the growers have revived the trade by using grafting techniques brought from Texas.

---

❷ Cap Canaille, Provence-Alpes
Less a conventional cape than a wall of towering sea-cliffs – at 395m (1,300 feet) Europe's highest cliff – this is one of the most superb viewpoints in France. It looks west to the mazy coastline of the *calanques*, with offshore islands and rock pinnacles seeming to float in the air, like dreamy hills in old Chinese paintings.

▶ *Continue into La Ciotat. Go right at the T-junction on to Avenue Victor Hugo, then left and left again along the seafront, following signs for Bandol.*

RECOMMENDED WALKS

The three magnificent rocky inlets west of Cassis – the *calanques* – and the wooded peninsulas which border them are easily reached by a network of footpaths. Park your car at the far end of the Avenue des Calanques and follow the marked paths to sheltered Port-Miou, the limpid waters and Aleppo pines of Port-Pin and the wild, needle-like rocks of En Vau.

Painters such as Matisse and Dufy enjoyed the Provençal charm of Cassis – and probably its wine, too

3 Bandol, Provence-Alpes
This is Cassis writ large, a resort with a marina, a fishing port and even more seafood restaurants. Boats sail from Bandol on cruises along the coast, but the most popular trip is to Bendor, a rocky island crammed with hotels and restaurants, beaches, sailing, diving and tennis clubs, an art gallery and an exhibition on wines and spirits from nearly 50 countries. There is a zoo, and along the coast is a maritime museum.

[i] *Allées Vivien*

▶ *Continue on the **D559** through Sanary-sur-Mer, then go left on the **D63** and follow signs to Toulon.*

naval museum, the Musée Naval.
Toulon has perhaps the most amazing suburban background of any city in Europe. The hillside districts behind the town centre suddenly rear up in the colossal limestone cliffs of Mont Faron. A one-way road system reaches the summit, the climb being up a steep incline with forbidding drops. As an option, a cablecar runs from Super Toulon. There are wonderful views from Mont Faron, pinewood picnic sites, a children's playground, a zoo and a comprehensive memorial exhibition on the 1944 liberation of Provence.

[i] *Avenue Colbert*

▶ *Leave Toulon on the **N98** to Hyères.*

5 Hyères, Provence-Alpes
Hyères is a town of colourful gardens. This is the oldest of all the modern Riviera resorts, although standing back more than most of them from the sea. The old quarter, reached through its original medieval gateways, is a place of cool narrow streets, historic buildings and an authentic atmosphere of people going about their daily business. Hyères is mature enough not to be any kind of tourist trap.
The museum takes the town's history back to the times of the Greeks and Romans – as *Olbia* it was a Greek colony,

4 Toulon, Provence-Alpes
With its interlocking harbours and a busy dockyard, Toulon is a famous and historic naval port. In World War II, in 1942, much of the French fleet was scuttled here, so that it would not come under German control. There is a great deal of civilian activity too. Ferries sail to Corsica and Sardinia, cargo ships use the freight quays, and smaller boats run scheduled services to the offshore islands as well as making shorter trips round the harbour. There is a well-stocked

FOR HISTORY BUFFS

As Captain Bonaparte, Napoleon first made a name for himself at the age of 24, when the Republican army attacked British-held Toulon in 1793.
Under withering enemy fire, his artillery battery bombarded a British strong-point at the fort now named after him, forcing the British ships to withdraw.

Toulon, France's second-largest naval base, is a surprisingly lively place

established by settlers from Marseille. There are some handsome old churches (St Louis associated with King Louis IX who landed at Hyères after crusading, and St Paul with its Romanesque front), and from the castle ruins in a hilltop park a panoramic view is revealed of the inland hills and the sea.

[i] *Rotonde, Jean-Salusse*

The cathedral of St Paul dominates the old town of Hyères

BACK TO NATURE

From Hyères Plage, on the D97 south of town, ferries run to the beautiful nature reserve island of Port Cros. Footpaths explore its bays and forests, and there is even an underwater offshore nature trail for swimmers with flippers and masks. The neighbouring islands of Ile du Levant and Porquerolles are also worth a visit. Both have small resort villages and good beaches.

▶ Leave Hyères on the **N98** as for Le Canadel. Watch for a left turn following the **N98** signed 'La Môle'. Turn right on the **D41** as for Bormes then, at a blind bend on a brow, left on the **RF32**, the Routes des Crêtes. Go straight on along this road, always on a tarred surface. Turn right at the Col de Canadel, away from La Môle, then left on the **D559** through La Croix-Valmer. Watch for 'Auberge les Sarments' sign, then immediately bear right off the **D559** to Gassin.

6 Gassin, Provence-Alpes
Sensitively restored in recent years, this hilltop village often attracts cooling breezes on hot summer days. There are lanes and stairways, houses with potted flowers and pocket-handkerchief gardens, a parish church barely illuminated by the modern abstract stained glass in its three tiny original windows, restaurants on a shaded terrace and, above all, views to the delicious miniature landscapes of the St-Tropez peninsula.

▶ Leave Gassin for Ramatuelle, turn left at a stop sign, right at a second stop sign, then left towards the **D98a**. At traffic lights, turn right on that road into St-Tropez.

BACK TO NATURE

On the left after Gassin, the Chemin du Radio Phare passes three old stone windmills on the way to a short circular walk outside the perimeter fence of a radio beacon. This is a splendid viewpoint, but the great attraction is the number and variety of brightly-coloured butterflies which flit around.

7 St-Tropez, Provence-Alpes
Publicity about the personalities – from the writers Guy de Maupassant and Colette to artists Henri Matisse, controversial writer, designer and film director Jean Cocteau and 'sex kitten' actress Brigitte Bardot – who have settled here, has always tended to hide the fact that this red-roofed town clustered beside a bay is an interesting place in its own right.

St-Tropez shops ask high prices, and the resort is full of deeply tanned characters in high summer fashion, who may be wealthy residents or simply day-trippers putting on an act – it can be fun to try to classify them. Needless to say, café and nightlife is abundant if you can afford the price and keep the pace.

An old chapel has been turned into a museum – the Musée de l'Annonciade – featuring paintings and sculptures by some of the notable artists who have lived here including Bonnard, Braque, Dufy and Utrillo, while lesser lights try to sell their canvases in an unofficial gallery by the harbour rails. The hexagonal 16th-century citadel is now a naval museum (Musée de la Marine) on several floors, where

you can peruse the exhibits
(which include a reconstructed
Greek galley) to the accompani-
ment of unearthly cries from the
local peacocks.

The fine sandy beaches are
4 to 5km (2½–3 miles) from St-
Tropez town, on the far side of
the headland on which it stands.
They are varied and very popular. Parking can be difficult.

[i] *Quai Jean-Jaurès*

FOR HISTORY BUFFS

Two processions, called
bravades, are held every year in
St-Tropez. The first, in May,
honours St Torpes, the town's
patron saint. A month later, the
second *bravade* celebrates the
defeat of a strong Spanish fleet
which tried to capture the
town in 1637. Fierce resistance
by the local militia drove it
away. Participants wear splendid uniforms and carry
blunderbusses – which are
fired (blanks only) at all oppor-
tunities.

▶ *Return along the D98a. At a
roundabout join the N98 as
for Fréjus, then under the
bridge take the right lane for
Port-Grimaud and left at the
roundabout to the 'Visiteurs'
car park.*

8 **Port-Grimaud,** Provence-
Alpes
In the 1960s this was simply a
wasteland of marsh and gravel
pits. Then the architect
François Spoerry created a
brand-new village on a lagoon
by the sea – a kind of Provençal
Venice with canals and peninsulas, bridges and water-buses,
shops, cafés, restaurants and
colour-washed houses, each
with its own boat mooring right
outside the door. Everything
was to be a modern expression
of traditional Provençal design.
In the wrong hands, Port-
Grimaud could have been a
tacky disaster. Instead, it is a
triumph.

▶ *Return to the roundabout,
go over the bridge then
turn right at the T-junction.
Continue straight on at the
next junction then left on the
D14 to Grimaud.*

9 **Grimaud,** Provence-Alpes
Further inland, the medieval
hillside town which gave Port-
Grimaud its name retains many
old buildings, notably the
houses in the arcaded street of
the Knights Templar, and the
massive Romanesque church of
St-Michel.

Above all, Grimaud, which
takes its name from the powerful Genoese Grimaldi family
(now rulers of Monaco), is dominated by the hilltop ruins of an
11th-century castle. It provides
a wonderful viewpoint.

[i] *I boulevard des Aliziers*

▶ *Leave Grimaud on the D558
then turn left on the D14.
Turn left on the mostly unsur-
faced D214 signed 'La Verne'.*

10 **Chartreuse de la Verne,**
Provence-Alpes
The road is lonely, slow and
dusty to this remote and
impressive monastery established by the Carthusians as
long ago as 1170. At the time of
the French Revolution it was
deprived of its revenues, and
the monks left secretly,
disguised as peasants. The
buildings then passed through
several hands, and are now
owned by a trust and are being
renovated. In 1983 another
order of monks – the Order of
St Bruno – moved in. There
are guided tours (for visitors
who are discreetly dressed)
showing the historic buildings
and the breathtaking view of
high ridges and deep valleys,
covered by the forest of the
Massif des Maures.

▶ *Rejoin the D14 and follow it
through Collobrières to
Pierrefeu. Turn right on the
D12 through Puget-Ville and
Rocbaron to Forcalqueiret. Go*

*left on the **D554** and continue to Méounes-les-Montrieux, then right on the **D2** via Signes, and right at Le Camp on the **N8** to Aubagne.*

SPECIAL TO...

Collobrières, near Chartreuse de la Verne in the Maures massif, has many varieties of the chestnut candies called *marrons glacés*. Two major producers in the village sell chestnut-based sweets, syrups and creams.

ⓘ Aubagne, Provence-Alpes
At the heart of this town, surrounded by a cat's-cradle of motorway bypasses, there are public gardens and cool tree-shaded squares. In one of them the tourist office pavilion houses a colourful display – using the painted clay-model figures called *santons* which are made in great numbers by craftsmen in the town – of scenes from the films of the writer and director Marcel Pagnol, a native of Aubagne. After the world-wide screening in the 1980s of new versions of his stories *Jean de Florette* and *Manon des Sources*, interest in Pagnol, who died in 1974, spread widely. Guided tours are organised round the real-life locations he used in the countryside near Aubagne. In the

FOR CHILDREN

On the N98 before Aubagne, the OK Corral has far more attractions than simply the Wild West elements its name suggests. As well as a 'western' street and railway, pony rides, cowboys and Indians, there are swooping roller-coasters which produce a total white-knuckle experience.

St-Tropez owes its popularity to its sheltered harbour and marina

western outskirts of the town, the Musée de la Légion Etrangère (Foreign Legion Museum) has displays on its years of service in the baking Sahara sands.

ⓘ *Avenue Antide Boyer*

▶ *Leave Aubagne on the **D2** and return to Marseille.*

RECOMMENDED WALKS

There is access at Collobrières to the long-distance footpaths which explore the deep wooded valleys and ridgetops of the Massif des Maures. For instance, GR90, offers a strenuous half-day hike out and back to the hermitage of Notre-Dame-des-Anges. Further on, Signes on the D2 is the starting point of forest and hill walks on the Massif de la Sainte Baume.

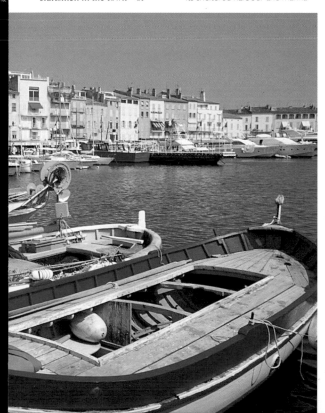

SCENIC ROUTES

The D559 leaves Marseille by the winding climb, under wooded cliffs and banks of valerian and broom, to the Col de la Gineste.
The climb to Cap Canaille – as well as the summit view – is one of the most spectacular on the coast.
Look for the views to the island of Bendor from the bay after Bandol.
Where clear of woodland, the RF32 on the way to the Col du Canadel has a glorious outlook to the sea.
The high road from Gassin to Ramatuelle looks over a beautiful settled landscape of woodlands, farms and farmyards.
The D14 to Collobrières gives a fine impression of the wooded ridges and deep lonely valleys of the Massif des Maures. Then from Pierrefeu towards Rocbaron, the D12 climbs sharply as it overlooks the vineyard plain it is leaving behind.

The Riviera &
its Hinterland

From Cannes and other coastal resorts, by way of artists' and craft-workers' villages, this tour climbs into the glorious mountain scenery that forms the backdrop to the Côte d'Azur. Limestone cliffs and ridges, spectacular valleys and ranges of faraway mountains reach a landscape climax in the magnificent Gorges du Verdon.

4/5 DAYS • 440KM • 273 MILES

ℹ Palais des Festivals, 1 la
Croisette, Cannes

► Leave Cannes on the **N7**
towards Golfe-Juan, then bear
right on the **N98** signed
'Antibes par Bord de Mer'. In
Juan-les-Pins watch carefully
for all the 'Cap d'Antibes' signs
and join the Cap d'Antibes
coast road, **D2559**.

❶ Cap d'Antibes, Côte
d'Azur
There are tiny family-style
beaches and boat moorings on
the east side of the Cape, which
also includes security-guarded
millionaires' retreats and, at the
Hôtel du Cap and the Eden Roc
restaurant, two of the most
exclusive establishments of
their kind on the coast. A fine
museum devoted to Napoleonic
and naval history – Musée
Naval et Napoléonien – occupies an old gun battery, perhaps
surprising visitors from the
United Kingdom with contemporary cartoons showing the
British as the enemy. Around
the Villa Thuret there is a
botanical garden, and right on
the summit of the Cape the
Sanctuaire de la Garoupe, a
seafarers' chapel beside the
lighthouse tower, which is a
marvellous viewpoint, houses a
collection of simple but affect-
ing thanks-offerings, often for a
safe return from a voyage.
American writers and artists
were attracted to the Cape from
the 1920s onwards. Scott
Fitzgerald's novel *Tender is the
Night* had its real-life setting
here. It is possible to trace the
exact course of the disastrous
car journey described in James
Thurber's *A Ride with Olympy*.
And Orson Welles once arrived
in a hurry for a cash-raising
meeting in the Hôtel du Cap,
having come by taxi all the way
from Rome!

► Continue on the **D2559** into
Antibes.

❷ Antibes, Côte d'Azur
The old town here, with its
narrow streets, cafés and restau-

Paintings in Notre Dame de
Bon Port, Cap d'Antibes

rants, is one of the most attractive and least pretentious on the
coast. Antibes' connection with
the ancient Greeks – it was
founded as *Antipolis* by Greek
colonists from Marseille in the
4th century BC – attracted the
Cretan writer Nikos
Kazantzakis, author of *Zorba the
Greek*, to settle here, as did the
British novelist Graham
Greene. While the archaeological museum in the old fortification of the Bastion St André
may look gloomy from the
outside, it has a wonderful
collection of thousands of
exhibits going back to Etruscan,
Greek and Roman times, many
recovered from the sea. The old
castle was a stronghold of the
powerful Genoese Grimaldi
family. With the little 'cathedral', it watches over the
bustling market place, and was
long since turned into the
Musée Picasso. The artist used
part of it as a studio for six amazingly fruitful months in 1946,
and now it contains many of his
– and other artists' – paintings
and ceramics, making it one of
the most important Picasso
collections anywhere. The so-
called cathedral is, in fact, a
church, with a Romanesque
tower and east end and 17th-
century façade.

ℹ 11 place du Général-de-Gaulle

**RECOMMENDED
WALKS**

On the south side of the Cap
d'Antibes, turn off the
Boulevard J F Kennedy for the
Sentiers des Douaniers – the
Excisemen's Path. Starting
alongside the wall of a private
estate, it leads to a beautiful
little park set among rocks
above the sea, with a lovely bay
stretching to the west.

► Leave Antibes on the **N98** as
for 'Nice par Bord de Mer'.
Take the left-hand lane, turn
left at the traffic lights for
Biot, then right and left on the
D4 to Biot.

FOR CHILDREN

Marineland, to the right of the
D4 on the way to Biot, has
penguins, seals, sea lions and a
dolphin show. Near by are a
butterfly jungle, a little
Provençal farm, water chutes
and an assault-course style of
mini-golf layout. This was
Europe's first marine park.

❸ Biot, Côte d'Azur
On the approach road to Biot, a
road to the right leads to the
Musée National Fernand Léger,
unmistakable thanks to the
huge abstract in multi-coloured

tiling which decorates its frontage. With more than 300 works on display, it celebrates the life of one of France's major 20th-century artists, and was opened in 1960 with fellow-artists Picasso, Braque and Chagall as its honorary presidents. The charming little town of Biot is largely given over to the shops and studios of painters, potters, woodworkers, embroiderers and craftworkers of many other kinds. Even the town maps are on painted ceramic tiles. Glassmaking is important here nowadays and it can be observed at the Verrerie de Biot near the southeast exit from the town. Gates and ramparts of the medieval town survive, and away from the tourist bustle there is a pleasant arcaded square beside a 15th-century parish church. The museum features mementoes of the days when the Romans and, later, the Knights Templar, were established here, and has a dazzling pottery display.

[i] *6 place de la Chapelle*

▶ *Continue on the **D4** via Valbonne to Grasse, turning right at a T-junction on the outskirts to follow the **D4** towards the town centre.*

4 Grasse, Côte d'Azur
Spread over a south-facing hillside with splendid views over a lovely plain towards the sea, Grasse enjoys a year-long calendar of concerts, drama, dance and exhibitions of every kind. The old town, crammed with 14th- to 18th-century buildings, is Italian in appearance and atmosphere. Around it, Grasse expanded with exuberant 19th-century architecture in typical French Riviera style.

Grasse has the most famous perfume industry in the world, and one museum, Musée International de la Parfumerie, traces its history as well as the processes by which huge amounts of flower petals are distilled down to tiny volumes of the ultimate essence. The Maison Fragonard, named after the rococo painter who was born in the town, is a perfume factory open to the public. The Musée d'Art et d'Histoire de Provence, housed in an 18th-century mansion, celebrates the art and history of Provence.

Another museum, the Musée de la Marine, has gathered an intriguing collection of ship models to illustrate the career of the 18th-century Admiral de Grasse, an ally of George Washington in the American

Biot is set attractively on a small hill rising in the centre of a valley

War of Independence. A statue on one of the town's outlook terraces recalls Washington's gratitude to him.

[i] *Place de la Foux*

> **FOR CHILDREN**
>
> There is no need for parents to worry that their offspring might get bored at The Musée International de la Parfumerie in Grasse because they organise special activities for children. As soon as they can gather 10 or more youngsters together, they have them making bubble bath, hand cream and Egyptian jewels.

▶ *Leave Grasse on the **D2085** as for Nice. At Pré-du-Lac turn left at the roundabout and immediately bear left on the **D3** to Gourdon. Turn right for the car park at the entrance to the village.*

5 Gourdon, Côte d'Azur
Some writers sneer at Gourdon for being a tourist trap, but this old Saracen stronghold, set on

the edge of a cliff which gives it tremendous views down into the valley of the Loup, goes about its business quietly. In the narrow lanes of restored and impeccably kept buildings, shops sell lavender, honey, herbs, perfumes, pottery, wines, basketwork and glassware, many of them produced locally.

The historic Château de Gourdon, with terraced gardens on the edge of the cliff, has architectural details from the 12th century onwards. Here you will see valuable furnishings, as well as collections of arms and armour, and 'naive' paintings by European and American artists.

> 🛈 *Place de l'Eglise*

▶ *Leave Gourdon on the D12 as for Caussols. In about 8km (5 miles) watch for a junction sign and then go sharp left under a sign giving advice to 'Visiteurs'.*

❻ **Plateau de Caussols,** Côte d'Azur

A notice at the turning off the D12 warns that gathering stones, mushrooms and snails is forbidden. Do not worry about the mild potholes on the early stretch of the road; the surface never deteriorates too badly. Here on the high limestone plain is a countryside not many casual tourists know: clumps of pines and rock outcrops, occasional sheep farms, isolated holiday homes, groups of beehives and, here and there, a survivor from the days of the *bories*, the stone-built shepherds' huts.

BACK TO NATURE

On the Plateau de Caussols, the rich limestone soil allows the growth of a riot of wildflowers. They flourish all over the natural pastureland, and colour the crevices of the hundreds of rock outcrops which are characteristic of the plateau. Orchids are particularly abundant from April to June.

There are mountain ridges to north and south, with the remote white buildings of the CERGA observatory high on the northern rim. Film buffs may recognise it as the setting of the Charles Bronson thriller *Cold Sweat*.

▶ *Turn right at a T-junction beside a postbox, following an old sign 'St-Lambert'. This is the D12 again. Turn sharp left as for Thorenc on the D112, then follow 'Thorenc' signs on the D5. Go left on the D2, left on the D2211, then right on the N85 to Castellane.*

❼ **Castellane,** Côte d'Azur

A modest little town on the Route Napoléon, Castellane lies in a constricted location where the River Verdon elbows its way through the hills. Directly overlooking the square is a massive

cliff, 184m (604 feet) high, on which the original settlement, dating from Gallo-Roman times, was built.

When the population decided, eventually, to settle in the valley, plague, floods and occupation in the time of the religious wars in the 16th century was their reward. Now the classic outing at Castellane is a walk up the steep and occasionally rough pathway to the 18th-century Chapel of Notre Dame du Roc, a magnificent clifftop viewpoint.

> 🛈 *8 rue Nationale*

▶ *Continue on the N85, go right on the D955. Then left on the N202 to St-André-les-Alpes.*

Perched high above the River Loup, Gourdon has stunning views of the coast

FOR HISTORY BUFFS

From near a car park on the D5 just before the summit of the Col de Castellaras, a steep footpath climbs to the hilltop ruins of Castellaras itself, a magnificently sited medieval fortress town. You will be able to make out the old castle, the barracks and the humble quarter where the peasants and their flocks took refuge in times of war. The whole town dominated the upper valley of the Loup.

8 St-André-les-Alpes, Côte d'Azur

This is a quiet little inland resort a world away from the hustle of the coast. But St-André was once a busy enough place. The village had four cloth mills, but all that remains of the industry is the canal which supplied their water-power. In the latter part of the 19th century it became the railhead of a line from Nice, and the place from which stagecoaches took passengers further on. This railway, now extended to Digne, is the last survivor of the old inland lines. St-André station is a halt on the year-round railcar

service, and there are summer excursions on the steam-hauled Train des Pignes (the Pine Cone Train).

St-André lies in an attractive valley that has helped it achieve its present-day renown as a centre for hang-gliding and free-fall parachuting.

i *Place Marcel Paslorelli*

RECOMMENDED WALKS

One walk from the centre of St-André-les-Alpes heads briefly south on the N202 before turning right for the steep climb to the 'lost' village of Courchons. Orange markers show where the footpath cuts out the hairpin bends of the Courchons road. Another route heads southeast up to the chapel of Méouilles overlooking the mountain-ridged reservoir of the Lac de Castillon.

▶ *Continue on the N202 to Barrême, then turn right on to the N85 and left on the D907, then in La Bégude-Blanche take the D953 to Riez.*

SPECIAL TO...

On the way to Riez you will pass through one of France's biggest lavender-growing areas. Naturally, this is fine country for bees, and a great deal of honey is also produced here. Maison de l'Abeille, on the approach to the town, houses a fascinating exhibition, explained by an enthusiastic owner, of modern and historic bee-keeping and honey-making.

9 Riez, Provence-Alpes

Two structures show how old the settlement of Riez is. A group of columns now standing isolated at the edge of the field was once part of a 1st-century Roman temple; and there is an early Christian baptistery (dating from some time in the 4th to 7th centuries), complete with the original font, inside a 19th-century building set up to preserve it.

The old town may have a faded look, but its streets

Surely one of nature's most delightful harvests – fields of perfumed lavender at Riez contain medieval doorways and Renaissance frontages, some in the course of restoration. In pre-Roman times, the settlement stood on the summit of the St Maxime hill overlooking the present-day town in the valley below. St Maxime, which is the site of an attractive chapel, is a pleasant place for a stroll. A popular Riez industry is the production of *santons*, characteristic Provençal painted clay figurines, originally made for the traditional Christmas crib, but now sold as souvenirs.

[i] *4 allées Louis Gadiol*

Moustiers has been famous for its pottery since the 17th century

---

BACK TO NATURE

After Riez, the Lapidaire Pierres de Provence on the D952 displays beautiful examples of rose quartz, agates, amethysts and other semi-precious stones. This is a fine area for minerals and gemstones, but much of it is protected as a geological reserve.

▶ *Leave on the D952 to Moustiers-Ste-Marie.*

10 Moustiers-Ste-Marie, Provence-Alpes

Any history of Moustiers pales before its amazing situation, clustered round the banks of a tumbling mountain stream at the foot of a huge gash in towering limestone cliffs. Footpaths climb to a spectacularly located church, Notre Dame de Beauvoir, set on a high rocky terrace. Across the break in the cliffs, and silhouetted against the sky, a chain supporting a gilded star was, according to tradition, first placed there by a crusader knight, who had sworn to do it when released from weary years of imprisonment.

The town is famous for its glazed pottery, or faienceware. The industry established in the 17th century died out for a generation or two, and restarted in the 1920s, but without equalling the delicacy of the

early designs, many of which are on show in the local museum, Musée des Faïences.

[i] *Rue du Seigneur de la Clue*

▶ *Continue on the D952 to La Palud. Go straight on through La Palud, then bear right on the D23, the Route des Crêtes. If you enjoy exposed and narrow roads with steep, unguarded drops, follow the D23 all the way back to La Palud and turn right on to the D952. If you do not enjoy this kind of road, go along the D23 to the first two or three belvederes, then retrace your route and turn right again on to the D952. Only the later part of the D23 is difficult.*

11 Gorges du Verdon, Provence-Alpes

Landscape superlatives are needed here, because this is France's equivalent, on a smaller scale, to the Grand Canyon in Colorado. The River Verdon, on its way to Castellane, runs through a huge ravine in the limestone mountains, with colossal drops, vertigo-inducing views, exciting low-level footpaths and the possibility of organised expeditions on foot and by canoe, raft or rubber dinghy, right through the heart of the gorge. There are magnificent, high-level roadside views from railed-off belvederes (look-out points), some of which, on the Routes

des Crêtes, have warnings not to throw stones off the edge – they might fall on walkers 715m (2,350 feet) below!

▶ *Continue eastwards on the D952. After a stretch of overhanging cliffs, turn right on the D955 to Comps-sur-Artuby and Draguignan.*

12 Draguignan, Provence-Alpes

Down from the mountains, and the vast military training area of Canjeurs which occupies the scrubland plateau south of the River Verdon, Draguignan marks a return to the milder landscapes of mid-Provence. There is a dignified old town here, and a fine museum, with thousands of exhibits connected with local industries, including a reconstructed olive oil mill. There is also an artillery museum, reflecting the military presence. Shaded squares and gardens fend off the sun. On the boulevard John Kennedy, the American military cemetery commemorates the mostly Franco-American Provençal landings of August 1944. In front of the memorial there is an imaginative tribute in the form of a massive relief map, in bronze and copper, illustrating the campaign.

[i] *9 boulevard Clemenceau*

► Leave Draguignan on the **D562** as for Grasse. Go left on the **D563** to Fayence.

13 Fayence, Provence-Alpes
Here is a classic back-from-the-coast village, facing southwards into the sun with its red-roofed houses stacked up a hillside that rises from the plain. Fayence has a very well-maintained 18th-century church, a good selection of craft studios and galleries, and terraces which act as splendid viewpoints. One very pleasant pastime here is to laze around them, look out over the plain and watch the gliders soaring from one of France's most important launching fields far below.

► Continue on the **D563** to Mons.

14 Mons, Provence-Alpes
The colonists from Ventimiglia in what is now Italy, who founded this little hilltop village in the 13th century, picked the location well. The spacious square, in fact a semi-circle, looks out over an extensive view from the islands off

The Gorges du Verdon offers a range of activities and natural beauty to take your breath away

Cannes to the Italian Alps, with suggestions that, on a really clear day, Corsica appears as a smudge on the horizon. Mons survived two outbreaks of plague and the fact that all its citizens deserted after a brigands' raid in 1468. It then dozed in the sun for centuries before it recently decided to emphasise its situation as one of the 'belvederes of the Côte d'Azur'. There is a maze of cool, narrow alleyways. The historic ramparts are still partly in place. Local arts and crafts are displayed in La Maison des Peintres. And the streets usually bear two names – in French and Provençal.

i Place St-Sébastien

FOR HISTORY BUFFS

After Mons, Roche Taillée, to the left of the D56, is a fine example of Roman civil engineering, a deep cutting in a limestone outcrop to take part of the 40km (25-mile) aqueduct which supplied the town of Fréjus near the coast. The aqueduct is still in use today.

► Leave Mons on the **D56** as for Callian, then go left on the **D37**. Follow the **D37** to the left for Montauroux at a T-junction where the right turn is signed 'Callian 0.5km'. Follow the 'Grasse' sign in Montauroux, still on the **D37**, cross the **D562**, then go left on the **D38** through Tanneron. At a five-road junction after Tanneron bear right for Mandelieu-la-Napoule, then watch for an abrupt left turn avoiding a road straight ahead signed 'Poney Club'. Take the **D92** to Mandelieu. Turn right on the **N7** then take the fourth exit at a roundabout signed 'Les Plages'. Go right at the T-junction as for Napoule, then keep in the right lane and return to Cannes.

SPECIAL TO...

From the Lac de St-Cassien to Mandelieu, the beautiful Tanneron massif is planted out with mimosa. In summer there is no trace of the brilliant yellow blooms which light up the winter hillsides.

SCENIC ROUTES

Approaching Gourdon, the D3 looks deep into the valley of the Loup, then reveals a stunning view of the village in the eagle's-eyrie location on the summit of a plummeting cliff.

FOR CHILDREN

In Mons, ask them to find the electricity meter for the house at 22 Su Lou Coustihoun.

Exploring the
Côte d'Azur

Often using steep and hairpinned roads, the route climbs spectacular valleys and wooded mountain ridges. Far from the hustle and
bustle of holiday crowds, the valley of the Gordolasque is a cleft in
the wildest part of the Maritime Alps, and the pilgrimage church of
Madone d'Utelle crowns a remote and atmospheric hilltop.

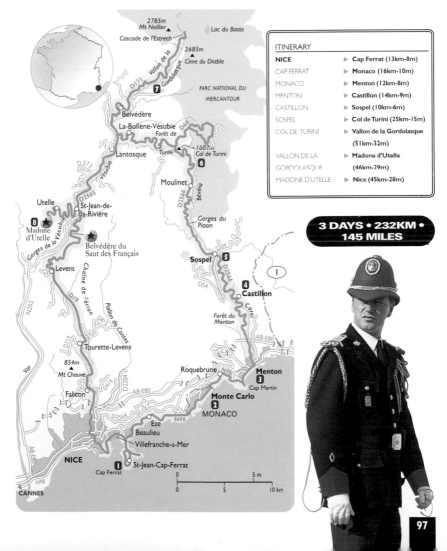

ITINERARY		
NICE	▶	Cap Ferrat (13km-8m)
CAP FERRAT	▶	Monaco (16km-10m)
MONACO	▶	Menton (12km-8m)
MENTON	▶	Castillon (14km-9m)
CASTILLON	▶	Sospel (10km-6m)
SOSPEL	▶	Col de Turini (25km-15m)
COL DE TURINI	▶	**Vallon de la Gordolasque**
		(51km-32m)
VALLON DE LA	▶	**Madone d'Utelle**
GORDOLASQUE		**(46km-29m)**
MADONE D'UTELLE	▶	Nice (45km-28m)

**3 DAYS • 232KM •
145 MILES**

TOUR
15   **Exploring the** Côte d'Azur

i *Avenue Thiers, Nice*

▶ *Leave Nice following the N98, the Corniche Inférieure, to Villefranche. Bear right for St-Jean-Cap-Ferrat.*

❶ **Cap Ferrat,** Côte d'Azur
Cap Ferrat is a cape extending about 3km (2 miles) south of Beaulieu. All the capes along the Côte d'Azur are favoured residential areas, with imposing villas in discreet well-wooded grounds. At Cap Ferrat one of the most majestic of these, once the home of the Baroness Béatrice Ephrussi-de-Rothschild, was built early this century to house a massive collection of furnishings, tapestries, costumes, paintings and porcelain.

The house and contents were left to the Académie des Beaux Arts and now form the Musée 'Ile de France'. It stands among 7 hectares (17 acres) of gardens, and the collection, although it has a strong bias to the 18th century, includes Impressionist paintings and oriental *objets d'art*. St-Jean-Cap-Ferrat, the resort village facing the towering cliffs that

march to Monaco and the Italian frontier, is on an arm of the cape going off to the east. It has two promenades, the upper one on the roof of a line of shops, cafés and restaurants looking out to the yachts and cruisers bobbing in the harbour.

i *59 avenue Denis Seméria*

FOR CHILDREN

Cap Ferrat Zoo, in a former estate of King Leopold II of the Belgians, raises many young animals, including llamas, kangaroos, gazelles and monkeys. Children enjoy its daily 'chimpanzee school'.

RECOMMENDED WALKS

On Cap Ferrat, the Maurice Rouvier walk is a promenade from the harbour to Beaulieu, while the Pointe St-Hospice walk from the Paloma beach circles a rocky peninsula below the villa gardens.

▶ *Return to Villefranche and bear right on the D125, then follow signs through Beaulieu for Monaco.*

FOR HISTORY BUFFS

On a rocky promontory in Beaulieu, which lies between Cap Ferrat and Monaco, the Villa Kérylos is a modern replica of a Greek palace of the 5th century BC, created early in the 20th century by archaeologist Théodore Reinach. Its pillars, mosaics, frescos and furnishings, marble and alabaster benefit from their location by the deep blue Mediterranean, and there are some granite antiquities among the reproductions.

---

❷ **Monaco**
If you are a first-time visitor to Monaco, forget any idea that it is some kind of comic-opera place where only high-society millionaires feel at home. This is an ancient and sovereign

Spectacular view over Monaco from the Jardin Exotique

Every year Menton hosts an elaborate lemon festival in February

state, ruled by the Grimaldi family for over 700 years. The Grimaldis originated in Genoa in Italy, one of their number seizing the Rock of Monaco in 1297.

Despite being so tiny – no larger than many a farm – the vastly wealthy principality is divided into four main districts: Monte Carlo, where the casino and the sumptuous Hôtel de Paris are located; La Condamine, around the harbour with its tens of millions of pounds' worth of yachts; the lovely old town on Le Rocher, the original Rock of Monaco, and Fontvieille, a new suburb.

Prince Rainier III's palace is reached from La Condamine up a steep ramp. It is mostly of the 16th and 17th centuries, and has several magnificent rooms open to the public, as well as a museum devoted to Napoleon, who was related to the Grimaldis. A fascinating archive collection documents centuries of Monagasque history. Throughout the palace and, indeed, throughout Monaco itself there are reminders of Princess Grace, the former film actress Grace Kelly whose fairytale marriage to Prince Rainier delighted the world.

Also in the old town are the elegant cathedral, built in neo-Romanesque style in the 19th century and containing the tomb of Princess Grace, and the Musée Océanographique, rising dramatically from the sea-cliffs. The latter, with an aquarium as well as fascinating museum exhibits, was directed by the famous underwater explorer Jacques Cousteau. Around it lie the beautiful St Martin gardens. They look down on the marina and Fontvieille, which is packed with housing and industry but has a large sports stadium and marina to its credit.

▸ *Leave Monaco on the* **N98** *as for Menton. In Roquebrune bear right for Cap Martin.*

BACK TO NATURE

Monaco's Jardin Exotique has a wonderful collection of sub-tropical plants, including 10m (35-foot) Mexican cacti, able to grow successfully because of the very warm microclimate. Below ground there are impressive limestone caverns at the Grotte de l'Observatoire.

SPECIAL TO...

Monte Carlo's Casino is the most famous in the world, with lush interior decorations and a gloriously baroque architectural style. Visitors may enjoy the public rooms without gambling, but a passport or some other identification is necessary, and no one under 21 is admitted.

ⓘ *Boulevard des Moulins*

▸ *Follow 'Menton' signs to the shore road, then keep right along the seafront to Menton.*

❽ Menton, Côte d'Azur
An old rhyme about the Riviera resorts claimed that 'Menton's dowdy, Monte's brass, Nice is rowdy, Cannes is class'. For years, Menton did have rather a faded air, brought about partly because its most faithful visitors were invalids and elderly people, from all corners of Europe. Now Menton has revitalised itself, but, nevertheless retains a less hectic pace than most other Côte d'Azur resorts. In addition, it has a lovely climate and Italian-style architecture; the Italian border is in its eastern outskirts.

Menton has beautiful gardens including the Jardin de la Serre de la Madone, laid out by the creator of Hidcote Manor gardens in Gloucestershire. In the town centre is a casino, fine museums, one of which is dedicated to the work of Jean Cocteau, and churches, promenades and squares. Around it lie the lemon groves – susceptible to very rare winter frosts – which give the town its most famous product. A Lemon Fair is held in February.

> [i] *Palais e l'Europe, avenue Boyer*

> ► *Leave Menton on the D2566 as for Sospel. Watch for the sharp right turn into Castillon.*

4 Castillon, Côte d'Azur

The original Castillon was wrecked in a 19th-century earthquake, and the rebuilt town destroyed during World War II. Their replacement is a charming modern village with lanes and stairways, a tiny square and a beautiful southern outlook, as well as shops and studios offering paintings,

sculptures, ceramics, leather-work, stained glass and jewellery.

> ► *Return to the D2566, bearing right to the Col de Castillon. Go through the tunnel and turn right to Sospel.*

5 Sospel, Côte d'Azur

Sospel is situated at the junction of two river valleys and is surrounded by exhilarating mountain scenery, yet still appears scruffy. However, there is an intriguing old quarter with houses alongside the River Bévéra which is crossed by an 11th-century toll bridge, and in the Église St Michel the town has a former cathedral complete

Sospel has a bohemian charm that inspires one to reach for paint-brush and canvas or camera

with grand baroque interior. At the railway station a group of coaches in a siding form a museum about the Orient Express. On the outskirts, Fort St Roch is an astonishing under-ground artillery installation, part of the Maginot Line of defences built in the 1930s between the Belgian border and Corsica and now a museum of the Resistance.

> [i] *Le Pont Vieux*

> ► *Leave Sospel on the D2566 via Moulinet to the Col de Turini.*

6 Col de Turini, Côte d'Azur

In the high pine and larch forests at 1,607m (5,270 feet) above sea-level, Turini is a winter sports resort and a cool bolt-hole in summer from the heat of the coast. Four roads radiate from the hamlet at the summit, one to the still-higher circuit of l'Authion, just inside the huge Parc National du Mercantour. There are magnifi-cent viewpoints here, as well as ruins of military fortifications battled over during the Revolution and in the last bitter days of fighting in 1944.

> ### SPECIAL TO...
>
> The Col de Turini is the most famous stage, every January, in the Monte Carlo Rally. You may see messages painted on the road – encouragement to top drivers from their fans.

> ### BACK TO NATURE
>
> Reached from the Col de Turini, the mountainous Parc National du Mercantour is home to chamois, ibex, ptarmi-gan and eagles. Alpine flowers and butterflies are at their best from June to August.

> ► *Leave the Col de Turini on the D70 through La Bollène-*

*Vésubie, where you should
turn sharp right following 'St-
Martin' sign. Go right on the
D2565 as for St-Martin-
Vésubie, then sharp right on
the D71, follow signs to
Belvédère and go right at the
T-junction for Gordolasque.
This is the narrow D171.
Follow it to a car park before
the bridge where the public
road ends.*

7 Vallon de la Gordolasque, Côte d'Azur

This dead-end valley road
follows a rocky mountain stream
past steep scree-slopes, crags
and boulder-runs where the
woodland cover peters out in
scattered pines and larches. The
public road ends at the 1,700m
(5,575-foot) Pont du Countet,
beside a relief map of the bare,

RECOMMENDED
WALKS

In the valley of the
Gordolasque, a long distance
footpath on the east bank can
be split into individual stretches
for shorter walks. Look for the
footbridges which cross the
river and take you past scree-
runs, boulder fields and thinning
pinewoods on the other side.

impressive upper valley still to
come. An easy stroll gives a
grand view of the dashing falls
at the Cascade de l'Estrech.

▶ *Return through Belvédère to
the D2565 and turn left as
for Nice. At St-Jean-de-la-
Rivière take the D32, the hairpinned climb past Utelle. Go
left on the D132 to Madone
d'Utelle.*

8 Madone d'Utelle, Côte d'Azur

The silence, air of tranquillity
and tremendous views make
the journey to this remote hilltop well worthwhile. Madone
d'Utelle has been a place of
pilgrimage since the 9th
century. The present church,
with its many thanks-offerings,
was built in 1806 and is the goal
of four major pilgrimages every
year. It shares the hilltop with a
mountain 'refuge' and a domed
orientation table which identi-
fies the major summits among
the all but unaccountable
mountain peaks included in the
glorious 360-degree skyline
view.

▶ *Return to St-Jean-de-la-Rivière
and turn right on the D2565.
After a 'Nice par Levens' sign,
bear left on the D19 and
follow it back to Nice.*

La Bollène-Vesubie is an enchanting village in the Col de Turini
region. For all its sophisticated
reputation, villages like this are
the real south of France

SCENIC ROUTES

From the immaculate villas of
the Cap de Nice, the N98
swings round to open up a gorgeous view of Villefranche bay.
Leaving Menton, the D2566
climbs past woodlands and
soaring limestone ridges which
stretch to the Italian border.
After the tunnel at the top of
the Col de Castillon, be ready
for a striking northwards view
past dramatic wooded ridges to
lonely skyline peaks.
Beyond Sospel the D2566
cuts through a seemingly
impenetrable mountain wall by
hairpinning up the Gorges du
Piaon. There is a remarkable
view back down the ravine
from the little Chapel of
Notre-Dame de la Menour,
reached by an arched staircase
bridge across the road.
The Col de Turini descends a
forested mountainside towards
the red-roofed village of La
Bollène-Vésubie.
As it rises, the hairpinned climb
to Madone d'Utelle opens up
more and more dramatic views.

Through
Historic Provence

The Romans left some of their most imposing monuments in the region they called *Provincia* – at Nîmes, Arles and Pont du Gard. Avignon retains the architectural grandeur given it by popes in voluntary exile from Rome. In the south, one of France's finest regional nature parks includes most of the Camargue.

3 DAYS • 306KM • 189 MILES

ITINERARY	
NÎMES	▶ **Pont du Gard (38km-24m)**
PONT DU GARD	▶ **Beaucaire/Tarascon** **(25km-15m)**
BEAUCAIRE/TARASCON	▶ **St-Michel-de-Frigolet** **(12km-8m)**
ST-MICHEL-DE-FRIGOLET	▶ **Avignon (15km-9m)**
AVIGNON	▶ **St-Rémy-de-Provence** **(25km-15m)**
ST-RÉMY-DE-PROVENCE	▶ **Les Baux-de-Provence** **(25km-15m)**
LES BAUX-DE-PROVENCE	▶ **Arles (21km-13m)**
ARLES	▶ **Méjanes (30km-19m)**
MÉJANES	▶ **Musée Camarguais** **(13km-8m)**
MUSÉE CAMARGUAIS	▶ **Maison du Parc** **(25km-15m)**
MAISON DU PARC	▶ **Saintes-Maries-de-la-Mer** **(5km-3m)**
SAINTES-MARIES-DE-LA-MER	▶ **Aigues-Mortes** **(32km-20m)**
AIGUES-MORTES	▶ **Nîmes (40km-25m)**

i 6 rue Auguste, Nîmes

▶ *Leave Nîmes on the **D979** as for Uzès. Turn right on the **D981**, then watch for a right turn following it to Pont du Gard.*

❶ Pont du Gard, Languedoc-Roussillon

In civil engineering the Romans thought big. Their settlement at Nîmes needed water, and the magnificent three-tiered aqueduct at Pont du Gard, built around 20BC, was the most spectacular section of the 50km (30 miles) of channels which brought it from faraway springs. The first and second levels of arched bridges are simply supports for the topmost water channel which now, out of use, is open to pedestrians. In the modern world, few utilitarian structures have such abiding elegance.

▶ *Continue to Remoulins. Go straight on along the **N86**, then follow signs for Beaucaire.*

❷ Beaucaire, Languedoc-Roussillon

Road traffic here defers to the Canal du Rhône à Sète (Rhône-Sète canal). Beaucaire's one-way street system circles an attractive canal basin where barges and holiday cruisers are moored. The two great interests of the town are bullfighting and music.

Beaucaire was where the Camargue style of bullfighting began, free from weapons and any taint of 'blood on the sand'. One statue in the town celebrates 'Clairon' – not a famous bullfighter, but a bull! Classical and jazz concerts are held at various venues all over the town throughout the season.

Beaucaire's part-ruined hilltop castle offers a good view over the lower Rhône, and the town museum holds many souvenirs of the days when traffic on the Roman highway – the *Via Domitia* – passed through between Italy and Spain. The town hosted a famous fair from

1217 to the mid-19th century and the museum has exhibits illustrating this.

i 24 cours Gambetta

▶ *Leave Beaucaire following signs to Tarascon.*

❸ Tarascon, Provence

The twin, and often the rival, of Beaucaire across the Rhône, Tarascon is famous for two fictional characters – the river monster called the Tarasqe, which is paraded through the town during the annual fair on the last Sunday in June, and Tartarin of Tarascon, the protagonist of *Aventures Prodigieuses de Tartarin de Tarascon* by Alphonse Daudet. The hero of these 'prodigious adventures' features in a musuem in the town. Tarascon has cool plane-tree avenues where the summer sun is held at bay. Its 15th-century castle on a dramatic riverside site displays valuable 17th-century tapestries and houses regular art exhibitions. Close by, the church dedicated to St Martha has a very impressive crypt which is the traditional burial place of Martha herself, the sister of Mary and Lazarus in the Bible story.

i 59 rue des Halles

▶ *Leave Tarascon on the **D970** as for Avignon. Turn right for St-Michel-de-Frigolet, looping over the **D970** on an elevated bridge.*

Practical and beautiful: the Roman aqueduct at Pont du Gard

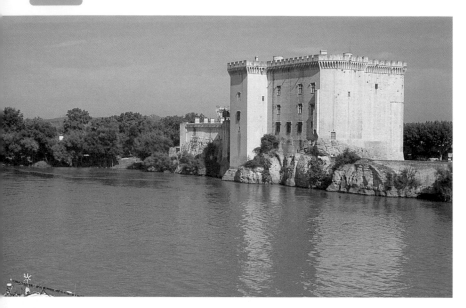

4 St-Michel-de-Frigolet, Provence

Among the trees, the spires and towers of a complex of abbey buildings suddenly comes into view. A religious community has lived here among the sweet scents of herbs and pinewood since as early as 1133, although there were some years in the 20th century when the monks were dispersed elsewhere. In the public areas of the abbey the buildings include a beautifully decorated basilica completed as recently as 1866. The old abbey farm is now a café; and items in the shop include the modern version of Père Gaucher's Elixir, which featured in one of Daudet's best-known stories.

▶ *Continue to Barbentane, where you should ignore the 'Toutes Directions' sign and go straight on, following the 'Château' sign, then turn right and follow signs into Avignon.*

5 Avignon, Provence

Avignon's heyday was in the 14th century, when the papacy moved the court here from Rome. The heart of the city is dominated by the grand 14th-century palace complex built by Popes Benedict XII and Clement VI and the towers, chapels, churches, cloisters and elegant courtyards which grew up to support it. What matters here is the architecture, since the restored buildings are mostly unfurnished, although Gobelin tapestries hang in the banqueting hall. Near by, the famous bridge of St-Bénézet stretches its remaining arches across the Rhône. Visitors from all over the world come to stroll 'sur le pont d'Avignon'.

The modern town has museums of all kinds, and a hectic summer programme of concerts, plays, dance, painting and sculpture exhibitions.

ⓘ *41 cours Jean-Jaurès*

▶ *Return from Avignon on the N570 as for Arles. Turn left on the D571, then right for St-Rémy-de-Provence on the D34, entering the town on the D571.*

6 St-Rémy-de-Provence, Provence

St-Rémy is a place that knows how to cope with the relentless summer sun of Provence. There are virtual tunnels of shady plane trees, and cooling water

The well preserved Château de Tarascon, sitting on the bank of the River Rhône

runs down channels in the alleyways of the old town. The Musée des Alpilles, named after the limestone sierra that rises to the south, contains exhibitions on St-Rémy's history and domestic life. Among townspeople commemorated is the 16th-century seer Nostradamus, whose birthplace can still be seen, but not visited. There is, however, a Nostradamus Museum in the nearby village of Salon de Provence.

On the outskirts of St-Rémy one road leads to a woodland lake at the foot of the Alpilles, another to the former Monastery of St Paul de Mausolée, converted into the mental home where Vincent van Gogh spun out his last demented days. In the countryside you may see amateur artists painting their own versions of the van Gogh scenes.

South of the town lie the extensive ruins of the Greek and Roman settlement of *Glanum*. Many of the artefacts discovered here are displayed in Le Centre Archéologie Antique in town.

i Place Jean-Jaurès

RECOMMENDED WALKS

From the tourist office in St-Rémy there is a walk through the outskirts of the town (finishing back on the main Boulevard Mirabeau), which visits the scenes of many of Vincent van Gogh's paintings – farms, poppy fields, plane and olive trees, and the quarry which appealed to him because of the Japanese-style arrangement of the rocks.

▶ Leave St-Rémy on the **D5**, then go right on the **D27a** to Les Baux-de-Provence.

⑦ Les Baux-de-Provence, Provence

On a ridge that towers above the southern plain, this hill settlement is split into two distinct parts, each of limestone masonry hard to distinguish at a distance from the living rock. The inhabited quarter, dating mostly from the 16th and 17th centuries, crams shops, museums, galleries, cafés, hotels and restaurants into its narrow lanes. The eerie 'Ville Morte' ('dead city') on the crown of the ridge was the medieval stronghold, which became famous for its 'Courts of Love', courtly rituals in which troubadours vied in composing ardent, flowery verses for aristocratic ladies. It is a now a ruin. In the 15th century Louis XIII crushed the power and influence of Les Baux, but the 'dead city' remains a haunting place with magnificent views over the surrounding countryside.

Just outside the town, on the D27, the Théâtre des Images offers a majestic audio-visual presentation. In chilly halls cut into the old bauxite quarries (Les Baux was where that aluminium ore was first discovered), 40 projectors continuously show historical and nature-based films.

BACK TO NATURE

All over the Camargue you will see the characteristic white horses, often ridden by *gardians* – the Camargue equivalent of cowboys. But look out for the foals. They are born black or grey, and may take as long as five years to grow a fully white coat.

FOR CHILDREN

The easiest thing to arrange in the Camargue is an escorted ride on one of the mysterious Camargue white horses, with a *gardian* to act as guide. Sessions as short as half an hour are offered, and many visit farms where bulls are reared for the ring.

i Hôtel de Manville

▶ From Les Baux-de-Provence, follow the signs to Arles, entering the town on the **N570**.

⑧ Arles, Provence

Phoenicians, Greeks and Romans all established themselves here, but it is the Romans who made Arles the capital of *Provincia*, who have left the most abiding monuments. The elliptical amphitheatre (Arènes) built by the Emperor Hadrian in the 1st century AD still survives, used, alas, for bull-fights in the Spanish style as well as the bloodless style of the Camargue; and you can attend concerts and festivals in the semi-circular Augustan theatre (Théâtre Antique). The town's summer calendar is crammed with events having an international flavour as well as those firmly rooted in the traditions of Provence. One of these is the parade of *gardians* – the

Carving on the main doorway of the Romanesque cathedral of St-Trophime, in Arles

Camargue 'cowboys' – on their white horses.

Arles is very well supplied with museums strong on paintings, sculptures and Provençal life. The former cathedral and cloisters of St-Trophime, one of the finest cloisters in the south of France, are decorated with beautiful stone carvings. A favourite walk is along the tree-lined avenue of Les Alyscamps, flanked by ancient tombstones, the remains of Arles' once widespread necropolis.

The Fondation Vincent van Gogh is a magnet for art lovers; it was in Arles that, after a fight with his friend Gauguin, he slashed off his own ear. A memorial to his tormented spirit stands in the quiet and shaded public gardens.

i Boulevard des Lices

FOR HISTORY BUFFS

In Fontvieille, 10km (6 miles) northeast of Arles, follow the 'Moulin de Daudet' signs to the restored windmill on an exhilarating viewpoint hill. This is the mill which featured in Alphonse Daudet's *Lettres de Mon Moulin*, required reading not only for generations of French schoolchildren, but also for those learning French abroad. It is now a museum devoted to Daudet's life and works. Many places on this tour – Beaucaire, Tarascon, Avignon and the Camargue among them – are mentioned in the 'Letters'.

▶ *Leave Arles on the **D570** as for Saintes-Maries-de-la-Mer. Go left on the **D36**, right on the **D36b**, then right on the **D37**. Turn left on the **C5** to Méjanes.*

⑨ Méjanes, Provence

In the very heart of the Camargue, and including some of the shoreline of the lagoon called Étang de Vaccarès, this estate doubles as a leisure centre and a farm. It has its own bull-ring, in which events are held every weekend during the summer, a restaurant and stables where horses may be hired for short or full-day rides.

▶ *Rejoin the **D37**. Turn right on the **D570** to the Musée Camarguais.*

⑩ Musée Camarguais, Provence

Based on an old sheepfold, the Camargue Museum is the best place to find out about the geology and history of this curious area and about the lives of the farmers and how intensive draining turned great areas of previously useless marsh into productive grazing and arable land. A walk from the museum follows the banks of a drainage canal dug as long ago as 1543, and shows the difference between reclaimed land and the original marsh. The museum is

one of the main centres of the Réserve Zoologique et Botanique de la Camargue (Camargue Regional Nature Park) which covers more than 83,000 hectares (205,000 acres) of the Rhône delta.

▶ *Return along the **D570** and watch for the Maison du Parc on the left of the road at Pont du Gau.*

⑪ Maison du Parc, Provence

Complementary to the Musée Camarguais, this centre explains and illustrates the fascinating wildlife of the park, with an audio-visual theatre and a display on all the brands used on the Camargue horses. Throughout, the emphasis is on the fragility of this marvellous habitat. The good advice is offered that anti-mosquito creams are a wise precaution for anybody exploring the Camargue, particularly in September and October; but to avoid the insects, there is indoor wildlife watching here too. The

picture windows at the rear of the centre overlook a pool where flamingos are often seen.

Close by, there is a privately owned Parc Ornithologique where many species of resident and migrant birds are on show.

▶ *Continue to Saintes-Maries-de-la-Mer.*

⑫ Saintes-Marie-de-la-Mer, Provence

Often packed with summer visitors, the former fishing village of Saintes-Maries takes its name from the tradition that the three Marys from the Bible story, together with Martha (the sister of Mary and Lazarus), sailed here from Palestine and began evangelising the Camargue.

But for the gypsy people of Europe the significant figure in the story is Sarah. In one version an Egyptian or Ethiopian servant who accompanied the Marys; in another, a local woman who helped them ashore. Sarah is venerated as the patron saint of gypsies. Her statue, dressed in rich robes, is paraded through the town during two festivals in May and October. For the rest of the year it rests in the claustrophobic undercroft of the 9th-century church, illuminated by candles which also throw an eerie glow on a head of Sarah sculpted from Silesian coal.

Just south of the church, the Musée Baroncelli concentrates on local and natural history and folklore.

ℹ️ 5 avenue van Gogh

FOR CHILDREN

Just beyond Saintes-Maries-de-la-Mer, look for the sign to the pier where *Tiki III*, a little Mississippi-style sternwheeler, starts its cruises around the mouth of the Petit Rhône. This is an ideal way to wander past the grazings of Camargue horses and bulls.

▶ *Follow 'Aigues-Mortes' signs from Saintes-Maries, keeping on the D38, D38c and D58.*

SPECIAL TO...

The watery landscape of the Camargue and the Mediterranean climate combine to offer perfect conditions for the cultivation of rice, in fact most of the rice consumed in France is grown here. Each September, the area celebrates the harvest with a Rice Festival, complete with a procession of *Gardians* and folk dancing. The Bouches-du-Rhône delta also produces 'solar' salt, so named because the sea water is collected in evaporation pools and dried by the sun.
Honey is another speciality, with 75% of France's production coming from this area. Lavender is just one of many varieties.

ℹ️ *Porte de la Gardette*

▶ *Return from Aigues-Mortes following 'Nîmes' signs on the D979, N313 and N113, avoiding the 'peage' signs, to Nîmes itself.*

SPECIAL TO...

Not only in the Camargue itself, but also in the inland towns, are regular and well-attended bullfights. However, these are not usually of the bloodstained Spanish variety that so many visitors find distasteful. Here the aim of the bullfighter (the *rasetteur*) is not to kill the bull but to get away unscathed with a rosette or some other favour that is tied to its horns. Bulls thus live to fight many times and become skilled operators. Some become as well known as the bullfighters.

Les Baux-de-Provence, one of France's most famous hill villages

🄱 **Aigues-Mortes,**
Languedoc-Roussillon
This town is an amazing survival, extended hardly at all beyond the original rampart walls constructed in the 13th century by Louis IX of France who called here on the seventh and eighth crusades. The walls, towers and fortified gateways remain in place. Inside them, a pleasant town retains the old medieval grid pattern of streets. A statue of St Louis looks down on the activity round the central square, just as his gilded statue graces the arcaded interior of the church. The best view of Aigues-Mortes is from the gallery of the Tour de Constance, once a political and religious prison, which overlooks the town and also puts it in a geographical context among the low-lying lagoons and lakes of the Camargue. But where is the sea? Over the years the Mediterranean has receded, stranding the town. In terms of the sea, Aigues-Mortes became what its name implies – the 'Dead Waters'.

SCENIC ROUTES

North of Nîmes the D979 crosses the limestone scrubland of the Garrigues, then descends to the gorges of the Gardon and continues through totally different country of fields and vineyards. On the way to Frigolet and Barbentane, to the south of Avignon, the road runs through pleasant pinewoods with long stretches of picnic sites.

BACK TO NATURE

Of the many species of birds which live in the southern part of the Camargue, the most often illustrated are the flamingos. Watch out also for herons and egrets standing motionless in the water before darting down to spear their prey. Bee-eaters are perhaps the most colourful – look for them perched beside roadsides.

THE ALPS TO ALSACE

Alsace, Savoie, Burgundy, Lorraine – these towns include four provinces, each with its own independent heritage, 'separate for centuries from that of France. On the French-German border, Alsace and Lorraine were long contended territories, and even after they merged with France, they were lost again during the years of German occupation following the disastrous war of 1870 until the Allied victory in 1918. The battlefields around Verdun and St-Mihiel were the scene of indescribable carnage during World War I.

For 2,000 years and more, the Rhône/Saône valleys have been major highways, and it is still easy to drive quickly and unseeingly through them. However, off the main route, there is a jigsaw of medieval fishponds, and small towns of great interest.

East of Grenoble lie the majestic passes of the Alps and one of the highest roads in Europe. An exploration of the country of the lost duchy of Savoie, shows how France's massive hydro-electric schemes are landscaped so as not to spoil the glorious mountain scenery in which they are set.

Alsace is a different country once again, France with German names, sweeping vineyards and a strong preoccupation with storks. The Vosges mountains here may pale beside the Alps, but their forests and often cloudy upland ridges have an individual appeal.

Driving conditions are very varied. There are roads across the plains, among great acreages of arable land. Others wind through the vine-clad foothills. But on the Col de l'Iseran and the upper reaches of the Col de la Croix de Fer, you are in genuine Alpine country. The first of these passes can be swept by icy winds, the second can create a curious vertigo. All the roads, though, cope with summer tourist traffic.

There is splendid vineyard country here, producing wines as different as Burgundy and the Rieslings of Alsace. Many sophisticated gourmets consider that the country's finest 'table' is in Lyon.

Nancy

If you are expecting some modest provincial town, Nancy will come as a surprise. At the heart of this historic capital of Lorraine, richly-gilded Place Stanislas is one of the most elegant squares in France. Look for the lovely late Gothic Palais Ducal containing the Musée Historique Lorrain, for the Église des Cordeliers with the tomb of the dukes of Lorraine, for the superb medieval gateway and former prison of the Porte de la Craffe, and for the beautiful buildings of the old town. The Musée de Fer illustrates the history of iron, for generations a major industry in Lorraine. You can watch the glass-blowers in the crystal works of Daum.

Lyon

Lyon is a handsome city. It has sweeping quays on two rivers, the Rhône and the Saône, whose waters converge in the southern suburbs. Many notable buildings stand on the Presqu'ile, the peninsula between the rivers. Here is the Musée des Beaux Arts with others devoted to textiles and decorative arts, printing and the history of banknotes. The 19th-century Basilica of Notre-Dame-des-Fourvière stands on the skyline above the streets of the old quarter in the loop of the Saône. A funicular links it with the lower town. Another climbs to twin Roman theatres still in use today.

The Lumière brothers, pioneers of moving film, worked in Lyon. There is a decorative mosaic, featuring famous figures such as Buster Keaton, near the Institut Lumière which regularly shows vintage films.

Grenoble

Grenoble, at the confluence of the Rivers Isère and Drac, is dominated by the soaring cliffs of the Massif de la Chartreuse. Cable cars whisk you to the viewpoint Fort de la Bastille, looking to the mountain ranges of Chamrousse and Vercors.

Beautifully sited, and with extensive parks and gardens, Grenoble offers music and drama, the Musée de Grenoble which contains paintings and sculpture, and has well-presented museums of science and technology, natural history, the Resistance and the region of Dauphiné.

Explore the gracious old quarter, admire Grenoble's modern architecture, and note its revived enthusiasm for the urban tram.

Strasbourg

Seat of the Council of Europe and the European Parliament, Strasbourg is also where Gutenberg, in the 15th century, invented modern printing. His memory is still revered.

The heart of the city is a river island. Look for the intriguing quarter called La Petite-France, where lovely old houses stand by the restored navigation canal.

Strasbourg has beautiful Renaissance and half-timbered buildings, a glorious cathedral and a cluster of museums in the 18th-century Château des Rohan. You can take a river cruise, stroll through botanic gardens and enjoy the Parc de l'Orangerie created in 1804 for Napoleon's Josephine.

Opposite: the cathedral of St-Etienne, in Toul, has a splendid Flamboyant frontage
Below: Nancy prides itself on its classical townscape

Visions of
War & Peace

Except for part of the valley of the Moselle, this tour avoids the industrial districts of Lorraine in favour of the agricultural south around Nancy. There are peaceful rural landscapes here, but they have bitter memories. The Franco-Prussian War of 1870 ravaged Lorraine, as did the battles of the 20th century.

3 DAYS • 300KM • 187 MILES

Verdun:
Champs de Bataille
5
Bras-s-
Meuse
6
Verdun
Eix   Eix
Haudimont
Forêt
de Sommedieue
REIMS
Ancemont
Woimbey
St-Mihiel
7
Woinville
8
Butte de
Montsec
Apremont-
la-Forêt
Gironville-s/s-
les-Côtes
Corniéville

LUXEMBOURG
Orne
Mont
St-Quentin
Scy-
Chazelles
Metz **3**
Ville-
s-Yron **4**
Gravelotte
VOIE DE LA LIBERTÉ
Harville   Mars-la-
Tour
Jouy-aux
Arches
Corny-s-M
Etang
de
Lachaussée
PARC RÉGIONAL
Lac de
Madine   Nonsard
DE LORRAINE
Pont-à-
Mousson
Saizerais
Liverdun Haut **2**
Aingeray
Lucey   Forêt   Parc de Haye
Velaine-   de
en-Haye   Haye
TROYES   Bruley
Toul **9**
DIJON   Maron
NANCY

0   5   10 m
0   5   10   15 km

i *14 place Stanislas, Nancy*

▶ *Leave Nancy as for Paris on the A31. Take the 'Parc de Haye' exit.*

❶ Parc de Haye, Lorraine
This extensive leisure park is laid out on the site of a World War II American army camp; so it is appropriate that its motor museum has both civil and military themes. You will see examples of Bugatti, Delahaye and Jaguar among the cars.

SPECIAL TO...

The most famous dish to come out of Lorraine is, of course, the quiche; other local delicacies include many kinds of sausages (beware of those of pale appearance - unless you like tripe!) and a tempting range of sweet pastries. There are the wines of the Moselle and the delicious fruity kirsch, but nothing quenches the thirst like the clear spring waters of the Vosges.

▶ *Turn right from the park exit following the D400 sign, then right through Velaine-en-Haye and Aingeray. Go left over the*

bridge on the D90b, through traffic lights, then left for Liverdun Haut.

❷ Liverdun Haut, Lorraine
Crowning a bluff above a wooded curve of the Moselle, and providing lovely views over the river, this little medieval town was once the favoured summer residence of the bishops of Toul. Many old buildings survive. The tourist office is in the 16th-century fortified gateway, and there is an arcaded square of the same period. Dedicated to St Euchaire, the church is basically 12th century. Look for the saint's tomb with his beheaded effigy. Euchaire was martyred at nearby Pompey in AD362.

i *Porte Haute*

BACK TO NATURE

See how the currents of air sweeping up the wooded ridge from the Moselle suit the birds of Liverdun Haut. Kestrels nest in the old buildings and hunt above the woodlands. Kites are here too, as well as swifts, swallows and martins darting around the streets.

Medieval Liverdun, once favoured by the bishops of Toul

▶ *Return to the D90b and continue through Saizerais. Go right on the D907 then, immediately after the 'Saizerais' board, turn left along Route de Villers. Go right at a give way sign, then left on the N57 to Metz.*

FOR HISTORY BUFFS

Jouy-aux Arches on the N57 takes it name from the high masonry arches, built almost 1,900 years ago in the reign of the emperor Trajan as part of the Roman aqueduct to Metz. Metz was already an old town when Julius Caesar conquered Gaul. The Romans fortified it, their walls forming the battlefield fortifications.

---

❸ Metz, Lorraine
Old fortifications are a reminder that Metz has been besieged, captured and relieved many times over the centuries, most recently in our own century. A memorial in the Place d'Armes recalls how, in 1918, Marshal Foch, Commander-in-Chief of the Allied armies on the

a landlord's and a labourer's farm, the 12th-century church and the simple château built in 1762 by the bishop of Metz.

SPECIAL TO...

Along the D903 near Verdun are certain kilometre stones which nominate the road the 'Voie de la Liberté' (Freedom Way). Allied troops swept the German forces along it in 1944.

FOR HISTORY BUFFS

Turn left along the Rue Robert Schuman in Scy-Chazelles, on the way from Metz to Ville-sur-Yron, to visit the modest home, now a museum, where the great French statesman (1886–1963) worked out his plans for a united Europe. Schuman played an important role in the creation of NATO, the Council of Europe and the European Coal and Steel Community, the first step towards the EU.
The Musée Militaire in Gravelotte recalls the disastrous Franco-Prussian War of 1870, which led to the downfall of Napoleon III.

Western front at the end of World War I, said that to see French troops on parade again at Metz was his greatest reward (the city had been in German hands for 47 years). Another memorial commemorates the liberation of Metz in 1944.

Despite being an industrial centre, Metz has colourful parks and gardens, a lake and attractive riverside areas. The cathedral (St-Étienne), of soft yellow stone, features a soaring interior with intricate stained glass, including an impressive rose window. Archaeology, art and history are all to be found under one roof at La Cour d'Or Musée d'Art et d'Histoire. The Renaissance section is particularly enchanting, as is Roman Metz, displayed through sarcophagi, pottery and architecture.

[i] Place d'Armes

▶ *Leave Metz by the N3 through Longeville. At traffic lights in Le Ban-St-Martin,*

Metz has been the prize of armies since Roman times

turn right on the D103w for Mont St-Quentin, following the hairpinned Rue Fort. Down from Mont St-Quentin, turn right at the Stop sign in the village (this is Scy-Chazelles), go left down Rue Leduchat and continue downhill at the next Stop sign. Pass Rue Robert Schuman on your left. At traffic lights turn right and follow 'Verdun' signs to Gravelotte, then go straight on along the D903 through Mars-la-Tour. Turn right on the D952, then left on the D132 to Ville-sur-Yron.

4 **Ville-sur-Yron,** Lorraine
In 1990, in this village tucked away among the fields, a fascinating trail was laid out which allows you to 'read' the architecture, building materials, history and way of life of a typical Lorraine agricultural settlement. It leads over the 19th-century bridge to the watermill,

▶ *Continue on the D132, then go left on the D15, which becomes the D26 to Harville. Rejoin the D903 as for Verdun. Go right on the D24, then left on the D24a and left on the N3 into Verdun. Turn right at the traffic lights as for Paris, then watch for a sharp right turn following 'Champs de Bataille' boards. This is the D112. Go left at the crossroads on to the D913, follow 'Ossuaire' signs, then go left as for Verdun.*

5 **Verdun: Champs de Bataille,** Lorraine
In 1916 the Germans launched a ferocious attack against the French lines northeast of Verdun: colossal artillery bombardments, mines, flame-

throwers and poison gas were all employed. In the next few months, literally hundreds of thousands of troops died in the trenches, but the French essentially held the line. After the war, the ground of the battlefields was so ravaged that it was forested over.

Along the D112 and the D913 you will find forts, trenches, memorials and utterly devastated villages. The hilltop Ossuaire (Ossuary) de Douaumont is the last resting place for the bones of 130,000 soldiers on both sides, and offers a regular audio-visual programme on life in the trenches. As you walk to the Fort de Douaumont, you might wonder why the French high command in 1915 decided to leave this greatest underground stronghold in Europe virtually unguarded.

► *Continue to Bras-sur-Meuse and turn left to Verdun.*

6 Verdun, Lorraine
Linked with other 'martyred towns' such as Hiroshima, Nagasaki, Coventry and Warsaw, Verdun is the Capital of Peace. Its vast underground citadel has tableaux of wartime

scenes, and of the sombre moment in 1920 when France's Unknown Soldier was chosen. He now lies under the Arc de Triomphe in Paris.

Attractively sited on a curve of the Meuse, Verdun enjoys riverside quays, a fine Romanesque cathedral and the former bishop's palace, gardens and sports grounds, as well as prehistoric displays, paintings, furnishings and ceramics in the 16th-century Hôtel de la Princerie. Try the *dragées* – the sugared almonds which have been made in Verdun to a secret recipe since the 13th century.

[i] *Place de la Nation*

► *Leave Verdun on the* **D34** *through Dugny, then go left on the* **D901** *to St-Mihiel.*

7 St-Mihiel, Lorraine
Best known in history for its strategic position in the St-Mihiel salient – the defensive ring created by the Germans in 1918 – this little town also has the notable Benedictine abbey church of St Michel, with a 12th-century Romanesque portal and, in its light and airy interior, 80 beautifully carved choir stalls from the time of

Louis XV. Here and in the Church of St Étienne, look for works by the local 16th-century sculptor Ligier Richier, a pupil of Michelangelo.

The Benedictines' library, itself a masterpiece of Lorraine design, survives with 8,000 valuable books and illuminated manuscripts.

[i] *Rue de Palais de Justice*

► *Leave St-Mihiel as for Chaillon. Go right on the* **D162** *and left on the* **D119** *through Woinville to Montsec. Turn right on the* **D12** *then follow 'American monument' signs.*

FOR CHILDREN

Turn left off the route at Woinville for Nonsard on the northeast shore of the reservoir called Étang de Madine. Here youngsters can enjoy mini golf, cyclocross and pedaloes, as relief from the grim memories of war all around.

The impressive Benedictine library in St-Mihiel

▶ Return to the **D12** and turn right. Go left on the **D908** to Toul.

SPECIAL TO...

On the D908 approaching Toul, turn off for Lucey and Bruley. Lucey's Maison du Polyculture illustrates old farming methods and equipment. Grape juice is pressed for visitors at the vine harvest. At Bruley the Centre du Promotion lets you sample local produce such as smoke-cured meats, Côtes de Toul wines – especially the rosé – and the famous Mirabelle plums.

9 **Toul,** Lorraine

Almost ringed by the Moselle, the Canal de l'Est and the canal linking the Marne with the Rhine, the fortress city of Toul once had the status of an independent enclave within the dukedom of Lorraine and, as

The town centre of Toul

the heart of a diocese and a free imperial city, was very important in medieval times. Old town gateways survive, as do the 17th-century walls, and the cathedral (St-Étienne) shows a splendid 15th-century Flamboyant frontage to the Place de Gaulle.

You should look at the decorated cloisters of the town's other principal church, St Gengoult. With all the water near by, Toul welcomes anglers, and the yacht basin is enlivened by the spray of a fountain in the centre.

[i] Parvis de la Cathédrale

RECOMMENDED WALKS

At Woinville, near Montsec, a roadside map will show you the network of local footpaths. Many are on the attractively wooded ridge of the Côtes overlooking the reservoir of Étang de Madine, and link up with other villages in the foothills.

8 **Butte de Montsec,** Lorraine

It was the Americans who smashed through the St-Mihiel salient in September 1918. The US 1st Army's memorial is a massive rotunda on this beautiful viewpoint summit overlooking the Étang de Madine, with a relief map illustrating the course of the battle. Ironically, American troops had to fire on the memorial to subdue a German machine-gun post here in 1944. It was later completely restored.

RECOMMENDED WALKS

On the return route to Nancy, from the D909 and the D92 before and after Maron, roads and tracks in the Forêt de Haye are linked up to make circular waymarked walks on the gentle gradients of the forest above the Moselle.

▶ Leave Toul on the **N4** as for Nancy. Go under the bridge, then right on the **D909** to Maron. Turn left on the **D92** and return to Nancy.

SCENIC ROUTES

From the farming plain after Velaine there are long views all around, including the beautiful setting of Liverdun above the far bank of the Moselle. At Gravelotte you begin to cross the vast arable plains of Lorraine, then along the D24 comes orchard country at the foot of low hills. From Montsec, the D12 runs through farm and orchard land, with occasional vineyards, below the wooded Côtes de Toul. After Toul, the D909 before Maron offers pleasant glimpses of the curves of the Moselle.

Secrets of the
Rhône Valley

The landscape changes from level plains scattered with ponds, to beautiful vineyards in the foothills and gentle forest passes. Wildlife parks display waterfowl and birds of prey. There is a spa, and one of the loveliest towns in the Lyonnais commemorates a saintly man whose life's work relieved the sufferings of the poor.

4 DAYS • 352KM • 219½ MILES

ITINERARY

LYON	▶	**Musée Henri Malartre** (17km-11m)
MUSÉE HENRI MALARTRE	▶	**Mont d'Or** (13km-8m)
MONT D'OR	▶	**Parc des Oiseaux** (32km-20m)
PARC DES OISEAUX	▶	**Villars-les-Dombes** (1km-½m)
VILLARS-LES-DOMBES	▶	**Châtillon-sur-Chalaronne** (16km-10m)
CHÂTILLON-SUR-CHALARONNE	▶	**Vaux-en-Beaujolais** (36km-22m)
VAUX-EN-BEAUJOLAIS	▶	**Amplepuis** (35km-22m)
AMPLEPUIS	▶	**Roanne** (30km-19m)
ROANNE	▶	**Chazelles-sur-Lyon** (90km-56m)
CHAZELLES-SUR-LYON	▶	**Charbonnières-les-Bains** (72km-45m)
CHARBONNIÈRES-LES-BAINS	▶	**Lyon** (10km-6m)

Dans cet endroit privilégié
de la campagne dombiste,
j'ai voulu faire de ce Parc,
un lieu d'accueil pour tous,
un havre de Paix et de Repos,
un livre ouvert sur la nature
où le visiteur se sente en
communion avec l'oiseau
et son environnement.
Jean - SAINT-CYR

Turn right on the **D89**. In St-Cyr, go right on the **D65**. Continue straight on uphill at the Stop sign, then keep right on the **D92** for Mont Cindre. After Mont Cindre, go straight on at a crossroads on the **D90** signed 'Fortin du Mont Thou'. Return to the cross-roads and turn right, then go right on the **D73** to Poleymieux-au-Mont-d'Or.

2 Mont d'Or, Rhône Valley
Follow the main route to Poleymieux over Mont d'Or ('Golden Hill') above Lyon, but be sure to stop off for occasional strolls, and to admire the views. There are several pleasant villages on the hillsides, as well as farms and woodlands. Mont Cindre, beside a telecommunications tower, is a favourite place for people from Lyon who take to the hills at weekends. Many of them enjoy the walk that starts at the hermitage. The best 360-degree panoramic view is from Mont Thou, as you walk over the grasslands beside a hilltop military camp.

[i] *Place Bellecourt, Lyon*

Lyon is a handsome city in the valley of the Rhône

FOR CHILDREN

The Parc de la Tête d'Or, on the banks of the Rhône in Lyon, has a lake, a small zoo, go-cart track, botanical gardens and pony rides.

▶ *Leave Lyon on the **D433** as for Neuville. Go through Caluire-en-Cuire, then turn right at 'Musée de l'Auto-mobile' sign and follow 'Musée' signs along a complicated route to the Musée Henri Malartre.*

1 Musée Henri Malartre,
Rhône Valley
In the attractive, high-set Château Rochetaillée and the exhibition halls in its grounds, is an impeccably maintained collection of really rare cars. The Hugot, Thieulin, Noël Beret and the very early steam-powered Secretand, displayed in the Musée Henri Malarte, are the only survivors of these makes in the world. The separate hall displays several Gordini racing cars, built by the dogged but perpetually broke French constructor after whom it is named.

Hitler's Mercedes is here, as well as examples of Packard, Lincoln and the 1912 Alco built by the American Locomotive Corporation. Look for the bizarre gyroscope-equipped 1926 Monotrace tandem car, and the huge battery-powered Stela which ran as a taxi in Lyon till 1953. There is also a strong collection of cycles and motorcycles (1898–1954).

▶ *Return by the same route to the **D433** and turn left. Go right over the suspension bridge into Couzon, then left on the **D51** into St-Romain.*

FOR CHILDREN

At the Maison d'Ampère in Poleymieux children are encouraged to try 18 of Ampère's original electrical experiments, including some with magnets. This is fun as well as a fine learning experience, and perfectly safe at the power levels employed.

FOR HISTORY BUFFS

In Poleymieux the Maison d'Ampère is devoted to the brilliant and engagingly eccentric Lyon-born physicist André-Marie Ampère (1775–1836), who gave his name to the standard unit of electric current. It also has an amazing display of historic electrical equipment.

▶ In Poleymieux-au-Mont-d'Or
bend right after gantry traffic
lights, still on the **D73**, and
continue via Curis-au-Mont-
d'Or to Neuville-centre on the
D16. Go straight on along the
D16e through Montanay,
then left at the T-junction (this
is the **N83**) through Mionnay.
Turn right into the Parc des
Oiseaux.

3 Parc des Oiseaux, Rhône Valley

Far more than simply the
ornithological park its name
suggests, this public estate near
Villars-les-Dombes takes full
advantage of its situation in
woodland circling an attractive
lake. Eagles, vultures, parrots
and parakeets have enclosures
in the woods, and there is a
tropical bird house, while peli-
cans, swans, geese and flamingos favour the water. The
guided tour, by 'tourist train',
takes 30 minutes. A walk round
to see the park in all its details
might occupy two hours. There
is an adventure playground and
a picnic area.

At the entrance to the park,
the Farmers' Market sells local
produce, and there is an exhibition about the different fish of
the region.

▶ Continue to Villars-les-
Dombes, eventually leaving
the village on the **D2** as for
Châtillon.

4 Villars-les-Dombes, Rhône Valley

With a fine Gothic church, a
road system which craftily
keeps through traffic away from
the narrow streets of the pleasant and colourful centre, and an
excellent natural history bookshop, Villars is where to start
any exploration of the curious
plateau district known as Les
Dombes.

Here there are a thousand
pools, lakes or meres dug as
fishponds from the 12th century
onwards. They are now split
between angling waters and
commercial fisheries for carp,
tench, roach and pike. Around
2,000 tonnes are taken every
year, to make this one of the
great inland fishery districts of
France. Ask locally about dishes
such as fillet of royal carp.

[i] *3 place Hôtel de Ville*

▶ Continue on the **D2** to
Châtillon-sur-Chalaronne.

Baby ostriches at the Parc des
Oiseaux – Villars-les-Dombes

....
BACK TO NATURE
....

Beyond Villars, the lakes and
ponds of Les Dombes are
havens for wildlife. On the
Étang Forêt and the Étang du
Château at Bouligneux you can
expect to see teal and mallard,
coots, herons and grebes.

5 Châtillon-sur-Chalaronne, Rhône Valley

Few small towns in France have
been awarded four stars in the
national *villages fleuris* ('villages
in bloom') competition, but
Châtillon deserves every one.
You should spend time admiring
the blaze of blossoms in parks
and gardens, beside the banks
of the River Chalaronne and its
tributary streams, in window
boxes and hanging baskets, and
decorating all the bridges.

Châtillon cherishes some
beautifully maintained buildings to match the flowers. The
covered market hall of 1670 is a
gem, some of the old town
ramparts survive, and the brickwork Church of St André dates
from the 16th century. The
famous Châtillon triptych of
1527 is displayed in the dignified town hall. Its three Biblical

scenes – the sleeping apostles, Christ taken from the cross and the Resurrection – are beautifully painted and restored.

Gathered in the intriguing old Apothecairerie is a fine collection of earthenware pots from which 18th-century pharmacists concocted their mixtures of gentian, sassafras, asafoetida and other plants. You can see where some of the prescribed salts ate away the painted surface of the pots!

RECOMMENDED WALKS

Three walks, mostly on country roads with occasional farm tracks, are suggested by the tourist office at Châtillon. One visits four of the little lakes for which the district is famous. The others go to the old castle ramparts and the banks of the Relevant stream.

prises here continue the *Clochemerle* name. This is one of the most beautifully located of the Beaujolais wine-growing villages. There is a lively fraternity of enthusiasts for wine, and much of it may be tasted locally at the Caveau de Clochemerle.

However, *Clochemerle* is perhaps best remembered for the ceremonial inauguration of the public toilet. La Pisotière de Clochemerle stands on a terrace above the beautiful wine-planted valley, and is still popular with visitors today.

▶ *Take the Lamure road, leaving Vaux on the 'Le Sottier poids lourds' road. This is the **D49**. Follow 'Lamure' signs – ignoring a left turn for Les Buissières – then go left on the **D44** to St-Cyr. Turn right on the **D504** to Allières, left on the **D485**, then right on the **D98** and over the level crossing. Go straight on through St-Just, then follow signs to Amplepuis.*

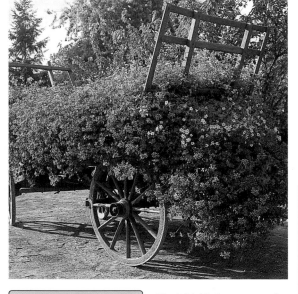

SPECIAL TO...

The slopes of Mont Brouilly, between Vaux-en-Beaujolais and Amplepuis, are packed with vineyards whose geometrical lines, at different angles, create a beautiful pattern on the hillsides. Available locally, *Côte de Brouilly* is one of the fine *crus* of Beaujolais wine, with many individual producers.

FOR HISTORY BUFFS

In Châtillon you can see the house where, in 1617, 'Monsieur Vincent' lived as the parish priest. Born in 1580, Vincent de Paul led an eventful early life, having been captured by corsairs on a voyage in 1605 and sold into slavery in Tunis. He was employed by the French royal family after his escape and before he came to Châtillon. Touched by the plight of the poor people of the town, he founded the first of his many charitable organisations, which led to the great Society of St Vincent de Paul (he was canonised in 1737).

The delightfully fragrant town of Châtillon-sur-Chalaronne

ⓘ *Place du Champ de Foire*

▶ *Leave Châtillon on the **D17**, which becomes the **D37** through Belleville and Cercié, then go left on the **D43** and left on the **D43e** to Mont Brouilly. Return to the **D43** and turn left. Turn right on the **D19**, then right on the **D49** to Vaux-en-Beaujolais.*

⓺ **Vaux-en-Beaujolais,** Rhône Valley

Gabriel Chevallier immortalised this village among the hillside vineyards as the fictional setting for his famous satirical novel *Clochemerle*, and several enter-

⓻ **Amplepuis,** Rhône Valley

In this little industrial town, the Musée Barthélémy Thimonnier celebrates a most heroic failure. Barthélémy Thimonnier was an apprentice tailor here. In 1825, having seen the laborious work of the seamstresses, he invented the sewing machine.

He was spurned in Paris. London businessmen paid him an insulting sum for his design. Soon after his dejected return to France, the sewing machine revolutionised the production of clothes. But by then

Thimonnier had died – still
poor, and still unknown.

[i] Place de l'Hôtel de Ville

▶ Leave Amplepuis on the **D8**,
then take the **D504** to
Roanne.

8 Roanne, Rhône Valley
Backing on to the Loire,
Roanne is also on a well-maintained canal along which visitor
cruises are run. It is an historic
textile town, and old techniques
of spinning and weaving are
demonstrated at the Écomusée.
If you enjoy ceramics, visit the
elegant château of the Musée
Déchelette, which has beautiful
displays of French and Italian
ware. Modern craftworkers
congregate in the Maison des
Métiers d'Art.
    Roanne keeps a foothold in
the wine business, although the
great days when it shipped
barge-loads of barrels to Paris
are long since gone. You can
taste some of the *Côte Roannaise*
wine in the town-centre *caveau*,
housed in a lovely little half-
timbered building.

[i] I cours de la République

SPECIAL TO...

Many gourmet centres were
originally on the main road
from Paris to the Riviera.
Roanne, on the N7, is now
bypassed by the traffic on the
Autoroute de Soleil, but it
remains a famous gastronomic
town. The restaurant of the
Troisgros brothers' hotel is
classed as one of the finest
tables in France.

▶ Leave Roanne on the **N7** as
for Lyon. Go right on the **D43**
as for Varennes then right on
the **D84** as for Vernay. As
soon as you enter Commelle-
Vernay turn left as for
Cordelle. Follow the **D56** and
N82 into Balbigny. Go right at
the traffic lights to Nervieux,
then left on the **D5** through

St-Étienne-le-Molard. Go left
on the **D8** into Montbrison,
left on the **D496**, then
straight ahead on the **N89**.
Go right to Chazelles-sur-
Lyon.

FOR CHILDREN

The Musée d'Allard on the
Boulevard de la Préfecture in
Montbrison, on the way to
Chazelles-sur-Lyon, has several
individual themes, but is best
known for its collection of
dolls and puppets from
countries all over the world.

9 Chazelles-sur-Lyon,
Rhône Valley
Off the main roads in the
wooded hills north of St-
Étienne, Chazelles owes a great

The countryside round Roanne
reflects its heyday as a major
producer of wine

deal to the crusaders who
brought back from the east the
secret of making felt. Chazelles
used this new-found expertise
to turn itself into a great hat-
making centre. The extensive
Musée du Chapeau explains,
with guided tours, audio-visual
presentations and working
machinery, all the techniques of
preparation, manufacture and
fashion. On display is a collection of more than 500 felt hats
of all styles, including a collection of chefs' *toques*. The
museum also devotes space to
the history of the town, from its
days as a junction of Roman
roads.

[i] 6 place Jean-Baptiste Galland

▶ *Leave Chazelles on the D103, which becomes the D2, to Ste-Catherine. Go straight on as for Mornant, then turn left on the D63 into Riverie and left on the D113 via St-André-la-Côte to St-Martin. Follow signs to Yzeron, go left as for Plan d'Eau, left on the D489 as for Duerne, then right on the D113. Continue straight on at Col de Malval, then at Col de la Luère go straight on along the D24 as for Lyon. Watch for a sudden left turn on to the D70. Go through Poillonnay then turn right on the D7 as for Lyon into Charbonnières-les-Bains, then left for Charbonnières-centre.*

BACK TO NATURE

Turn left at Col de Malval for the Parc de Courzieu. Here, not only are wolves, lynx and wildcats on show, but free-flying displays by eagles, vultures and falcons also take place in a thousand-seat auditorium.

🔟 Charbonnières-les-Bains, Rhône Valley

Lyon is one of several French cities to have a totally different-looking spa town just beyond its outskirts, well away from the familiar busy streets. The first mineral spring here was traditionally discovered by a donkey on its last legs, which regained its vigour by drinking from it.

Whatever its origins, Charbonnières developed into a full-scale spa and health resort with thermal baths, a pump house, a casino and elegant villas in discreetly wooded

RECOMMENDED WALKS

Stop off on the way from Chazelles to Charbonnières and in St-André-la-Côte, or from a left-hand bend on the route beyond it, take the waymarked path to the Signal de St-André. In clear weather the dramatic view extends from a series of hill villages to the mountain wall of the Alps.

grounds. It has good sports facilities, shaded footpaths and a fine array of shops.

  ⓘ *18 avenue Charles de Gaulle*

▶ *Follow 'Lyon-centre' signs and return to Lyon.*

SCENIC ROUTES

From Mont Cindre wonderful views open up of Lyon, the Rhône valley and the Alps. After Châtillon there is a splendid outlook to the hillside vineyards of Beaujolais. On the D504 to Roanne, look for the gorgeous hilltop setting of Thizy. The Lac de Villarest reservoir is very attractive from the D56 between Roanne and Chazelles; a view of wooded gorges with an abandoned castle standing on a flooded rock. There is a magnificent valley view to the right of the D113 after Riverie, on the way from Chazelles to Charbonnières.

Vineyard in the Beaujolais region

The French Alps

This is essentially a mountain tour among the wild and magnificent landscapes of the French Alps. Check the *ouvert-fermé*
(open/closed) signs – in most years the route is not fully open till
mid-June – and be ready for some steep gradients and exposed
hairpinned climbs.

**4 DAYS • 472KM
294 MILES**

ITINERARY	
GRENOBLE	▶ **La Grande Chartreuse** (27km–17m)
LA GRANDE CHARTREUSE	▶ **Chambéry (42km–26m)**
CHAMBÉRY	▶ **Aix-les-Bains (15km–9m)**
AIX-LES-BAINS	▶ **Annecy (47km–29m)**
ANNECY	▶ **La Clusaz (30km–19m)**
LA CLUSAZ	▶ **Beaufort (55km–34m)**
BEAUFORT	▶ **Bourg-St-Maurice (25km–16m)**
BOURG-ST-MAURICE	▶ **Val-d'Isère (29km–18m)**
VAL-D'ISÈRE	▶ **Col de l'Iseran (18km–11m)**
COL DE L'ISERAN	▶ **Modane (55km–34m)**
MODANE	▶ **St-Jean-de-Maurienne (30km–19m)**
ST-JEAN-DE-MAURIENNE	▶ **Col de la Croix de Fer (27km–17m)**
COL DE LA CROIX DE FER	▶ **Défilé de Maupas (13km–8m)**
DÉFILÉ DE MAUPAS	▶ **Grenoble (59km–37m)**

[i] 14 rue de la République,
Grenoble

▶ Leave Grenoble for Le Sappey
on the **D512**, then continue
to St-Pierre-de-Chartreuse.
Turn left and follow signs to
the Musée de la Grande
Chartreuse, using the one-way
system.

❶ La Grande Chartreuse,
Rhône-Alpes
High on the west side of the
Massif de la Chartreuse stands
La Grande Chartreuse, the
grand mother house of the
Carthusian monks, on ground
that is under snow for more than
half the year. Its founder, St
Bruno, built the first monastery
here in 1084.
    The monks lead an austere
life of study, meditation, soli-
tude and prayer. No visitors are
allowed in La Grande
Chartreuse itself, and cars may
not use the road to it. However,
a fine museum has been created
at La Correrie, by the end of the
public road. It explains and
illustrates the monastic life, as
well as the history of the Order
and the difficulties experienced
by the monks here (they were
expelled from the monastery
during the Revolution, and
again between 1903 and 1940).

The famous Chartreuse
liqueurs, the profits from whose
sales fund the Order's charitable
works, are distilled elsewhere.

▶ Return to St-Pierre-de-
Chartreuse and turn left to
rejoin the **D512**. Follow this
road and the **D912** to
Chambéry.

❷ Chambéry, Rhône-Alpes
Why the elephants, you may
wonder, on the great fountain in
the pleasant centre here? They
commemorate the Duc de
Boigne, who made his military
reputation and his fortune in the
East, before retiring to
Chambéry to indulge his
passion for town planning.
    Above the arcaded streets
and courtyards of the old quarter stands the castle of the
dukes of Savoie, whose territory
stretched from Lake Geneva to
the Mediterranean and included
regions of modern Italy.
    The Italian connection
persists in the Musée des
Beaux-Arts, which has a splendid display of Italian paintings.
Local history collections are
housed in the Musée Savoisien.
Opened in 1995, Galerie
Eureka is an exciting science
centre, designed to appeal
particularly to young visitors.

Fontaine des Éléphants, one of
the sights of Chambéry

Three main galleries are
devoted to mountains, new
scientific developments and
temporary exhibitions.
    In the cathedral (look for
more elephant motifs), some
interior details such as the
apparently vaulted ceiling are
actually 19th-century attempts
at *trompe l'œil* paintwork.

[i] 24 boulevard de la Colonne

▶ Leave Chambéry for Aix-les-
Bains on the **N201**.

BACK TO NATURE

Approaching Aix-les-Bains, the
N201 runs beside the shore of
Lac du Bourget. Just before
Tresserve, stroll over to look on
the reed beds and watch the
comings and goings of the great
crested grebes. Coots, pochards
and little grebes can also be
seen on the water, and there are
grey herons around the margins.

---

❸ Aix-les-Bains, Rhône-
Alpes
Starting at the banks of the Lac
du Bourget, the most extensive

mountain lake in France, the town rises from a cruise-boat harbour and a lakeside promenade to a very stylish town centre. Aix-les-Bains is an elegant and well equipped spa resort. Its springs were known to the Romans, and later patrons were Napoleon's family and Queen Victoria.

Colourful gardens, old and new-style fountains and pleasant woodland walks are scattered around. Top-class sports facilities are provided, especially winter sports on the lake, and the mountains are always in view. Relics of Roman times include a Temple of Diana and a restored archway facing the Thermes Nationaux. Guided tours – on which you are encouraged to wear a toga – explore the Roman remains, the original baths and the statues preserved in the Musée Lapidaire.

On a hillside boulevard, the Musée Faure houses a valuable art collection. Look for fine paintings and sculpture by Degas, Pissarro, Rodin and Corot.

[i] *Place Maurice Mollard*

▶ *Continue on the N201, then go right on the D911. Turn left on the D31, right on the D5 and go straight on as for le Châtelard on the D911. Turn sharp left on the D912 over Col de Leschaux. Go left on the N508 to Annecy.*

4 Annecy, Rhône-Alpes
You can see how dearly the Annéciens love their pure and beautiful mountain-rimmed lake (Lac d'Annecy). They have spurned any encroachment on the lakeside parks and gardens which are areas of general relaxation as well as wonderful mountain viewpoints; and they make an attractive feature of the rivers and canals which thread through the lovely old quarter of the town.

Lake cruises are a favourite excursion here, but in a place ideally laid out for aimless

strolling around, or for clip-clopping along in the calèches (open carriages) which ply for hire, there are also specific attractions on land. Visit the castle museum, for instance. Go to prison – or, at least, to the Palais de l'Ile, the old jail, mint and courthouse (which now houses a small history museum). The restored château houses a local museum.

In the evenings, the old town (pedestrianised) is lively and chattering as its pavement restaurants and cafés fill up. Then the lights reflect in the waters lapping quietly by.

[i] *Centre Bonlieu, 1 rue Jean-Jaurès*

▶ *Leave Annecy for Veyrier-du-Lac on the D909. Continue through Thônes to La Clusaz.*

5 La Clusaz, Rhône-Alpes
Here is the first of many Alpine ski resorts on this tour, occupying a valley site crammed between jagged peaks. In summer when, as throughout the region, the weather can be very changeable, La Clusaz seems to be waiting impatiently until the snows return, bringing with them thousands of winter sports enthusiasts.

However, summer visitors are by no means neglected. The Bureau des Guides will introduce you to rock-climbing in half-day courses, and grass skis are available for hire. You can also, briefly or at length, try your hand at canoeing, fishing, skating, tennis, horse- or pony-

Aix-les-Bains is a great centre for boat trips on the Lac du Bourget riding, fencing, archery, pistol-shooting and pottery. Folklore groups enliven the evenings.

In among the typical shops, chalets, bars, cafés, hotels and restaurants of a ski resort, La Clusaz has a most attractive modern church. Look for the beautiful stained-glass windows, illustrating work in the mountains, fields and forests.

ⓘ *Parc de l'Église*

SPECIAL TO...

Before La Clusaz you will begin to see signs to the farms where the delicious traditional Savoie cheeses are produced. Most popular is *Reblochon* – check for the green '*fermier*' label guaranteeing that it is farm-made. Look also for *Tomme de Savoie* and the strong goat's-milk *Chevrotin des Aravis*.

RECOMMENDED WALKS

La Clusaz has a network of summer walks, some from the top stations of cable-car and chairlift lines. Ask at the tourist office, where you can also book for guided walks to lakes and mountain viewpoints, good areas for alpine flowers and the secret trails of the old *contrebandiers* (smugglers).

FOR CHILDREN

La Clusaz has a summer toboggan run called the *luge d'été*. Youngsters (and adults) have a choice of two smooth metal pistes sweeping down the hillside for 800m (2,620 feet). Here also, on summer evenings, there are free shows in the village by jugglers, clowns and puppeteers.

▶ *Continue on the **D909** over the Col des Aravis to Flumet, then go straight ahead on the **D218B** over the Col des Saisies and follow signs to Beaufort. Go through Beaufort as for Bourg-St-Maurice.*

FOR HISTORY BUFFS

At the breezy summit of the Col des Saisies, on the stretch between La Clusaz and Beaufort, look for the monument to the daring exploit in August 1944, when a daylight wave of RAF planes parachuted arms and ammunition to the Resistance fighters of Savoie.

🄶 **Beaufort,** Rhône-Alpes
At Beaufort, a village in a spruce-clad mountain valley, you may wonder where the road can possibly go next. In fact,

it slices through the amazing rock cleft of the Défile d'Entreroches, then up a steep hairpinned pass with magnificent views of the valley left behind.

A good excursion centre, Beaufort is the heart of the Beaufortain district. In its co-operative you can watch the making of 'the prince of Gruyères' – Beaufort cheese, produced with milk from the upland farms – and even help in the process.

Eastwards, the Lac de Roselend reservoir lies in a deep depression among the mountains. Then the road battles up through 10 hairpin bends towards a notch in the skyline. This is an exciting landscape of mountain torrents, scree slopes and high snow-filled gullies. Wildflowers put on their brave summer display.

ⓘ *On the D925 in Beaufort*

La Clusaz is one of Haute Savoie's oldest and biggest ski resorts

▶ *Continue to Bourg-St-Maurice.*

7 Bourg-St-Maurice,
Rhône-Alpes
Bourg-St-Maurice lies in a spectacular setting overlooked by cliffs and tiers of chalets. Green in summer, the hill slopes to the southeast are in the easily-reached skiing area of Les Arcs, upgraded for the 1992 Winter Olympics.

Down in the town itself there is a woodland park beside the compensation reservoir of a hydro-electric scheme. Bourg-St-Maurice is good for sports such as white-water canoeing and rafting. Horse and pony trips can also be arranged. There is a minerals and crystals display, and another co-operative where Beaufort cheese is made.

The satellite village of Vulmis, along a steep road to the southwest, has a chapel with beautiful 15th-century frescos.

And at Hauteville-Gondon, to the south, you will find a costume museum and an unexpectedly baroque 17th-century church.

⊡ *Place de la Gare*

FOR CHILDREN
Bourg-St-Maurice has installed a modern funicular railway. Children will enjoy the ride as the train climbs above the river then plunges into a mountain tunnel on its way up to the ski areas of Les Arcs.

▶ *Leave Bourg-St-Maurice on the **N90** to Séez. Go right on the **D902** to Val-d'Isère.*

8 Val-d'Isère, Rhône-Alpes
The resort of Val-d'Isère lies 1,850m (6,068 feet) above sea level and is one of the most famous locations on the European ski-racing calendar. Cable cars climb from its narrow valley setting to reach spectacular viewpoint summits such as Bellevarde at 2,827m (9,270 feet). The eastern mountain ridge, marking the frontier with Italy, soars to over 3,350m (11,000 feet).

Val-d'Isère is simply a series of long lines of apartment blocks, chalets, shops, hotels and restaurants. Many of the latest buildings, though, are quite sensitively designed in traditional mountain-country idiom.

Summer sports facilities are more for weekly residents than for transients, although horse and pony hire, archery and tennis lessons and mountain biking may be tackled in shorter bursts.

⊡ *Maison de Val-d'Isère*

▶ *Continue on the **D902** to Col de l'Iseran.*

9 Col de l'Iseran, Rhône-Alpes
When the road over the Col de l'Iseran was opened in 1937, it had taken 20 years to build. At 2,770m (9,085 feet) in the wildest country, it was the highest road in Europe. Today, only a handful surpass it. The Iseran is usually under impenetrable snow till mid-June, but even a month later chill winds may sweep down from the still higher glaciers and snowfields.

In clear weather the Iseran is exhilarating, although the climb is on a broken surface. There is a summit shop. An austere, four-square chapel stands a little way apart. This is the only through road which penetrates the huge nature reserve of the Parc National de la Vanoise. The mountain scenery is magnificent, and the descent is fortunately on a much better-surfaced road.

▶ *Continue on the **D902**. In Bessans follow the 'Chambéry' sign. Go through Lanslevillard,* which you will see directly across the valley. Another excursion worth making is to the complex of forts at l'Esseillon, built in the 1820s to defend the forgotten kingdom of Piedmont-Sardinia against possible invasion from France.

i Place du Replaton

▶ Leave Modane on the **N6**, then turn left into St-Jean-de-Maurienne.

⚂ **St-Jean-de-Maurienne,** Rhône-Alpes

Although the world's most modern aluminium factory is sited here, it is well away from the charming heart of St-Jean-de-Maurienne, you will see a sweep of pasture land dotted with hamlets and farms, rising above the town.

The town square dips down to a fine modern war memorial outlined against the northern mountains. During the holidays, schoolchildren act as earnest and well-informed guides to the cathedral and the one-time bishop's palace whose elegant salon and connecting rooms house a comprehensive museum of costume. Displays include traditional women's dresses from villages round about, showing how each place had its individual style. The Opinel company based here exports its wooden-handled clasp knives all over the world. The factory museum shows how its extensive range is produced.

i Place de la Cathédrale

▶ Leave St-Jean for Col de la Croix de Fer on the **D926**.

then, in Lanslebourg-Mont-Cenis, join the **N6** as for Chambéry. In Sollières, turn right on the **D83**. In Sardières, go right as for Hôtel du Parc, then left past La Monolithe. Turn right at the T-junction, rejoining the **D83** to Aussois, then go straight ahead on the **D215** to Modane.

BACK TO NATURE

Pause after Sardières, on your way to Modane, to look at the *monolithe*, a huge isolated limestone pillar soaring to 83m (272 feet) in the heart of a pinewood. This strange weathered feature is not uncommon here. You will see more of them among the pines further on.

⚈ **Modane,** Rhône-Alpes

This is where the busy road and rail tunnels to Bardonecchia in Italy begin. The 12.8km (8-

Val-d'Isère has developed into a popular summer and winter resort

mile) road tunnel opened in 1980. Go to the old ornamental rail tunnel entrance above the town, and you will see the coats of arms of the main cities on the Calais-Paris-Rome line.

Modane had a hard time in World War II. It was heavily bombed by the Allies in 1943, in an attempt to disrupt the German-Italian rail supply system, and the Germans fired colossal demolition charges at the rail tunnel entrance in 1944. You can still see a concrete blockhouse, intact but flung askew by the tremendous force of the explosion.

There is a glorious view from here, over Modane in its deep winding valley to the skyline of the Vanoise peaks. The town is an access point to the mountain footpaths of the Vanoise. Local walks include a hairpinned climb to the Fort St Gobain

---

SPECIAL TO...

Transhumance – the bringing down of sheep from the lush summer mountain pastures – is still practised in the Maurienne. However, nowadays, the flocks arrive by train.

🔟 Col de la Croix de Fer,
Rhône-Alpes

Take care in the five rock tunnels above the stunning Arvan gorge, with the needle peaks of the Aiguilles d'Arves on the skyline. Alpine meadows towards Entraigues, and the little ski resort of St-Sorlin, come and go. Then comes the narrow and dizzying zigzag road up the boulder fields to the summit of the pass. Here you can relax by the restaurant, note the cross of iron which gave the col its name, and marvel at the outlook over a sea of Alpine summits. To the south-south-east, the 3,983m (13,065-foot) peak of La Meije is just in view.

▶ Beyond the col, turn left as for Grenoble.

🔟 Défilé de Maupas,
Rhône-Alpes

The final exposed climb to the Croix de Fer may have left you wondering what lies on the other side. In fact, the descent is on a road of a much higher stan-

Grenoble is a modern city dedicated to superlative winter sports

dard, although the grandeur of the mountain scenery and of the majestic gorge which takes the route back down to a lower level is even more impressive.

Pause at the Barrage de Grand'Maison. Displays here explain how this is the top reservoir of the most powerful hydro-electric scheme in France, fed by cascades from the permanent snowfields.

FOR HISTORY BUFFS

On the return route to Grenoble, the 17th-century château at Vizille houses a comprehensive museum of the French Revolution. In 1788, a year before the Revolution, the three Estates – nobles, clergy and commoners – met in this castle to denounce Louis XVI's suppression of parliament and proclaim individual liberty. With tableaux, sculptures, paintings and posters as well as weaponry, the museum stresses the artistic environment of revolutionary France no less than the events and personalities.

▶ Continue downhill. Avoid the road for Le Verney and take the road signed 'Hydrolec'. Turn left as for Grenoble, then join the **N91**. Go through Le Péage de Vizille, then turn right to Vizille-centre on the **D101**. Continue to Uriage on the **D524** and return to Grenoble.

SCENIC ROUTES

From Grenoble to Chambéry the route, runs over a massif of hills, forests, deep-cut valleys and towering limestone cliffs.
On the D34, after Aix-les-Bains, look for the dramatic valley of the Chéran, overlooked by the rock pillars called the Fairies' Chimneys.
The superlative mountain landscapes beyond La Clusaz include glimpses on the eastern horizon of Mont Blanc.
Even the spectacular climb to the Col de la Croix de Fer is surpassed by the descent through precipitous gorges to the N91.

The German
Connection

From the Rhineland plain south of Strasbourg to the viewpoint roads high in the Vosges mountains, this tour explores some of the most beautiful areas of Alsace. There have been vineyards in the eastern foothills of the Vosges since Roman times. At higher altitudes lie forests and upland pastures covered by winter snows.

3/4 DAYS • 420KM • 260 MILES

ITINERARY

STRASBOURG	► **Mont Ste-Odile** (42km-26m)
MONT STE-ODILE	► **Ste-Marie-aux-Mines** (52km-32m)
STE-MARIE-AUX-MINES	► **Thann** (105km-65m)
THANN	► **Mulhouse** (24km-15m)
MULHOUSE	► **Écomusée de Haute Alsace** (13km-8m)
ÉCOMUSÉE DE HAUTE ALSACE	► **Guebwiller** (10km-6m)
GUEBWILLER	► **Colmar** (35km-22m)
COLMAR	► **Kaysersberg** (41km-25m)
KAYSERSBERG	► **Riquewihr** (10km-6m)
RIQUEWIHR	► **Sélestat** (26km-16m)
SÉLESTAT	► **Strasbourg** (63km-39m)

i 17 place de la Cathédrale,
Strasbourg

▶ Leave Strasbourg for
Eckbolsheim on the **D45**.
Continue to Ergersheim, then
take the **D30** to Molsheim.
Follow the 'Strasbourg' sign,
then take the **D422** and **D35**
through Rosheim to Ottrott.
Turn right in Ottrott on the
D426, then follow the **D426a**
to Ste-Odile.

SPECIAL TO...

Molsheim, to the southwest of
Strasbourg, was the home of
Bugatti, the marque which
epitomises *pur sang* (the thor-
oughbred ideal) in car design.
Cars are no longer built in
what is now the Messier-
Bugatti factory, but Bugatti
owners regularly make the pilgrimage to Molsheim.

❶ Mont Ste-Odile, Alsace
You may be surprised by the
press of traffic on this out-of-
the-way woodland hilltop. The
cluster of buildings here is one
of France's great pilgrimage
centres: the historic convent
which guards the tomb of Saint
Odile.

Odile, abbess of the original
religious house of this splendid
site, died around the year 720.
The present buildings, in fine
order, are from much later
centuries, including the 20th.
With cloister and courtyard
gardens, an excellent paved
walk around viewpoint terraces,
a pilgrims' hall and several individual chapels, this is a place of
beauty, dignity and repose. The
site appealed to earlier civilisa-
tions, too. As you approach the
summit, look for carefully
worked masonry of the imposing Mur Païen (Pagan Wall)
constructed in prehistoric times.

▶ Return downhill, bear slightly
left and follow signs to
Champ du Feu. Go straight
ahead there and follow signs
to Villé. Turn right on the **D39**

RECOMMENDED
WALKS

At Mont Ste-Odile you can
step into the network of waymarked trails which explore
this beautifully wooded hill.
Some were originally pilgrims'
paths, others follow the Pagan
Wall, and all offer splendid
views to the valleys.

as for St-Dié. In Fouchy, go left
on the **D155** to Col de
Fouchy, then follow signs to
Lièpvre and go right to Ste-
Marie-aux-Mines on the **N59**.
Approaching Ste-Marie, avoid
the tunnel.

Strasbourg, capital of Alsace and
sophisticated seat of government

❷ Ste-Marie-aux-Mines,
Alsace
From the 16th century onwards,
this little town was famous for
the richest seams of silver in
France. You can join a guided
tour of the old St Bartélemy
mine. Safety helmets and
waterproof capes are provided,
and you start by walking in
through a hillside tunnel to the
levels and galleries beyond.

The Maison du Pays (not
quite the 'country house' which
the local English translation
suggests) houses the Musée
Minéralogique, and also mounts
displays on the mining era and

BACK TO NATURE

To the right of the D430 after the Col de la Schlucht, the university-run Jardin d'Altitude du Haut-Chitelet, at nearly 1,228m (4,030 feet), displays hundreds of mountain plant species from all over the world. Beyond the Col de la Schlucht, watch for buzzards soaring over the open ground. The pine forests are home to the bulky capercaillie. Biggest of the grouse family, it is reduced to something like 160 pairs in the whole of the Vosges. Several species of woodpecker are found in the forests, along with crested tits and Bonelli's warblers.

on the spinning, dyeing, weaving and hosiery which, combined, formed Ste-Marie's other 'boom' industry.

Look for the restrained baroque style of the Church of La Madeleine, for intriguing old buildings such as the towered Pharmacie by the main square, and for the little public gardens which include one, beside the town hall, with a floral peacock on display.

[i] *Place du Prensureux*

▶ *Leave Ste-Marie-aux-Mines as for Le Bonhomme. Turn right at Col des Bagenelles to Col du Bonhomme. Turn left on the N415. At the roundabout go right on the D48 to Orbey, then follow signs 'Les Lacs' and 'Lac Blanc'. Go left on the D418 to Col de la Schlucht. Turn right on the D417 as for Épinal and almost immediately left on the D430 to Le Markstein. Continue straight ahead on the D431 to le Grand Ballon, then follow signs to Thann.*

3 **Thann,** Alsace
On the banks of the fast-flowing River Thur, overlooked by a hillside Cross of Lorraine, Thann was wrested back from German control by Marshal Joffre's troops in 1914. The text of his emotional proclamation is carved on a war memorial.

Superb carvings on the choir stalls in Thann's Gothic cathedral

Thann's history is even more complex than that of other places in Alsace, as it was Austrian territory from 1324 to 1648.

The splendid collegiate Church of St Thiébaut features immensely detailed sculptured façades and portals, polychrome roof tiling and superb carved-oak choir stalls. Look there for the figures of the gossip, the fiddler and the spectacled man. Thann's local history museum is in the arcaded corn market (Halle aux blés) of 1519. Two towers survive from its medieval ramparts, and several fine buildings from the 16th century onwards remain.

[i] *6 place Joffre*

▶ *Leave Thann on the N66. Go over the autoroute and continue to Mulhouse.*

FOR CHILDREN

At Le Grand Ballon, the highest point in the Vosges mountains, the youngsters will enjoy a whoosh down the *luge d'été* summer toboggan ride; but in chilly weather make sure they wrap up well.

4 **Mulhouse,** Alsace
Despite its parks and gardens, zoo and yacht basin and attractive old quarter, 'Moo-loose' is an industrial town which may take some time to grow on you. Look round its museums, and you will realise that this is one of the most amazingly well-endowed towns in Europe as regards museums of technology.

History, fine arts, painted wall-coverings and printed fabrics all have extensive museums of their own, but the Musée des Beaux-Arts is an excellent starting-point. Railway enthusiasts should head for the excellent Musée Français du Chemin de Fer. Close by, the Musée du Sapeur-Pompier has a fine display of fire engines.

However, the pride of Mulhouse is the Musée National de l'Automobile, the most stupendous motor museum in the world. On display are over a hundred Bugattis, whole collections of Rolls-Royces, Alfa Romeos, Maseratis, Mercedes-Benz, Gordinis and the rest – more than 500 splendid vehicles of almost 100 different makes. The fine tradition continues, as new Peugeots are also made in Mulhouse.

⊡ *9 avenue Maréchal-Foch*

▶ *Leave Mulhouse as for Guebwiller on the **D430**. Turn on to the **D430bis** and follow 'Écomusée' signs.*

⑤ Écomusée de Haute Alsace, Alsace

Occupying a roomy site on the Alsace plain, here is a fascinating replica village of more than 60 traditionally styled buildings – houses, farms, barns and workshops – created to show the domestic life of past generations, as well as the work of the blacksmith and cart builder, baker, clog-maker and weaver, and all the half-forgotten farming trades.

Favourite local dishes are offered in the restaurants, and Alsace wines are served. There is a keen interest in wildlife conservation: storks, for instance, are encouraged to nest.

During the 1990s a major project was the restoration of the potassium mine whose buildings are passed on the approach road.

▶ *Return to the **D430** and continue to Guebwiller.*

⑥ Guebwiller, Alsace

A place full of squares, and bright with window-boxes, Guebwiller is partly built of a soft local stone which gives the Église St-Léger, for instance, a warmer 'feel' than most French churches. St-Léger also has stately arcaded aisles and some worthwhile stained-glass windows.

Overlooked by hillside vineyards, the town enjoys some beautiful parkland. The Parc de la Marseillaise features fine examples of cypress, lime, cedar and sequoia trees.

Guebwiller was the birthplace of the 19th-century ceramic artist Théodore Deck. Examples of his work, and historical mementoes of the district, are on display in the Musée du Florival.

⊡ *73 rue de la République*

▶ *Continue on the **D430** as for Le Markstein. Turn right on the **D40** to Soultzmatt, left on the **D18bis** to Osenbach, then right on the **D40** again. Bear right to Gueberschwihr, turn left as for Hattstatt, then join the **N83** for Colmar, and enter it on the **D30**.*

⑦ Colmar, Alsace

In colour, design, construction, layout and state of preservation, Colmar is one of the world's most beguiling towns. The narrow streets, some darting off at eccentric angles, are lined with colour-washed half-timbered houses of the 16th and 17th centuries, most of them banked with flowers.

Look in particular for the balconied Maison Pfister of 1537, the riverside houses of the Quai de la Poissonnerie and 'La Petite Venise' (Little Venice) to which they lead, and for the lovely cluster of buildings by the pastry shop at the corner of Rue Kléber. The 15th-century Koïfhus – the old customs house, used as the town hall – is topped by glorious polychrome roof tiling.

Colmar's fine town hall

Colmar has a museum and art gallery in the old Dominican convent of Unterlinden (Musée d'Unterlinden), noted for its 16th-century altarpiece by Matthias Grünewald – the Isenheim Altarpiece. The sculptor Auguste Bartholdi was born here, in a courtyard house which is now a museum recalling that his most famous work was the Statue of Liberty.

i *4 rue Unterlinden*

Take the first left under the archway, follow the 'Toutes Directions' sign, then turn left and continue to Kaysersberg.

8 Kaysersberg, Alsace
As you stroll through this attractive little flower-decked medieval 'city', past the *caves* of wine growers and liqueur distillers, you will encounter many houses, gateways, bridges, towers and chapels of the 13th to 15th centuries.

9 Riquewihr, Alsace
Enclosed in 16th-century ramparts, this charming old town is the 'pearl of the Alsace vineyards'. Wine cellars stock the produce of its Riesling, Muscat, Tokay and Gewürztraminer grapes.

Local history is the concern of the Musée Dolder. The Tour des Voleurs (Thieves' Tower) houses an 'authentic' torture chamber. Installed in a princely palace, the Musée d'Histoire

RECOMMENDED WALKS

The hilltop resort of Les Trois-Épis, between Colmar and Kaysersberg, concentrates on sports and open-air activities. Ask at the tourist office about the 50km (31 miles) of footpaths on its invigorating woodland ridges.

The Église Ste-Croix has a magnificent altarpiece of 1518. Other works of religious art are displayed in the local museum.

Kaysersberg is twinned with Lambaréné in Gabon because of the town's links with Dr Albert Schweitzer. He was born in Kaysersberg in 1875 and spent most of his working life at his hospital in West Africa. A room in his birthplace is preserved in his memory.

i *38 rue du Général de Gaulle*

▶ Leave Kaysersberg as for Ribeauvillé on the **D28**. Go left at the roundabout and left on the **D3** to Riquewihr.

Kaysersberg, once the home of kings, is now a small wine-growing centre

des PTT d'Alsace includes lavish displays of stage coaches, maps, models, uniforms, electric and wireless telegraphy systems, telephones, teleprinters and a miniature of the *Ariane* space rocket, telling the story of 2,000 years of message deliveries since Gallo-Roman times.

i *2 rue de la ère Armée*

▶ Leave Riquewihr for Ribeauvillé and Bergheim. In Bergheim, go left on the **D42** as for Haut Koenigsbourg.

▶ Leave Colmar as for Épinal on the **D417**. Turn right to Gunsbach, then right at the crossroads on the **D10**. Go left on the **D11** to Trois-Épis, then right to Ammerschwihr.

SPECIAL TO...

The population of storks, which have nested for centuries on the rooftops and chimneys of Alsace, dwindled alarmingly in the 1970s. However, the birds are strongly established once again.
After Riquewihr, turn left as for Hunawihr to visit the Centre de Réintroduction des Cigognes.

findare beautiful medieval, Renaissance and 18th century houses and public buildings, the Romanesque Church of Ste-Foy and the later Gothic Church of St-Georges. The town's water towers are unexpectedly ornate.

Sélestat is the main centre where modern Alsace artists show their paintings, and its 15th-century Bibliothèque Humaniste, housed in the old corn market (Halle aux blés),

Sélestat's greatest glory is its Humanist library

is one of the most valuable libraries of books and manuscripts in France.

i   10 boulevard Leclerc

▶ *Leave Sélestat on the D424 as for Marckolsheim. At the roundabout, turn left on the D468 and return to Strasbourg.*

Turn right on the D159 and continue to Sélestat, entering it on the N83.

FOR CHILDREN

Off the D159 on the way to Sélestat, the Montagne des Singes allows 300 Barbary apes to roam in 20 hectares (50 acres) of forest. At the nearby Volerie des Aigles, in the grounds of a castle, eagles, vultures, kites and falcons give flying displays.

🔟 **Sélestat,** Alsace
Unremarkable in its suburbs, Sélestat becomes much more interesting as you explore its historic centre. Here you will

FOR HISTORY BUFFS

On the way to Sélestat, turn left off the D159 for the spectacular hilltop castle of Haut-Koenigsbourg. The 12th-century fortress was destroyed in the 17th century, and was completely restored early this century on the orders of Kaiser Wilhelm II. It looks like a film set, and was in fact used by the great director Jean Renoir for *La Grande Illusion*.
On the return route to Strasbourg, turn right into Marckolsheim then left on the D10 to the Musée de l'Abri, recalling the bypassing of the Maginot Line by the Germans in 1940, and the fierce fighting that took place there in 1944.

SCENIC ROUTES

Early on, the D45 opens up long views over villages and vineyards to the forested range of the Vosges.
On the way to Thann, the D48 rises through beautiful miniature landscapes in the valley of the Petite Lièpvre. After the Col de la Schlucht, admire the 'top of the world' views over the deep western valleys from the 'Route des Crêtes', then on to the descent of Le Grand Ballon.
From the approach to Guebwiller, you are in the delicious foothills country of the 'Route du Vin'. The flat return to Strasbourg is enhanced by unexpectedly bright and flower-filled villages.

THE NORTH, BURGUNDY & CHAMPAGNE

This area of northern France, just back from, or along the coast, has long been fought over, and frequently devastated by war. Here you will find historic battlefields, including Crécy, Valmy and Sédan, from the World War I Somme campaign, whose British and Commonwealth victims are remembered in dignified parkland memorials such as Vimy Ridge.

Huge areas of land are occupied by arable farms. This is the country's bread-basket, and the source of many of its fine vegetables. Here and there, modest woodlands break up the view, and the high points are more likely to be the water towers known grandly as *châteaux d'eau*.

Elsewhere, there are full-scale state forests, including some of the most beautiful in France. The forest around Fontainebleau attracted the royal and imperial courts. Then it was the turn of the 19th-century artists to enjoy the forest and the atmospheric towns and villages close by. Some of France's most lavish state residences are here: Fontainebleau, Rambouillet, Pierrefonds.

Near the border, France shares with Belgium the lovely winding, wooded river valleys of the Ardennes. Other hill country includes quiet areas off the Paris-Riviera autoroute and the mazy lanes of the Morvan.

You can hardly miss the vineyards in the foothills of the Côte d'Or and the great champagne estates round Reims. On the coast you will find resorts as different as stylish Le Touquet and simple Le Crotoy by the Somme. Inland towns, such as Pierrefonds, Compiègne and Moret-sur-Loing, have their following too.

You will encounter the long-lost melding of French and English history – Richard the Lionheart conferred with the French king at Vézélay before they set off to lead their joint army in the Third Crusade. And you can learn how Revolutionaries pursued and captured the fleeing Louis XVI, how artists such as Millet shrugged off the studios of Paris and came to paint from real life in the countryside.

Calais

Under English occupation for more than 200 years, Calais has always looked across the Channel. The Dover-Calais route was the first Continental service to be operated by a steamship, the *Rob Roy*, in 1821. One of the most famous sights is Rodin's great statue of the Burghers of Calais, who pleaded with Edward III of England to spare the town after its surrender in 1347. There is a confidently ornate town hall, a fine arts museum displaying the lacework for which Calais is famous, and a little parkland museum of the town's travails in World War II.

Amiens

Amiens is centred on the majestic Cathédrale Notre-Dame, largest of all the Gothic churches in France. Even its grubby exterior cannot hide the wonderful fretted upper reaches. Inside, there are beautifully carved oakwood choir stalls.

Museums and galleries concentrate on local art and history: Amiens is the capital of Picardy. Quaysides and inlets of the Somme thread through the northern suburbs, and there is an eastern quarter of market gardens first cultivated in medieval times.

Reims

Reims is not just outwardly the city of champagne. Millions of francs' worth lies in cellars underground. Visitors are welcome at the champagne houses which even commissioned stained-glass panels of the different vineyard areas for the cathedral. Two of the old city abbeys have been turned into museums. You can see where the German capitulation order was signed in 1945. And Reims has a major motor museum devoted entirely to French marques.

Chalon-sur-Saône

Baseball in France? Yes, in a beautiful park at Chalon-sur-Saône, which also features a magnificent riverside garden with 25,000 roses from Europe, America, Japan and the Himalayas.

By the Saône, visit the museum commemorating the pioneer of photography, Nicéphore Niepce. Exhibits range from his first camera of 1822 to the Apollo equipment taken to the moon.

There is an exhibition centre for the 44 vineyard villages known collectively as the Côte Chalonnaise. On the little St Laurent island, the topmost gallery of the Tour du Doyenné is an unusual viewpoint over the town.

Chartres

Chartres is, first and foremost, its cathedral, Notre Dame, whose twin towers are seen for miles across the plain. Connoisseurs consider that the stained-glass windows at Chartres are the finest in the world. An art gallery concentrates on stained glass of classical and modern designs, and there are studios where present-day artists work.

Look for the Maison Picassiette with its décor picked out in fragments of glass and china. Admire the paintings, sculptures and tapestries in the fine arts museum, and stroll by the quays, mills and wash-houses on the River Eure.

Opposite: Flavigny sits on a rocky outcrop above wooded valleys
Below: *caves* of Moet & Chandon

The English
Connection

This tour from Calais, busiest of all the French car ferry ports, visits resorts both sophisticated and family-style. The chalk headlands match the white cliffs of Dover, which can be seen on a clear day, glistening in the sun. Behind the coast there are inland river valleys where quiet villages doze in the shelter of gently wooded hills.

3 DAYS • 272KM • 170 MILES

ITINERARY	
CALAIS	▶ **Sangatte (11km-7m)**
SANGATTE	▶ **Cap Blanc-Nez**
	(3km-2m)
CAP BLANC-NEZ	▶ **Boulogne-sur-Mer**
	(39km-24m)
BOULOGNE-SUR-MER	▶ **Le Touquet (32km-20m)**
LE TOUQUET	▶ **Domaine du**
	Marquenterre
	(45km-28m)
DOMAINE DU	▶ **Le Crotoy (10km-6m)**
MARQUENTERRE	
LE CROTOY	▶ **Crécy-en-Ponthieu**
	(26km-16m)
CRÉCY-EN-PONTHIEU	▶ **Montreuil (32km-20m)**
MONTREUIL	▶ **Desvres (28km-18m)**
DESVRES	▶ **Calais (46km-29m)**

ⓘ *12 boulevard Clemenceau, Calais*

▶ *Leave Calais on the D940 through Sangatte.*

SPECIAL TO...

West of Calais there are several smaller fishing ports. One local speciality is *moules* (mussels), often sold from stalls outside the fishermen's homes.

❶ Sangatte, Pas de Calais
Already familiar to anyone who has taken the Channel Tunnel route to France, Sangatte is the huge landward base on the French side.

ⓘ *Route Nationale*

▶ *Continue on the D940 to Cap Blanc-Nez.*

❷ Cap Blanc-Nez, Pas de Calais
This sweeping chalk headland is introduced by a fine windswept statue of the pioneer French aviator, Hubert Latham, who was famous, like Blériot, for his 'audacious flights' above the Channel. Turn right for the splendid viewpoint memorial to the French sailors of the World War I Dover Patrol. Turn left for the Musée du Transmanche, devoted to the history of the Channel Tunnel, including the earliest schemes involving horse-drawn carriages, as well as the final successful project.

BACK TO NATURE

The chalk cliffs around Cap Blanc-Nez and Cap Gris-Nez are a nesting ground for gulls and fulmars which skim the waves and soar on the up-currents of air. Kestrels also nest here, and you may be lucky enough to see one hovering over the grassy clifftops before plunging on its prey. The clifftop flora is outstanding during the summer months.

Calais' ornate *Hôtel de Ville* (town hall)

▶ *Continue on the D940 through Audinghen, where the D191 on the right leads to Cap Gris-Nez. Beyond Wimereux the left turn signed 'vers A16' leads towards the Colonne de la Grande Armée. The D940 continues to Boulogne-sur-Mer.*

FOR CHILDREN

Nausicaa (National Marine Centre), claims to be the largest marine complex in Europe. Its vast array of aquariums contains no fewer than 4,000 fish, and the centre also has film shows and exhibitions, a library, bookshop and café.

❸ Boulogne, Pas de Calais
France's most important fishing port has a bustling and complex harbour front. Every morning fishermen's stalls offer the freshest possible produce of the sea.
   Turn uphill through the busy shopping streets, and you will come to one of the best-preserved historic citadels in the north of France. The castle

museum covers a bewildering variety of subjects including archaeology, ethnology, painting and sculpture and local souvenirs from the time of Napoleon. A pleasant stroll round the towers and fortified gateways of the preserved 13th-century ramparts, which enclose the medieval Haute Ville, gives views of the catamarans below discharging and loading.

ⓘ *Forum Jean-Noël*

FOR HISTORY BUFFS

On the outskirts of Boulogne, the Colonne de la Grande Armée is a towering monument topped by a statue of Napoleon in characteristic pose. He assembled his army here in 1803 for an invasion of Britain which never took place.

▶ *Leave Boulogne on the N1, then take the D940 and N39 to Le Touquet-Paris-Plage.*

4 Le Touquet, Pas de Calais
Le Touquet grew up in the 19th century, largely as a haven for British gamblers taking advantage of the more lenient French gambling laws. Developed jointly by French and British interests Le Touquet has unparalleled facilities for all kinds of sport, including a huge annual motor-sport 'enduro' race on its extensive sands. There are three well-kept golf courses.

Some of the seafront apartment blocks contrast hideously with the few remaining 19th-century buildings there, but the heart of the town has retained a certain elegance. Discreet wooded footpaths are threaded through the pine- and birch-woods of the handsome residential suburbs.

[i] Palais de l'Europe, place de l'Hermitage

FOR CHILDREN

Aqualud on the seafront at Le Touquet is a modern swimming pool complex. Its water fountains and a 90m (98-yard) curving chute are great fun for the children; adults might enjoy the sauna.

FOR CHILDREN

On the D940 south of Le Touquet, the extensive fun park at Bagatelle features a roller-coaster ride which finishes with a belly-flop into a lake, a mono-rail, a mirror maze, roundabouts, an aviary and a zoo.

Le Touquet is a fine example of a turn-of-the-century seaside resort

▶ Leave Le Touquet following Berck and Hesdin signs, and rejoin the **D940** as for Rue. Turn right, following signs to Domaine du Marquenterre.

5 Domaine du Marquenterre, Picardy
Reached by a rather rough approach road, this private estate is one of the finest bird reserves in Europe. La parc ornithologique de Marquenterre was created behind a screen of pine trees on land reclaimed as recently as the 1970s from the estuary of the Somme. Residents and migrants include ducks, geese, swans, gulls and waders, hoopoes, avocets, spoonbills, storks and dozens of other species of shore, lake and salt-marsh. Entry is free and you may rent binoculars.

▶ Return from the Domaine and follow signs to Le Crotoy.

6 Le Crotoy, Picardy
Very much a French family resort, Le Crotoy has a good beach, fishing and yacht harbours by the River Somme. Fresh fish and shellfish are available from roadside stalls and in the restaurants. You should take care before imitating the locals' casual-seeming gumbooted strolls across the tidal inlets. Make sure not to be caught by the incoming tide. The old station is a terminus for the summer railway whose steam-hauled trains explore the pleasant countryside inland.

[i] I rue Carnot

RECOMMENDED WALKS

Local tourist offices have maps of the network of walks inland from Le Crotoy, in the lovely pastureland behind the Somme estuary. They wander past fields, woodlands and water channels in what was unproductive marshland just a few generations ago.

▶ Leave Le Crotoy by 'Sortie Ville' signs. Turn right on the **D940**, then left on the **D140** to Noyelles. Turn left over a level crossing, then left on the **D111** through Nolette to Crécy-en-Ponthieu.

7 Crécy, Picardy

On the exit from the village a view point tower (Le Moulin Édouard III) stands at Edward III's traditional vantage point over the battlefield of Crécy in

FOR HISTORY BUFFS

At Nolette, between Le Crotoy and Crécy, one of the most unusual cemeteries in France commemorates the 96,000 members of the Chinese Labour Force employed by the Allies during World War I. Its base was near by, and 870 of the Chinese, who died in an epidemic, are buried here. Another hero of the Battle of Crécy was the blind King John of Bohemia, brother-in-law of the French king, Philippe VI. A cross marks the spot on the battlefield where he is said to have fallen. A tradition that this king's emblem was adopted by the Black Prince as the Prince of Wales' Feathers is a romantic fiction.

1346, when his English archers routed the French cross-bowmen in one of the most decisive battles of the Hundred Years' War. Edward's son, the Black Prince, who was no more than a boy, won his spurs here.

▶ Continue on the **D111** to Dompierre, then go left on the **D224** which becomes the **D192**. After the Abbaye de Valloires turn sharp right to Moulin de Maintenay, right at a roundabout and left on the **D139** to Montreuil.

8 Montreuil, Pas de Calais

Formerly Montreuil-sur-Mer, the town is now 14km (9 miles) from the sea. It retains many picturesque houses on cobbled and steeply cambered streets; some of the action of Victor Hugo's *Les Misérables* is set here. A statue of Sir Douglas Haig is a reminder that the British commander-in-chief in World War I made his headquarters near by. Montreuil's historic ramparts provide a beautiful hour-long walk, partly edged with trees and giving splendid sunset views. The abbey church dates back to the 11th century.

i 21 rue Carnot

▶ Leave Montreuil on the **N39**, then take the **N1** as for

Le Crotoy is a bustling fishing and yacht harbour on the River Somme

Boulogne. Bear right off the **N1** for Ixent, then follow the **D127** to Desvres.

9 Desvres, Pas de Calais

The square here is the site of regular morning markets, but since the 18th century the main business of the town has been in faïence or glazed pottery. Several workshops welcome visitors, and there is a purpose-built pottery museum.

i Rue Jean Macé

▶ Leave Desvres on the **D127**. Turn right on the **N42** and then take the **D224** to Ardres. In Ardres turn left on the **N43** and return to Calais.

SCENIC ROUTES

After the D940 climbs out of Sangatte it swoops up and down hill through immaculately tended farmland.
Further south, bypassing Rue, the D940 crosses lovely pastoral country given artificial horizons by line upon line of stately poplars.

Towns of
Picardy

Centred on the cathedral city of Amiens, this tour is through districts often missed by visitors to France. It features wide rural landscapes in areas such as the Picardy plateau, goes through the fringes of the northern industrial belt and takes in elegant towns.

4 DAYS • 553KM • 345 MILES

ICI EST TOMBÉ
POUR LA FRANCE
LE 21 MAI 1940
SILVESTRE DE SACY
MARCEL
CAPITAINE AVIATEUR

ITINERARY	
AMIENS	▶ **Samara** (19km-12m)
SAMARA	▶ **Grottes de Naours** (16km-10m)
GROTTES DE NAOURS	▶ **Battlefields of the Somme** (45km-28m)
BATTLEFIELDS OF THE SOMME	
ARRAS	▶ **Arras** (37km-23m)
ARRAS	▶ **Vimy Parc Memorial** (13km-8m)
VIMY PARC MEMORIAL	▶ **Douai** (27km-17m)
DOUAI	▶ **Centre Historique Minier** (10km-6m)
CENTRE HISTORIQUE MINIER	▶ **Laon** (105km-65m)
LAON	▶ **Blérancourt** (45km-28m)
BLÉRANCOURT	▶ **Pierrefonds** (26km-16m)
PIERREFONDS	▶ **Compiègne** (21km-13m)
COMPIÈGNE	▶ **Ermenonville** (46km-29m)
ERMENONVILLE	▶ **Beauvais** (86km-54m)
BEAUVAIS	▶ **Amiens** (57km-36m)

ⓘ *6 bis rue Dusevel, Amiens*

▶ *Leave Amiens on the N235 through Picquigny, then go right on the D191 to Samara.*

❶ Samara, Picardy
Laid out among scrubland, marsh and ponds, Samara is a fascinating historical park which looks at thousands of years of human life and activity in the valley of the River Somme. There are accurate representations of ancient dwellings and demonstrations of prehistoric trades such as flint cutting. There is a botanical garden and arboretum, an excavated Celtic town and displays covering both the distant past and what life may be like in the future.

ⓘ *Place du Général de Gaulle, Picquigny*

▶ *Continue on the D191 to St-Sauveur, go left on the D97 at 'Grottes de Naours' sign, left on to the D933 to Flesselles, straight on along the D111 to Naours, right on the D60, then sharp left to the Grottes de Naours.*

Amiens, a pleasing mixture of ancient riverside streets and modern development

❷ Grottes de Naours,
Picardy
Burrowed into a wooded hillside above the village, the Underground City of Naours (Grottes de Naours) is one of the most amazing places in France. About 30 tunnels and 300 separate rooms – including chapels and stables – have been used as refuges in times of danger and invasion from the Gallo-Roman era to the 18th century. They were the haunt of salt smugglers and used as stores for the British Army in World War II.

▶ *Return from the car park, go left at the Stop sign and follow the D60 to Contay. Turn right on the D919, immediately left on the D23 to Franvillers and left on the D929 through Albert. Go left on the D20, right on the D151 to Thiepval, left on the D73 and follow signs to Beaumont-Hamel memorial park.*

❸ Battlefields of the Somme, Picardy
The countryside hereabouts is scattered with war graves and monuments recalling the first day of July 1916, the opening of the Battle of the Somme. Among the most impressive are

Sir Edward Lutyens's massive brick-and-stone memorial at Thiepval; the Ulster Tower also near Thiepval; and the Newfoundland Memorial Park at Beaumont-Hamel, where almost the whole of the 1st Newfoundland Regiment were mown down by enemy machine-gun fire and shrapnel. The circuit of Remembrance is a 60km (38-mile) route, taking in all the major sites.

At the Château de Personne, the purpose-built Historial de la Grande Guerre (Museum of the Great War) illustrates life at the front and behind the lines. Its halls display over 25,000 items, including weapons and military equipment, and there are displays on the civilian war effort and a collection of Otto Dix etchings.

▶ *Continue on the D53 to Mailly-Maillet. Turn right on the D129, then right on the D919 to Arras.*

❹ Arras, Picardy
Arras, the capital of Artois, would be a finer place if its two most spectacular squares – la Grand Place and la Place de Héros – had gleaming stonework to match the elegance of their arcaded build-

ings. The Hôtel de Ville (town hall) is a handsome affair, and there is a good view from its belfry. Part of the former Benedictine Abbaye de St-Vaast is now a cathedral (18th- to 19th-century); in the south wing of the abbey is a well-stocked fine arts museum with extensive collections of French and Flemish paintings, medieval wood carvings and a superb display of local porcelain and tapestry.

⬛ *Place des Héros*

▶ *Leave Arras on the **N425**, then take the **D937** as for Béthune. Turn right on the **D55** following the 'Memorial Canadien' sign to Vimy Parc.*

5 **Vimy Parc Memorial,** Picardy
One of the largest war memorial areas in France, Vimy Parc commemorates, in particular, the tremendous assault of 9 April 1917 when all four divisions of the Canadian Corps stormed the German defences on Vimy Ridge. Keep to the paths, as there is still a chance of encountering unexploded shells and ammunition. Guided tours explore the underground galleries. On the crown of the ridge, the Mémorial et Parc Canadien, whose soaring pillars bear the maple leaf of Canada and the fleur-de-lys of France, is the most majestic of all the monuments raised after the Great War.

The Vimy Parc·Memorial honours the 75,000 Canadians who died in 1917

▶ *From the memorial, return down the **D55** as for Arras, then go left at the first junction following the 'Gendarmerie' sign. Turn right on the **N17** to Thélus, left on the **D49**, right on the **D33**, go under a bridge, then turn left and join the **N50** dual carriageway to Douai.*

6 **Douai,** Picardy
An industrial town brightened by judiciously placed gardens, flowery roundabouts and avenues of trees, Douai is, at its heart, an island bounded by the River Scarpe and its associated canals, lined with old quaysides. The most impressive building is the ornate Gothic belltower, completed in 1410. Escorted tours show visitors the view from the top, over the town, and also the fine interior of the historic Hôtel de Ville.

⬛ *70 place des Armes*

SPECIAL TO...
....
The belfry at Douai houses the largest carillon in France, using no fewer than 62 individual bells. Douai's official carillonist is the 34th in a line which started in 1391. Douai also owns the first mobile carillon in France, with 50 bells.

▶ *Leave Douai on the **N45**. In Lewarde turn right on the **D135** and follow 'Centre Historique Minier' signs on to the **D132**.*

7 **Centre Historique Minier,** Picardy
On the site of the old Delloye pit (Fosse Delloye) near Lewarde, you will find an extensive indoor, outdoor and underground museum dedicated to coal-mining in the north of France. Former miners guide visitors round displays about the geology and exploitation of the coal-seams, the machinery and processing plant used in the mines, and the working conditions of miners through the centuries.
Finally, you can descend into one of the original pits where 450m (490 yards) of galleries have been reconstructed as they would have been in their heyday.

▶ *Continue on the **D132** to Bouchain. Go right on the **D943**, left on the **N30**, then right to Haspres. Go left for Saulzoir and right before the FINA station, leaving Haspres on the **D955** to Solesmes. Then follow signs to Le Cateau-Cambrésis. Leave Le Cateau on the **D12**, which becomes the **D27**, then follow the **D946** and the **D967** to Laon.*

8 **Laon,** Picardy
The attractions of Laon are partly in its situation, partly in the architecture of the old city (Ville Haute) surrounded by medieval ramparts and imposing entrance gates. Laon lies on a long narrow ridge which dominates the surrounding plain and is an excellent natural viewpoint. The many-towered 12th- to 14th-century cathedral, one of the great Gothic edifices of France, has a nave of immense grandeur and some beautiful medieval stained-glass windows. Beside an old garden chapel of the Knights Templar (Chapelle des Templiers), the museum holds extensive

archaeological and arts collections.

☐ *Place du Parvis*

▶ *Leave Laon on the **D7** for St-Gobain. Go left on the **D13**, then right on the **D5** to Coucy. Join the **D937** as for Folembray, then turn left on the **D934** to Blérancourt.*

9 Blérancourt, Picardy
Headquarters during World War I of the American volunteer ambulance corps, the pavilions, restored ground floor and gardens of the largely dismantled Château de Blérancourt are now the national Museum of Franco-American Co-operation. Notable Americans such as George Washington, Benjamin Franklin, John Paul Jones and Thomas Jefferson are honoured. There is a substantial library, as well as many documents and souvenirs of battles in which the two nations fought side by side, notably in the two World Wars.

▶ *Leave Blérancourt on the **D935**, which becomes the **D335**, to Pierrefonds.*

10 Pierrefonds, Picardy
Drive slowly down the hill into Pierrefonds, so as not to miss

the first stunning glimpse of the massive castle which towers over this engaging island resort. Handsome villas in discreet wooded grounds overlook a lake, which rowing boats and pedaloes share with the coots and mallards. The Parc Rainette is home to a herd of stately fallow deer. However, it is the château which dominates the town. Napoleon I bought it in ruins, but it was Napoleon II who commissioned the great architect Viollet-le-Duc to oversee its transformation into a grand imperial residence. Guided tours show off the whole lavish project; one room is dedicated to the architect himself, but the château itself is his memorial.

☐ *Place de l'Hôtel-de-Ville*

▶ *Leave Pierrefonds on the **D973** as for Compiègne. Go right on the **D547** to Vieux Moulin, then left on the **N31** and right on the **V4** to Clairière de l'Armistice. Then follow signs to Compiègne.*

11 Compiègne, Picardy
Here is a dignified and spacious town with a fine riverside frontage on the River Oise, spreading parkland and suburbs

to south and west where villa gardens drift into the glorious Forêt de Compiègne. Louis XV and Louis XVI commissioned the building of a palace here, facing a wide cobbled square. It was completed in the fateful year of 1789. After the Revolution, Napoleon I had it rebuilt, and later still it was the favourite residence of Napoleon III and Empress Eugénie.

Open to the public, the royal and imperial apartments recall all these personages, and there is a separate Musée du Second Empire. A first-class motor and carriage museum (Musée National de la Voiture et du Tourisme) includes splendid exhibits of vehicles from the horse-drawn age, and cars which are a reminder that, although Germany was the birthplace of the automobile, the French were livelier designers and experimenters.

Other memorable museums in Compiègne are the Musée Vivenel, which includes fine collections of archaeological items and classical ceramics, and the Musée de la Figurine.

☐ *Place de l'Hôtel de Ville*

For 200 years until AD987, Laon was actually capital of France

and white 'A1' signs. Join the
A1 autoroute as for Lille. Parc
Astérix is reached by the first
exit. After Parc Astérix take
the next autoroute exit as for
Senlis. After the toll booths
follow the 'Creil' sign on the
N330, then the Beauvais
signs via Clermont into
Beauvais itself.

FOR CHILDREN

Parc Astérix, off the A1, on the
way from Ermenonville to
Beauvais, is an expensive but
massive theme park based on
the adventures of the ancient
Gauls – Astérix, Obélix and
Toutafix – made famous by
Goscinny and Underzo.

🔢 Beauvais, Picardy
One victim of World War II was
the tapestry industry at
Beauvais, removed elsewhere
and never brought back. The
Galérie Nationale de la
Tapisserie, a gallery of French
tapestries from the 15th century
onwards, is one of the sights of
the town. Stained glass was
another Beauvais craft, and
much of it survives, both in the
Church of St-Etienne and as a
feature of the superb interior of
the cathedral (St Pierre), which
has a tremendous height for the
area of its base. The cathedral's
astronomical clock, gilded and
astonishingly complicated, was
completely restored in 1989.

Beside the cathedral, the old
bishop's palace houses the
Musée Départementale de
l'Oise, the principal museum in
the *département* of the Oise
region. There are wide-ranging
displays of classical and
contemporary art, art nouveau
and art deco, as well as a glorious exhibition of ceramics.

i 1 rue Beauregard

▶ *Leave Beauvais on the **D901**
as for Abbeville, then take the
D149 as for Crèvecoeur-le-
Grand and the **D11/D210**
back to Amiens.*

▶ *Leave Compiègne on the
D332 as for Meaux. In Crépy-en-
Valois follow 'Paris' signs and take
the **D136** into Nanteuil, ignoring
the bypass. Watch the navigation
here. About 55m (60 yards) after
a Fiat garage, turn right following
the sign 'Ermenonville Tourisme'.
Go left on the **D922**, then right
on the **N330** through
Ermenonville.*

🔢 Ermenonville, Picardy
Ermenonville has been done no
favours by the planners, who
have signposted the road here
as being a convenient way to
bypass other towns. Traffic is
usually heavy. However, the
town itself has one haven of
tranquillity. To the left of the
main road is a park, introduced
by a carved stone which trans-
lates as 'here begins the course
of a sweet and rustic leisure'
with woodland paths, ponds and
streams.

Beyond Ermenonville is a
small zoo (Zoo Jean-Richard).
The Abbey of Chaalis, just

The elegant town of Compiègne

north of the town, in a gracious
parkland which contains one of
France's finest rose gardens, is a
classical 18th-century château
on the site of an old Cistercian
monastery.

i 1 rue René de Girardin

▶ *Turn sharp left for
Mortefontaine. Join the **D922**
and in Plailly follow the blue*

RECOMMENDED
WALKS

Ask at the tourist office
in Pierrefonds for the
Itinéraires circuits pédestres
booklet describing four
waymarked walks in the
eastern part of the Forêt de
Compiègne. One follows an
ancient Roman road, another
goes past the Empress
Eugénie's hunting pavilion.

A Taste of
Champagne

Although Reims itself is the heart of champagne country, in the early part of the tour you will find many vineyards occupying sloping fields on the edge of the Montagne de Reims, south of the city. Arable plains stretch north to the hill and river country which France shares with Belgium in the Ardennes.

ITINERARY		
REIMS	▶	**Montagne de Reims** (17km-11m)
MONTAGNE DE REIMS	▶	**Châlons-en-Champagne** (54km-34m)
CHÂLONS-EN-CHAMPAGNE	▶	**Valmy (34km-21m)**
VALMY	▶	**Ste-Menehould** (10km-6m)
STE-MENEHOULD	▶	**Varennes-en-Argonne** (28km-18m)
VARENNES-EN-ARGONNE	▶	**Parc de Vision de Belval** (45km-28m)
PARC DE VISION DE BELVAL	▶	**Sedan (47km-29m)**
SEDAN	▶	**Charleville-Mézières** (20km-12m)
CHARLEVILLE-MÉZIÈRES	▶	**Musée de l'Ardennes** (45km-28m)
MUSÉE DE L'ARDENNES	▶	**Rethel (47km-29m)**
RETHEL	▶	**Reims (39km-24m)**

3/4 DAYS • 386KM • 240 MILES

_i_ *2 rue Guillaume de Machault, Reims*

▶ *Leave Reims on the **N31** as for Soissons. Turn left on the **D27** to Gueux, then left on the **D26** through Vrigny. Turn right into Ville-Dommange, follow 'Courmas' sign, then go right to the Chapelle de St-Lié.*

❶ Montagne de Reims,
Champagne-Ardenne

From the viewpoint below the Chapelle St-Lié there is a glorious outlook down over the vineyards on the lowest slope of the wooded hills south of Reims, and of the city itself, separate on the plain. Many of the villages are the home of champagnes little known abroad – Rilly for *Vilmart*, Ludes for *Blondel*, Villedommange immediately below for *Champagne de la Chapelle*. St-Lié, a church on the summit of a wooded hill sacred from pagan days, is being sympathetically restored.

The hilly woodlands and the villages are all included in the Parc Naturel Régional de Montagne de Reims. Many waymarked walks have been laid out in it. St-Lié is on the *sentier petite montagne* which meanders along the north-facing slopes.

▶ *Return to the **D26** and turn right. Follow this road, not always numbered on signs, through Villers-Allerand, Ludes, Rilly-la-Montagne and Verzenay to Verzy. In Verzy, watch for a right turn on the **D34** to Louvois and Condé. Go left on the **D1** to Châlons-en-Champagne.*

BACK TO NATURE

On the way to Châlons, turn left off the D34 for Les Faux de Verzy. These are bizarrely mutated beeches, first mentioned in monastic writings of the 6th century, with thin corkscrewed trunks and umbrella-like foliage.

❷ Châlons-en-Champagne,
Champagne-Ardenne

This is an old-established town whose main street is on the line of the Romans' Via Agrippa that runs from Milan to Boulogne. As its name suggests, the town does have extensive champagne cellars to be visited. The largely 13th-century cathedral (St Étienne) with lovely stained glass which you can easily admire, because it is at less than the usual neck-craning angle, has a march of flying buttresses and a later north front uncomfortably out of tune with the rest. You may find Notre-Dame-en-Vaux just as interesting. In a cloister museum reached by a lane beside this multi-towered church, more than 50 carved columns featuring saints, prophets and medieval personalities are on display. Châlons has many waterfronts along the River Marne and the canals connected with it. Look for the series of parks and formal gardens called the Jards.

_i_ *3 quai des Arts*

▶ *Leave Châlons on the **N3** as for Metz. After Auve, watch for a left turn signed for Valmy. This is the **D284**. Turn right for Moulin de Valmy.*

FOR HISTORY BUFFS

In the village of L'Épine, on the N3 after Châlons, the pilgrim-age church is an astonishing miniature cathedral in Flamboyant Gothic style. It houses a statue of the Virgin found miraculously unharmed in a burning thorn bush (*épine*).

❸ Valmy, Champagne-Ardenne

The reconstructed windmill (*moulin*) on the hilltop at Valmy, marks the site of the most significant engagement in the war which Revolutionary France fought against the Prussians and Austrians. Plaques show the line-up of troops on 20

September 1792, when General Kellermann's inexperienced French army faced the battle-hardened Prussians under the Duke of Brunswick. Expecting an easy victory, the Prussians were in fact repulsed, and the young Revolutionary forces proved they could defend the homeland. Within a few hours, the Republic was proclaimed. The French troops, and Kellermann himself (by a spirited statue) are commemorated in the little village of Valmy.

ⓘ *Maison du Meunier*

▶ *Continue on the D284, follow signs to Braux-Ste-Cohiere, then follow sign 'Vers N3'. Go left on the N3 to Ste-Menehould.*

4 Ste-Menehould,
Champagne-Ardenne
A statue of Dom Pérignon recalls the fact that this Benedictine monk, to whom we owe the modern method of blending different wines into

champagne, was born here in the 17th century. Incongruously, perhaps, you will find many shops selling a quite different speciality – pigs' trotters.

At the now-restored Maison de Poste, the ill-fated Louis XVI and Marie Antoinette were recognised and subsequently arrested by Revolutionaries.

At Ste-Menehould you will witness the unusual sight of a river flowing in different directions. Thanks to canal works, the Aisne splits into two channels which encircle the town and join up again after it. Since the Auve joins the Aisne here, Ste-Menehould has many pleasant waterways.

Its plateau location and a woodland fringe keep the old upper town almost out of sight, but a good self-guided walk links it with the lower town, whose elegant public buildings were raised after a disastrous fire in 1719.

A picturesque windmill (*moulin*) still operates in Verzenay

ⓘ *5 place Général Leclerc*

▶ *Continue on the N3. In Les Islettes turn left for Varennes, following the D2 and then the D38.*

5 Varennes-en-Argonne,
Champagne-Ardenne
In June 1791, when Louis XVI and his family fled secretly from Paris to try to join loyal troops at Metz, it was in Varennes that their coaches were stopped. Arrest, trial and the guillotine followed. The Musée d'Argonne is an excellent local museum, which describes the drama, and gives a balanced account of a king who forcefully supported the Americans in the War of Independence but made many political blunders at home. It also has intriguing displays on the old crafts and industries of the Forest of Argonne, and on the devastating effect on the district of World War I.

French and American flags fly at the entrance to the little grassy park leading to the pillared Pennsylvania Monument. It was troops from that US state who liberated Varennes in 1918.

ⓘ *Musée d'Argonne*

▶ *Leave Varennes on the D946. Turn right on the D6 to Buzancy, left on the D947, then right and left on the D155 to Fossé, taking care on the bumpy roads. Go left on the D55, left on the D4 and follow it right as for Beaumont, to the Parc de Vision de Belval.*

6 Parc de Vision de Belval,
Champagne-Ardenne
In 350 hectares (865 acres) of woodland and clearings, with a lake to accommodate its ducks and geese, this extensive wildlife park houses around 400 wild animals belonging to species which either still live in the northern forests or are known to have lived in them within the last 2,000 years.

Because the red, roe and fallow deer, the wild boars, the moufflons, the bison and the other animals all live in semi-freedom inside the boundary fence, visitors drive slowly along the viewing roads, follow a fenced-in walking route or travel on the little 'train', whose locomotive is a thinly-disguised tractor. The only animal kept in a separate secure enclosure is a brown bear, which might otherwise become testy if annoyed!

▶ *Continue on the **D4** through Beaumont, then go straight on to the **D30** as for Le Chesne. Beyond Les Grandes-Armoises, after the bend sign, take the first right to pass an '8t' sign. Turn right at the Give Way sign. This is the **D977**. Follow the signs to Sedan.*

RECOMMENDED WALKS

After joining the D977 for Sedan, turn right on the D230 into the Forêt de Mont-Dieu. The Circuit de la Chartreuse walk wanders through the forest and overlooks the historic monastery of Mont-Dieu.

Sedan, dominated by its fortress, has had a turbulent history

❼ **Sedan,** Champagne-Ardenne
Some quarters of the town are fairly depressing, but Sedan can barely dispel the memories of its past. This is where Napoleon III capitulated to end the Franco-Prussian War of 1870. In World War I the huge Château-Fort, in area the biggest castle in the whole of Europe, was a brutal forced-labour camp. And in the next war, this was where the Germans burst through the French lines in the invasion of 1940. Now the castle houses a museum on Sedan's military history, and there is a guided tour.

Away from these melancholy recollections, Sedan is famous for its high-quality woollen rugs; the workshop where rugs are still made as they were a century ago is open to visitors. There are pleasant promenades by the River Meuse.

[i] *Place du Château*

▶ *Leave Sedan for Floing on the **D5** and continue on this road to Charleville-Mézières. Avoid the autoroute.*

---

❽ **Charleville-Mézières,** Champagne-Ardenne
Two once-separate towns, around loops of the River Meuse, have merged here. Mézières to the south is virtually on two islands. Within its 16th-century ramparts, the Flamboyant Gothic Church of Notre-Dame d'Espérance will surprise you with its abstract and geometrical stained-glass windows by René Dürrbach, a collaborator of Picasso's.

At Charleville the elegant, arcaded Place Ducale remains virtually as it was completed in 1628 (pity about the faded and obsolete shop signs).

The grand watermill (Vieux Moulin) on the Meuse is a local museum (Musée de l'Ardennes), partly dedicated to the poet Arthur Rimbaud, who was born at Charleville.

[i] *22 place Ducale*

FOR CHILDREN

Charleville-Mézières is the world capital of puppetry. Its Institut International de la Marionette has details of the summer puppet festival.

▶ *Leave Charleville on the* **D988** *and follow signs to Monthermé along the* **D989**. *In Monthermé watch for a sharp left turn on the* **DI** *to Revin. Go left on the* **D988** *as for Les Mazures, then Renwez and turn left at the junction with the* **D140** *into the Musée de l'Ardennes.*

❾ Musée de l'Ardennes,
Champagne-Ardenne

As much a museum 'in' the forest as 'of' the forest, this 5-hectare (12-acre) area of woodland is devoted to showing – partly with the aid of cheery wooden sculptures – the traditional crafts and harvesting methods of a few unmechanised generations ago. Strolling round, you will see how birchwood brushes were made, how oak bark was peeled, how charcoal burners went about their trade, the kind of huts woodcutters lived in, and a selection of axes and single- and two-man saws.

The museum holds occasional wood-chopping contests, where competitors test their speed and accuracy as they axe their way through felled logs.

▶ *Continue on the* **D40**. *Go straight through Lonny. Turn right into Sormonne and left on the* **D978** *as for Laon. Go left on the* **D985** *and continue to Rethel.*

FOR CHILDREN

Before Rethel turn left off the D978 after Lonny for a neat little karting centre with two circuits for children of different ages. Low-powered karts are available for the real youngsters, and first-time drivers are patiently shown how to go about it.

❿ Rethel, Champagne-Ardenne

An inscription at the bridge over the River Aisne here is a simple list of seven years between 1411 and 1940 – the years when war came to Rethel. In the 1930s the town hall was proudly re-created in Renaissance style; then in May 1940 more than three-quarters of the buildings in Rethel were flattened. But the town bobbed up again, as it always has.

The fine old Church of St-Nicholas was restored and the local museum was restocked. Walks along the river and the nearby canal were opened up, including the tree-lined Promenade des Isles.

There are sports facilities here for everything from tennis and rugby to show-jumping and archery, and the modern swimming pool is partly under cover, partly in the open air.

Rethel is famous for its local culinary speciality – the *boudin blanc*, a white sausage made from pork, eggs, shallots and seasoning.

SCENIC ROUTES

From the beautifully kept village of Gueux, the D26 runs along the foothills of the Montagne de Reims, through vineyards below the forest ridge.
Beyond Varennes the route follows a pleasant rural landscape, sometimes on the shallow valley floor. The D6 gives long views over fields and wooded hills.
After Monthermé the deep, sinuous and thickly wooded valley of the Meuse gives the finest scenery in the French Ardennes.

⬚ *Mairie, avenue Gambetta*

▶ *Leave Rethel on the* **N51** *to Reims.*

Monthermé is a popular resort in the Meuse valley

TOUR
24

The Heart
of Burgundy

North of Chalon-sur-Saône, this tour runs through the famous Burgundy vineyards. Then it crosses upland areas off the usual tourist track, and wanders through the farm and forest country of the extensive Parc Naturel Régional du Morvan.

3 DAYS • 408KM • 255 MILES

▶ Leave Chalon on the **N6** as
for Beaune. Turn right on the
N74, left on the **C2** to
Puligny-Montrachet, then take
the **D113b** to Mersault. Go
straight ahead on the **D23**,
turn right on the **D17**,
continue through Pommard
and go left into Beaune.

❶ Beaune, Burgundy
Thousands of visitors come
every year to Beaune. Many go
to the Hôtel-Dieu, opened in
1443 as a charitable hospital.
Containing displays which show
how the nuns looked after their
aged patients in years gone by,
as well as Rogier van der
Weyden's stunning 15th-century
altarpiece of the *Last Judgement*,
the building is a ravishing
mixture of polychrome tiling,
intricate window details and
appealing galleries. Beaune is
honeycombed with wine cellars,
some of them in the town walls.
The Musée du Vin de
Bougogne occupies an old town
mansion of the dukes of
Burgundy, while the Athenaeum
is a cultural centre linking wine,
literature and local history.

Magnificent tapestries hang
in the Church of Notre-Dame.
Beaune also has a fine arts
museum and the Musée Marey
is a tribute to Beaune-born
pioneer of moving pictures,
Étienne Jules Marey.

i Rue de l'Hôtel-Dieu

SPECIAL TO...

Puligny-Montrachet, Meursault
and Pommard are vineyard villages of the Côte d'Or, whose
white burgundies are held in
high regard. More than a dozen
grand crus and *premiers crus*
come from Puligny-Montrachet,
while the Meursault growers
are keenest on welcoming visitors. Details of wine tours are
available from the tourist information in Beaune.

▶ Leave Beaune on the **D18**
going north, passing Pernand-
Vergelesses. Continue on the
D18 through Changey, turn
right on to the **D8**, then take
the **D25F** and the **D25** to
Bruant. Go left on the **D8**
again, fork right on the **D104**,
right on the **D104b** to

Magnificent Gothic architecture
characterises medieval Beaune

Ternant, then take the **D35** to
Pont-de-Pany. Go left on the
D905, and immediately after
leaving Pont-de-Pany turn
right over the autoroute to
Mâlain. Continue through
Baulme-la-Roche. Turn left on
the **D10** to Gissey-sous-
Flavigny. Bear left at the
roundabout, past Café de
l'Oze, on to the **D10e** to
Hauteroche. Turn sharp right
and follow signs to Flavigny,
entering it on the **D9**.

FOR HISTORY BUFFS

Look for the dolmens in the
woodland left of the **D104b**
before Ternant. These great
balanced-stone chambers
remain impressive and mysterious after 6,000 years.

❷ Flavigny-sur-Ozerain,
Burgundy
History has moved on, isolating
this little medieval hilltop town.
Park outside, study the
labyrinthine medieval street
plan and feel the centuries drift

151

away as you stroll through an ancient gateway, along narrow streets and alleyways, to the 13th-century church in the square. Local farm produce is sold here. Guided tours are arranged of an eerie 8th-century crypt. There are farm-track walks on the plateau, one to a site said to be a Roman camp from Julius Caesar's time.

[i] Place de l'Église

SPECIAL TO...

Lliquorice is Flavigny's most famous product. The old abbey makes aniseed in many forms – sweets, candies and flavourings. The genuine article – *véritable marque des anis* – is on sale in local groceries.

▶ Continue on the **D9** and **D954** to Semur-en-Auxois.

8 **Semur-en-Auxois,**
Burgundy
Semur occupies a pinched-in red granite promontory at a hairpin bend on the River Armançon. Its 18th-century Pont Joly looks to banked up houses and massive rampart towers of the Château Flée.

The 13th-century Church of Notre-Dame features an eccentrically narrow nave and good stained-glass windows including a rather frank account of the work of the butchers' guild. There are medieval houses and a rampart walk. From the Pont Joly, Semur probably looks its best floodlit or at sunset.

The Church of St-Lazare, Avallon, has fine carvings on its doorway

[i] 2 place Gaveau

▶ Continue on the **D954** and **N6** to Avallon.

FOR HISTORY BUFFS

At Époisses, on the **D954** on the way to Avallon, pause to visit the dry-moated château, with its dovecote exhibition and 13th-century parish church. Madame de Sévigny was a frequent visitor to the château. Even when the château itself is closed, you can visit its grounds, which form a Burgundy village in miniature.

4 **Avallon,** Burgundy
Many of the old rampart walls, towers, bastions and gateways survive in the very agreeable old town. Perimeter walks and stairways look down on the attractive valley of the River Cousin.

Avallon is packed with fascinating old buildings, such as the clock tower of 1456, formerly a town gate, through which a street leads to the well-endowed Musée de l'Avallonnais and the 12th-century Church of St-Lazare. Part of St-Lazare houses the etchings for 20th-century artist Georges Rouault's harrowing but highly regarded series of prints entitled *Miserere*.

At the Château Montjalin you can see how the other half drives, or, more correctly, are driven. The collection of limousines here includes many cars used by world celebrities and politicians.

[i] 4 rue Bocquillot

▶ Continue on the **N6** as for Auxerre, then turn left on the **D951** to Vézelay.

5 **Vézelay,** Burgundy
Climbing sinuously to a hilltop, the main street of this little town passes artists' studios, galleries and displays of semi-precious stones before it reaches the Basilica of Ste-Madeleine,

one of the all-time glories of
Romanesque design. The
church, a great pilgrimage goal
when it was believed to contain
the remains of Mary Magdalen,
survived fire, plunder and
virtual destruction during the
Revolution, to be completely
restored in the 19th century.
Look for its splendid doorways,
intricately carved capitals,
impressive crypt and the view
from the tower, but most of all
for the mellow light that pours
into the interior.

[i] Rue St Pierre

Stylised carving over a doorway at
the Basilica of St Madeleine

RECOMMENDED WALKS

Ask at the tourist office in
Vézelay about the seven
waymarked walks in the countryside 'under the hill'. Each is
described in an individual leaflet
which includes a map, walking
directions and information.

▶ Leave Vézelay on the **D957**
to St-Père, then go right on
the **D958** to Pierre-Perthuis.
Turn left on the **D353** and
immediately right following
'Les Ponts' sign. Go through
Précy-le-Moult, then turn right
on the **D36** which becomes
the **D20**. At a crossroads, turn
right on the **D944**. In St-
Martin-du-Puy, watch for a
sharp left turn to Quarré-les-
Tombes. In Quarré, turn right
through Les Levaults on the
D10, then right on the **D211**.
Go straight ahead on the **D6**
to the Maison du Parc.

6 St-Brisson, Burgundy
On the edge of St-Brisson, a
fine old red-roofed farm
complex is the headquarters of
the Parc Naturel Régional du
Morvan, the Morvan being the
wooded mountain region
between the rivers Loire and
Saône. The Maison du Parc
illustrates wildlife, crafts,
conservation and the rural way
of life. The grounds include a
herb garden, animal enclosures,

a waterfowl pond, and pathways
down to the lake. Also here is
the Musée de la Résistance,
which tells the story of the
Morvan's secret war in World
War II.

[i] Maison du Parc

▶ Return from Maison du Parc,
take the first left, go left at
the T-junction through St-
Brisson, then bear right on
the **C1** and continue to
Montsauche-les-Settons. Go
left on the **D37**, then left on
the **D193**. Keep Lac des
Settons on your right, then
watch for a sharp right turn
following the 'Rive Gauche'
sign. At the give way sign turn
left on the **D520** and
continue to Château-Chinon.

FOR CHILDREN

Lac des Settons beside the
D193 is a fine recreational
reservoir with wooded bays,
beaches and picnic sites. The
youngsters can try out
pedaloes and generally splash
around.

7 Château-Chinon,
Burgundy
Capital of the Morvan, Château-
Chinon rises to a parkland with
walks and drives and gorgeous
views over the surrounding
countryside.

The Musée du Costume also
has displays on local arts and
traditions. In the Musée du
Septennat you will find an exhibition of the ceremonial gifts
lavished at home and abroad on
François Mitterand during his
first term as President of
France. Previously a local politi-
cian here, he donated them all
to the *département*.

[i] Place Notre Dame

▶ Leave Château-Chinon on the
D978 to Autun.

8 Autun, Burgundy
Founded by the Emperor
Augustus as *Augustodunum*,
Autun retains Roman archways
such as the Porte St-André and
the Porte d'Arroux, still used by
traffic and pedestrians. The
Musée Rolin, housed in a 15th-
century mansion, specialises in
Roman exhibits, and the original riverside theatre is still in
use. Look for the majestic portal
of the 12th-century Cathédrale
St-Lazare, the medieval rampart
walk, the immaculate military
academy, and the 18th-century
Lycée Bonaparte where
Napoleon was a pupil.

[i] 2 avenue Charles de Gaulle

▶ Leave Autun following signs to
Chalon-sur-Saône.

The Historic
Centre of France

Many strands of French life and history combine in this tour from Chartres – the palace of Fontainebleau, the castle at Rambouillet, Barbizon and Moret-sur-Loing. You will find pleasant roads which run through cool shady woodlands, and others which cross skyline-to-skyline arable plains, wide open to the summer sun.

2/3 DAYS • 312KM • 194 MILES

ITINERARY

CHARTRES	▶	**Rambouillet (46km-29m)**
RAMBOUILLET	▶	**Milly-la-Forêt (82km-51m)**
MILLY-LA-FORÊT	▶	**Barbizon (13km-8m)**
BARBIZON	▶	**Fontainebleau (17km-11m)**
FONTAINEBLEAU	▶	**Moret-sur-Loing (16km-10m)**
MORET-SUR-LOING	▶	**Grez-sur-Loing (15km-9m)**
GREZ-SUR-LOING	▶	**Pithiviers (50km-31m)**
PITHIVIERS	▶	**Chartres (73km-45m)**

☐ *Place de la Cathédrale, Chartres*

▶ *Leave Chartres on the **N154**. At the traffic lights, turn right for St-Prest and continue on the **D6** to Maintenon. Turn right to Épernon. Turn right on the **D176**, then continue through Droue to Émancé. Go as for Orphin, turn left on the **D62** to Gazeran, then follow the signs to Rambouillet.*

❶ Rambouillet, Île de France
This is France's 'presidential town'. Its elegant château, standing among extensive woodlands, lawns and water gardens, is an official residence of the president, but is open to visitors most of the year. Louis XVI commissioned two buildings in the grounds – the ornamental dairy called the Laiterie de la Reine, and the Chaumière des Coquillages ('Cottage of Shells') with its wall covering of seashells, mother-of-pearl and tiny pieces of marble. Also in the grounds you will see the Bergerie Nationale, famous for its pedigree Merino rams. There is a museum here on the husbandry and breeding of sheep. Rambouillet's racecourse is southeast of the town. Beyond it (take the D27), a wildlife reserve shelters red, roe and fallow deer.

☐ *8 place de la Libération*

RECOMMENDED
WALKS

After you have left Rambouillet, where the D24 crosses the D91, turn left, following the 'Cascades' sign to the woodland walks, to the left of the road, leading by a jumble of rocks down to a river ravine and its falls.

▶ *Leave Rambouillet as for Paris, join the **N10** dual-carriageway, and turn off through Le Perray-en-Yvelines on the **D910**. Go right on the **D24** and continue to Cernay-la-Ville. Turn left on to the **D306**, then sharp right on the **D72**, left on the **D61**, then right **D72** again to Clairefontaine-en-Yvelines. Go left on the **D27** and follow 'Dourdan' signs, turning right on the **D149**. Go left on the **D836** to Dourdan, then take the **D116** before rejoining the **D836** and taking the **N191** through Étampes. Go right on the **D837** and into Milly-la-Forêt.*

❷ Milly-la-Forêt, Île de France
Expertly trimmed, shade-providing trees; a 15th-century market hall; red-tiled houses; and a wondering stream with wash-house quays: all these combine to give this village a timeless appearance.

The artist, poet and dramatist Jean Cocteau is buried in the little 12th-century chapel of St-Blaise-des-Simples, which he had previously decorated. The *simples* are medicinal herbs, which remain a preoccupation of Milly today. On the Nemours road you can visit the Conservatoire National of medicinal and aromatic plants and plants used by industry.

☐ *60 rue Jean Cocteau*

SPECIAL TO...

In Le Perray, after Rambouillet, the Musée des Vieux Métiers is a working forge with a collection of traditional blacksmith's tools and equipment. You can hardly miss the 9m (30-foot) model of the Eiffel Tower.

▶ *Follow 'Fontainebleau' signs on the **D837**. In Arbonne, bear left as for Melun. Turn right on the **D64** to Barbizon.*

❸ Barbizon, Île de France
In the mid-19th century, a group of landscape artists centred on the painter Théodore Rousseau, made this village their base.

Rodin called Chartres Cathedral the 'Acropolis of France'

They were to become known as the Barbizon School. Greater figures, such as the Realist painter Jean François Millet, whose *Angelus* was painted near by, were also Barbizon men.

In Rousseau's house, fascinating maps and illustrations shows the village as it was then. Upstairs in his north-light studio is a collection of little gems of landscape art.

The artists' often frugal meals were taken at the village inn run by old Monsieur Ganne. Now the Auberge du Père Ganne houses an atmospheric museum in which it is easy to imagine that the next person at the door is a hungry painter, ready for dinner after a day's sketching in the countryside.

$\boxed{i}$ *55 grande Rue*

▶ *Leave Barbizon by the Grande Rue and enter the Forêt de Fontainebleau. Turn right at a T-junction following the 'Fontainebleau par route forestière' sign. Go right at the Stop signs for Franchard (this is the D301), then left on the N152 and at the busy roundabout take the N6 for the town of Fontainebleau.*

4 **Fontainebleau,** Île de France

Everything else in this elegant town defers to the spectacular palace in its parkland of lakes, wooded and formal and landscape gardens. A discreet plaque acknowledges John D Rockefeller Jr's generous funding of the palace restoration. The Musée Napoléon houses a massive exhibition on the Bonaparte family. Do not confuse this with the Musée Napoléonien d'Art et d'Histoire, in the town itself, which features grand displays on the French military through the ages.

$\boxed{i}$ *4 rue Royale*

BACK TO NATURE

Planted with pines, oaks, birches, chestnut trees, hornbeams and – especially – glorious beechwoods, the Forêt de Fontainebleau is one of the most beautiful and most carefully protected woodlands in Europe. It covers about 25,000 hectares (61,775 acres), most of them open to the public.

▶ *Return to the busy roundabout and take the D58 as for Bourron-Marlotte. Go straight ahead on the D148, then turn left on to the D104 to Moret-sur-Loing.*

5 **Moret-sur-Loing,** Île de France

This very appealing little place is an 'ancient and royal city' which once stood on the French frontier, fortified against Burgundy on the far side of a beautiful stretch of the River Loing. Fine medieval gateways, Renaissance and later buildings survive.

By the river, La Grange Batelière is the home of the Clemenceau family, open at weekends to tell the story of France's famous World War I president. Moret also celebrates its connection with the Impressionist painter Alfred Sisley.

$\boxed{i}$ *4 bis place de Samois*

▶ *Leave Moret on the D302, then immediately turn right at traffic lights for Nemours.*

Napoléon was responsible for Fontainebleau's sumptuous interior

Watch for another right turn as for Nemours along the D40. Go right on to the D40d, then left into Grez-sur-Loing.

FOR CHILDREN

As you approach Grez-sur-Loing, look on the right for Tacot des Lacs, a full-scale railway, with trains like the 1900 steam locomotive *Clémentine* running trips through scrubland and across the River Loing.

❻ Grez-sur-Loing, Île de France

Here is a lovely stretch of the Loing with gardens, boathouses, weeping willows and flotillas of geese and mallards. Swallows and damselflies dart above the water, swifts in the higher air. Beyond the old arched bridge rises a pale 12th-century tower.

In the 1870s, Robert Louis Stevenson joined the Bohemian summer colony at Grez. Later, Frederick Delius composed much of his music here.

Stroll to the austere and lofty medieval church, and along the hollyhock lane from the little

Place Jolivet. The artists have gone, but the appeal of this charming village never fades.

▶ *Leave Grez as for La Chapelle-la-Reine, taking the D104. After the junction sign watch for a left turn to Larchant. Go right as for La Chapelle on the D16. Turn left on to the D36 and follow signs to Jacqueville. Bear right then left following the 'Malesherbes' sign on the C7. Take care at the level crossing. At the give way sign, go left on to the N152 to Malesherbes. Take the D948 as for Puiseaux, then go right on the D25 through Pinçon and Briarres. Continue through Aulnay-la-Rivière to Pithiviers.*

FOR HISTORY BUFFS

Malesherbes, on the way to Pithiviers, has two castles worthy of a visit on its outskirts. The Château de Malesherbes, off the Puiseaux road, is furnished as it was immediately before the Revolution. Off the D132, the many-turreted Château de Rouville overlooks the valley of the Essone.

Moret-sur-Loing is a favourite destination for Parisians at 'le Weekend'

❼ Pithiviers, Île de France

Famous for its fine almond cakes, Pithiviers has a very interesting local museum, housed in the former 18th-century Hôtel-Dieu, which explains the local cuisine and its cooks' pioneering use of saffron – the region was once of European importance for saffron-growing

Historic steam locomotives from as early as 1870 run on the last 4km (2½-mile) stretch of a light railway opened in 1892. An exhibition displays some elegant old coaches and tells the story of France's branch lines.

[i] *Mail Ouest*

▶ *Leave Pithiviers on the D927 to Allaines. Now follow the signs to the D12 and join the D10 to Voves. Turn right on to the D17 as for Auneau and enter the one-way traffic system in Voves. At the two-way sign turn into a side road on the left. Go right at the Stop sign and return to Chartres.*

PRACTICAL INFORMATION

ACCIDENTS
If you are involved in an accident you must complete a *constat l'amiable* before moving the vehicle. It must be signed by the other party, and in the event of a dispute or a refusal to complete the form, you should immediately obtain a *constat d'huissier*, a written report from a bailiff (*huissier*).

The police are only called out when someone is injured, a driver is under the influence of alcohol or the accident impedes traffic flow. (See also **warning triangles/hazard warning lights**.)

BREAKDOWNS
If your car breaks down, try to move it to the side of the road so it obstructs the traffic flow as little as possible. Place a warning triangle to the rear of the vehicle at a suitable distance. You are advised to seek local assistance as, at present, there is no nationwide road assistance service in France.

On autoroutes, ring from emergency phones located every 2km (mile) to contact breakdown service. (See also **warning triangles/hazard warning lights**.)

CAR HIRE AND FLY/DRIVE
If you are not taking your own car, you can make arrangements to hire before departure. Many package holidays include car hire as an option. The main car hire companies are represented in France.

CHILDREN
Children under 10 are not permitted to travel as front seat passengers, with the exception of babies or very young children in an approved rear-facing child seat. Children under the age of 10 in the rear must use a child seat or restraint if fitted. Note: under no circumstances should a rear-facing restraint be used in a seat with an airbag.

MOTORING IN FRANCE

CRASH HELMETS
Visiting motorcyclists and their passengers must wear crash or safety helmets.

DIMENSIONS AND WEIGHT RESTRICTIONS
Private cars and towed trailers or caravans are restricted to the following dimensions: height – no restrictions, but 4m is a recommended maximum; width – 2.5m; length – 12m (excluding any towing device).

DOCUMENTS
A valid full driver's licence is required, and the minimum driving age is 18. Visitors may use temporarily imported motorcycles of up to 80cc at 16. An international licence is not required for visitors from the US, UK or Western Europe. You also require the vehicle's registration document, plus a letter of authorisation from the owner, if they are not accompanying the vehicle, and the current insurance certificate (a green card is not mandatory but remains internationally recognised and can be helpful). A nationality plate or sticker is also required.

DRINKING AND DRIVING
The laws in Europe regarding drinking and driving are strict and the penalties severe. They include stiff fines and police escort back to a ferry terminal. The best advice is, as at home, if you drink don't drive.

DRIVING CONDITIONS
Keep to the right (*serrez à droite*).

Though main roads have priority (*passage protégé*), right of way is otherwise given to vehicles coming in from the right (*priorité à droite*).

The *priorité* rule no longer applies at roundabouts with signs bearing the words '*Vous n'avez pas la priorité*' or '*Cédez le passage*', which means you give way to cars already on the roundabout.

Mountain tours call for a properly serviced and not overladen car. Especially in these areas, petrol stations may be far apart.

On the Clermont-Ferrand, Pau and Grenoble tours, roadside notices displaying either *Ouvert* (open) or *Fermé* (closed) will show the road conditions ahead.

FUEL
You will find comparable grades of petrol in France, with familiar brand names along the main routes. You will normally have to buy a minimum of 5 litres (just over a gallon) but it is wise to keep the tank topped up, particularly in remote areas.

Some garages may close between noon and 3pm, but fuel is generally available, 24-hours on motorways. Prices on motorways will normally be higher than elsewhere; self-service pumps will be slightly cheaper.

Leaded gas (*essence super*) is now only sold in one grade (98 octane), while unleaded is sold in two: 95 octane (*essence sans plomb*) and 98 octane (*super sans plomb*). Diesel is much cheaper and readily available. Credit cards are generally accepted, but in rural areas some garages may not accept them.

INSURANCE
Fully comprehensive insurance, which covers you for some of the expenses incurred after a breakdown or an accident, is advisable.

LIGHTS
It is obligatory to use headlights, as driving on sidelights only is not permitted. In fog, mist or poor visibility during the day, either fog lamps or

dipped headlights must be switched on in addition to side-lights. It is compulsory for motorcyclists riding machines exceeding 125cc to use dipped headlights during the day. Failure to comply with these regulations will lead to an on-the-spot deposit (see below, **police fines**).

It is recommended that visiting motorists equip their vehicles with a set of replacement bulbs. Drivers able to replace a faulty bulb when requested to do so by the police will not avoid a fine, but may avoid the cost and inconvenience of a garage call-out. Yellow tinted headlights are now no longer necessary.

MOTORING CLUB
The AA is affiliated to the Automobile Club National (ACN) whose office is at 75009 Paris, 5 rue Auber (tel: 44515399).

POLICE FINES
Police in France impose an on-the-spot deposit for minor traffic offences and subsequently levy a fine which may be the same as, or greater or lesser than, the deposit. If the fine is not paid, legal proceedings will usually follow. Once paid, a fine cannot be recovered, but a receipt should be obtained as proof of payment.

ROADS
France has a very comprehensive network of roads, and surfaces are generally good; exceptions are usually signposted *Chausée deformée*.

SEAT BELTS
It is compulsory to wear seat belts if your car is fitted with them.

SPEED LIMITS
In dry weather a higher speed limit applies than in wet weather. Unless otherwise indicated, maximum speed limits are as follows, with wet-weather limits in *italics*.
Built-up areas 50kph (31mph).

Outside built-up areas on normal roads 90kph (56mph) *80kph (49mph)*; on dual carriageways separated by a central reservation 110kph (69mph); also motorways without tolls.
Toll motorways 130kph (80mph) *110kph (69mph)*.

The beginning of a built-up area is indicated by a sign with the place-name in blue letters on a light background; the end is signified by a thin red line diagonally across the place-name sign. Unless otherwise signposted, follow the above speed limits.

Note: the minimum speed in the fast lane on a level stretch of motorway during good daytime visibility is 80kph (49mph), and drivers travelling below this speed are liable to be fined.

In fog, when visibility is reduced to 50m (55 yards), the speed limit on all roads is 50kph (31mph).

Both French residents and visitors to France who have held a driving licence for less than two years, must not exceed 80kph (49mph) outside built-up areas, 100kph (62mph) on dual carriageways separated by a central reservation and 110kph (69mph) on motorways.

TOLLS
Tolls are payable on many motorways in France. Toll booths will not accept travellers' cheques, but some credit cards are accepted.

WARNING TRIANGLE/ HAZARD WARNING LIGHTS
The use of a warning triangle or hazard warning lights* is compulsory in the event of an accident or breakdown. As hazard warning lights may be damaged or inoperative, it is advisable to carry a warning triangle. The triangle must be placed on the road 30m (33 yards) behind the vehicle, or further, if necessary, to allow for bends in the road, and clearly visible for 100m (110 yards).

*If your vehicle is equipped with hazard warning lights, it is compulsory to use them if you are forced to drive temporarily at a greatly reduced speed. However, when slow moving traffic is established in an uninterrupted lane or lanes, this only applies to the last vehicle in the lane(s).

ACCOMMODATION
Listed below is a selection of hotels which can be found along the routes of each tour.

Prices
Hotel charges are divided into three price brackets:
Expensive £££ – £60 or more
Moderate ££ – between £35 and £60
Budget £ – up to £35
These are the rates for a double room for one night.

TOUR 1
CAEN Normandy
Quatrans *£*
17 rue Gémare (tel: 02 31 86 25 57; fax: 02 31 85 27 80)

GRANDCAMP-MAISY
Normandy
Duguesclin £
4 quai Crampon (tel: 02 31 22 64 22; fax: 02 31 22 34 79)

TOUR 2
HONFLEUR Normandy
Hostellerie Lechat ££
3 place Ste-Catherine(tel: 02 31 14 49 49; fax: 02 31 89 28 61

TOUR 3
LE MONT ST MICHEL
Normandy
Mouton-Blanc ££ Grande Rue (tel: 02 33 60 14 08; fax: 02 33 60 05 62)

ST MALO Brittany
Hôtel de France et de Chateaubriand ££
Place Chateaubriand (tel: 02 99 56 66 52; fax: 02 99 40 10 04)

DINARD Brittany
Reine-Hortense ££–£££
19 rue de la Malouine (tel: 02 99 46 54 31; fax: 02 99 88 15 88)

DINAN Brittany
Arvor ££
5 rue Pavie (tel: 02 96 39 21 22;
fax: 02 96 39 83 09)
Avaugour ££
1 place du Champs-Clos
(tel: 02 96 39 07 49; fax: 02 96
85 43 04)

TOUR 4
QUIMPER Brittany
Novotel ££
17 rue Dupoher, pond de
Poulguignan (tel: 02 98 90 46
26; fax: 02 98 53 01 96)
La Tour d'Auverge ££
13 rue des Réguaires
(tel: 02 98 95 08 70; fax: 02 98
95 17 31)

TOUR 5
CLERMONT FERRAND
Auvergne
Galleni £
51 rue Bonnabaud (tel: 04 73 93
59 69; fax: 04 73 34 89 29)
Mercure £££
Clermont-Ferrand Centre 82
bd. François Mitterand (tel: 04
73 34 46 46; fax: 04 73 34 46 36)

TOUR 6
LIMOGES Limousin
La Caravelle ££
21 rue Armand-Barbès
(tel: 05 55 77 75 29; fax: 05 55
79 27 60

TOUR 7
LA ROCHELLE Poitou-
Charente
Les Brises ££
Chemin de la Digue de
Richelieu (tel: 05 46 43 89 37;
fax: 05 46 43 27 97)
**Hôtel de France et
d'Angleterre ££**
20 rue Rambaud (tel: 05 46 41
23 99 [800/528-1234 in USA];
fax: 05 46 4115 19)

SAINTES Poitou-Charente
Hôtel de l'Avenue £
114 av. Gambetta
(tel 05 46 74 04 91; fax: 05 46 74
32 16)

ANGOULEME Poitou-
Charente
Mercure Hôtel de France ££
1 place des Halles (tel: 05 45 95
47 95; fax: 05 45 92 02 70)

TOUR 8
NANTES Loire Atlantique
Hôtel Graslin ££
1 rue Piron (tel: 02 40 69 72 91;
fax: 02 40 69 04 44)

SAUMUR Loire Valley West
Anne d'Anjou ££
32 quai Mayaud (tel: 02 41 67
30 30; fax: 02 41 67 51 00)

ANGERS Loire Valley West
Mall £
8–10 rue des Ursules (tel: 02
41 25 05 25; fax: 02 41 86 91
20)

TOUR 9
TOURS Loire Valley Central
Le Central ££
21 rue Berthelot (tel: 02 47 05
46 44; fax: 02 47 66 10 26)
Manoir £
2 rue Traversière (tel: 02 47 05
37 37; fax: 02 47 05 16 00)

ORLÉANS Loire Valley
Central
Hôtel d'Arc ££
37 rue de la République (tel: 02
38 53 10 94; fax: 02 38 81 77 47)
St-Martin £
52 bd. Alexandre-Martin (tel:
02 38 62 47 47; fax: 02 38 81 13 28)

TOUR 10
BORDEAUX Gironde
Continental ££
10 rue Montesquieu (tel: 05 56
52 66 00; fax: 05 56 52 77 97)
Hôtel de Sèze £–££
23 allées de Tourny (tel: 05 56
52 65 54; fax: 05 56 44 31 83)

MIMIZAN Aquitaine
Hôtel Club Atlantis £
19 rue de l'Abbaye (tel: 05 58
09 02 18; fax: 05 58 09 36 60)

TOUR 11
PERIGUEUX Aquitaine
Hôtel Bristol ££
39 rue Antoine-Gadaud (tel: 05
53 08 75 90; fax: 05 53 07 00 49)

LES EYZIES Aquitaine
Centre £
Place de la Mairie (05 53 06 97
13; fax: 05 53 06 91 63)
Les Glycines ££
Rte de Périgueux (tel: 05 53 06
97 07; fax: 05 53 06 92 19)

GRAMAT Midi Pyrénées
Château de Roumégouse £££
On the N140, Rignac (tel: 05 65
33 63 81; fax: 05 65 33 71 18)

ROCAMADOUR Midi
Pyrénées
**Beau-Site et Le Jehan de
Valon ££**
Cité Médiévale (tel: 800/528-
1234 in the US, or 05 65 33 63
08; fax: 05 65 33 65 23)
Domaine de la Rhue ££
(tel: 05 65 33 71 50; fax: 05 65
33 72 48)

TOUR 12
PAU Midi Pyrénées
Gramont ££
3 place Gramont (tel: 05 59 27
84 04; fax: 05 59 27 62 23)
Le Postillon £
Place de Verdun, 10 cours
Camou (tel: 05 59 72 83 00)

LOURDES Midi Pyrénées
Adriatic ££
4 rue Baron-Duprat (tel: 05 62
94 31 34; fax: 05 62 42 14 70)
Grand Hôtel de la Grotte ££
66–68 rue de la Grotte
(tel: 05 62 94 58 87; fax: 05 62
94 20 50)

TOUR 13
MARSEILLE Provence-Alpes
New Hôtel Vieux-Port ££
3 bis rue Reine-Elisabeth
(tel: 04 91 90 51 42; fax: 04 91
90 76 24)
**La Résidence du Vieux-Port
££**
18 quai du Port (tel: 04 91 91 91
22; fax: 04 91 56 60 88)

TOULON Provence-Alpes
La Corniche ££
1 littoral Frédéric-Mistral
(at Le Mourillon) (tel: 04 94 41
35 12; fax: 04 94 41 24 58)
New Hôtel Tour Blanche ££
boulevard de l'Amiral-Vence
(tel: 04 94 24 41 57; fax: 04 94
22 42 25)

ST-TROPEZ Provence-Alpes
Ermitage av Paul-Signac £££
(tel: 04 94 97 52 33; fax: 04 94
97 10 43)
La Tartane £££
Rte des Salins (tel: 04 94 97 21
23; fax: 04 94 97 09 16)

TOUR 14
CANNES Côte d'Azur
Le Florian £
8 rue Commandant-André
(tel: 04 93 39 21 82; fax: 04 92
99 18 30)
La Madrilène ££
15 bd Alexandre III (tel: 04 97
06 37 37; fax: 04 97 94 38 78)
Provence ££
9 rue Molière (tel: 04 93 38 44
35; fax: 04 93 39 63 14)
Villa de l'Olivier ££–£££
5 rue des Tambourinaires
(tel: 04 93 39 53 28; fax: 04 93
39 55 85)

ANTIBES Côte d'Azur
Le Cameo £
Place Nationale (tel: 04 93 34
24 17)

GRASSE Côte d'Azur
Les Arômes ££
115 rte de Cannes (tel: 04 93 70
42 01)

TOUR 15
NICE Côte d'Azur
Villa Eden £
99 bis promenade des Anglais
(tel: 04 93 86 53 70; fax: 04 93
97 67 97)

MENTON Côte d'Azur
Aiglon ££
7 av de la Madone (tel: 04 93 57
55 55; fax: 04 93 35 92 39)

TOUR 16
NIMES Languedoc-Roussillon
New Hôtel La Baume ££
21 rue Nationale (tel: 04 66 76
28 42; fax: 04 66 76 28 45)

AVIGNON Provence
Angleterre ££
29 bd Raspail (tel: 04 90 86 34
31; fax: 04 90 86 86 74)

ARLES Provence
Calendal £
22 place du Docteur-Pomme
(tel: 04 90 96 11 89; fax: 04 90
96 05 84)

AIGUES-MORTES
Languedoc-Roussillon
Hostellerie de Remparts ££
6 place Anatole-France
(tel: 04 66 53 82 77; fax: 04 66
53 73 77)

TOUR 17
NANCY Lorraine
Albert-1er-Astoria ££
3 rue de l'Armée-Patton (tel: 03
83 40 31 24; fax: 03 83 28 47 78)

VERDUN Lorraine
Le Coq Hardi ££–£££
8 av de la Victoire (tel: 03 29 86
36 36; fax: 03 29 86 09 21)

TOUR 18
LYON Rhône Valley
Bayard ££
23 place Bellecour (tel: 04 78 37
39 64; fax: 04 72 40 95 51)

ROANNE Rhône Valley
Hôtel Restaurant Artaud ££
133 av de la Libération, Le
Coteau (tel: 04 77 68 46 44; fax:
04 77 72 23 50)

TOUR 19
GRENOBLE Rhône Alpes
Angleterre ££–£££
5 place Victor-Hugo
(tel: 04 76 87 37 21; fax: 04 76
50 94 10)

AIX-LES-BAINS Rhône
Alpes
Ariana ££
Av de Marlioz, à Marlioz
(tel: 04 79 61 79 79; fax: 04 79
61 79 00)

ANNECY Rhône Alpes
Au Faisan Doré ££
34 av d'Albigny (tel: 04 50 23 02
46; fax: 04 50 23 11 10)

TOUR 20
STRASBOURG Alsace
Hôtel de l'Ill £
8 rue des Bateliers (tel: 03 88 36
20 01; fax: 03 88 35 30 03)
Rohan £££
17–19 rue du Maroquin (tel: 03
88 32 85 11; fax: 03 88 75 65 37)

COLMAR Alsace
Hostellerie de Maréchal £££
4–5 place des Six-Montagnes-
Noires (tel: 03 89 41 60 32, fax:
03 89 24 59 40)

TOUR 21
CALAIS Pas de Calais
George-V ££
35 rue Royale (tel: 03 21 97 68
00; fax: 03 21 97 34 73)

LE TOUQUET Pas de Calais
Résidence Hippotel £
Av de l'Hippodrome (tel: 03 21
05 07 11; fax: 03 21 05 44 88)

MONTREUIL Pas de Calais
Auberge d'Inxent £
318 rue de la Vallée, Inxent
(northeast of Montreuil) (tel: 03
21 90 71 19; fax: 03 21 86 31 67)

TOUR 22
AMIENS Picardy
Le Carlton ££
42 rue de Noyon (tel: 03 22 97
72 22; fax: 03 22 97 72 00)

LAON Picardy
**Hôtel de la Bannière de
France ££**
11 rue Franklin-D.-Roosevelt
(tel: 03 23 23 21 44; fax: 03 23
23 31 56)

TOUR 23
REIMS Champagne-Ardenne
**Best Western Hôtel de la
Paix ££**
9 rue Buirette (tel: 800/528-
1234 in the US, or 03 26 40 04 08)
Grand Hôtel du Nord £
75 place Drouet-d'Erlon (tel: 03
26 47 39 03; fax: 03 26 40 92 26)

TOUR 24
BEAUNE Burgundy
Hostellerie de Bretonnière ££
42 Faubourg Bretonnière
(tel: 03 80 22 15 77)

AVALLON Burgundy
Moulin des Ruats ££
Vallée du Cousin (tel: 03 86 34
97 00; fax: 03 86 31 65 47)

AUTUN Burgundy
Hostellerie du Vieux Moulin £
Porte d'Arroux (tel: 03 85 52 10
90; fax: 03 85 86 32 15)

TOUR 25
CHARTRES Île de France
Poste ££
3 rue du Général-Koenig
(tel: 02 37 21 04 27;)

FONTAINEBLEAU Île de
France
**Hôtel-Restaurant Legris et
Parc ££**
36 rue Paul-Séramy (tel: 01 64
22 24 24; fax: 01 64 22 22 05)

TOUR INFORMATION

The addresses, telephone numbers and opening times of the attractions mentioned in the tours, including the telephone numbers of the Tourist Information Offices are listed below tour by tour.

TOUR 1

i Place du Canada, Caen. Tel: 02 31 27 90 30.

i Place du Groupe Lorraine, Arromanches. Tel: 02 31 22 36 45.

i Pont St Jean, Bayeux. Tel: 02 31 51 28 28.

i Place du Château, Valognes. Tel: 02 33 40 11 55/02 33 95 01 26.

i 10 rue des Ecoles, Barneville-Carteret. Tel: 02 33 04 90 58.

i 4 cours Jonville, Gran-ville. Tel: 02 33 91 30 03.

i Place des Costils, Villedieu-les-Poêles. Tel: 02 33 61 05 69.

i Place du Marché, Bagnoles-de-l'Orne. Tel: 02 33 37 85 66.

i Place du Tripot, Clécy. Tel: 02 31 69 79 95.

1 Pegasus Bridge
Musée Pegasus Bridge
Tel: 02 31 44 62 54.
Open Apr–Oct daily 9.30– 12.30, 2–6; Jul–Aug 9–7.

2 Arromanches
Musée du Débarquement
Place du 6-Juin. Tel: 02 31 22 34 31.
Open Feb–Oct daily, 9.30– 4.30 (9–7 May–Sep) .

3 Bayeux
Musée de la Bataille de Normandie
Boulevard Général-Fabian-Ware. Tel: 02 31 92 93 41.
Open daily, May–Sep 9– 6.30; Oct–Apr 10–12, 2–6.
Musée de la Tapisserie
Centre Guillaume le Con-

quérant, rue de Nesmond. Tel: 02 31 51 25 50.
Open daily, mid-Mar–mid-Oct 9–6.30; mid-Oct–mid-Mar 9.30–12.30, 2–6.
Musée Baron Gérard
1 rue la Chaine.
Tel: 02 31 92 14 21.
*Open daily, Jun–mid-Sep 9– 7; winter 10–12.30, 2–6.
Closed 2 weeks in Jan.*

4 Plage d'Omaha
Musée Omaha
Rue de la Mer, St-Laurent-sur-Mer. Tel: 02 31 21 97 44.
Open mid-Feb–Mar daily 10–12.30, 2.30–6; Apr–Jun 10–6; Jul–Sep 9.30–7.30.

5 Valognes
Hotel de Beaumont
Rue du Versailles-Norman.
Tel: 02 33 40 12 30.
Open Easter weekend, then Jul–mid-Sep daily 2.30–6.30 (also 10.30–12.30 on Tue).
Musée de l'Eau de Vie et des Vieux Métiers
Rue Belouze. Tel: 02 33 40 26 25.
Open daily (ex Tue) 10–12, 2–6 (closed Sun am).
Musée Cidre et Calvados
Rue du Petit Versailles, and rue Pelouze. Tel: 02 33 40 22 73 or 02 33 40 18 87.
Open Apr–Oct Mon, Wed–Sat 10–12, 2–6, Sun 2–6; also Tue Jul–Aug .

7 Granville
Musée du Vieux Granville
2 rue Lecarpentier. Tel: 02 33 50 44 10.
Open in season Wed–Mon 10–12, 2–6; out of season Wed, Sat, Sun 2–6.
Aquarium du Roc
Tel: 02 33 50 19 83.
Open Apr–mid-Sep daily; Feb–Mar & Oct–mid-Nov daily in school holidays.

8 Villedieu-les-Poêles
Atelier du Cuivre
54 rue du Général Huard.
Tel: 02 33 51 31 85.
Open daily 9–5.30 (from 10am Sun). Closed for lunch.
Maison de l'Etain
15 rue du Général Huard.
Tel: 02 33 51 05 08.
Open daily 9–5.30 (from 10am Sun). Closed for lunch.
Fonderie des Cloches
10 rue du Pont Chignon.
Tel: 02 33 61 00 56.
Open mid-Feb–mid-Nov Tue–

Sat 8–12, 1.30–5.30; mid-Jun–mid-Sep also Sun & Mon.
Maison de la Poeslerie et de la Dentellerie
25 rue du Général Huard.
Tel: 02 33 90 20 92.
Open Easter–mid-Nov daily 10–12, 2–6.30 (Tue pm only).

10 Clécy
Musée Hardy
Place du Tripot. Tel: 02 31 69 79 95.
Open Easter–Sep daily 10–11.30, 2–5.30.
Musée du Chemin de Fer Miniature
Les Fours à Chaux. Tel: 02 31 69 07 13.
Open Easter–Sep daily 10– 12, 2–6; Oct–Nov & Mar–Easter Sun 2–6.

Back to Nature
Maison de la Mer
Place du 6 Juin, Courseulles-sur-Mer.
Tel: 02 31 37 92 58.
Open daily 9–1 &2–7.

For History Buffs
Musée des Troupes Aéroportées
Place du 6 Juin, Sainte-Mere-Eglise. Tel: 02 33 41 41 35.
Open Feb–mid-Nov daily 9–6 or 6.45, closed for lunch out of season; mid Nov–mid Dec weekends 10–12, 2–6.

For Children
Le Village Enchanté
Bellefontaine. Tel: 02 33 59 01 93.
Open daily 10–6).

Special to...
Musée des Sapeurs-Pompiers
16 bd Albert Christophe.
Tel: 02 33 38 10 34.
Open Apr–Oct daily 2–6.
Maison de la Pomme et de la Poire
La Logeraie, Barenton.
Tel: 02 33 59 56 22.
Open late Mar–Oct daily 9.30–12.30, 2–7.

TOUR 2

i Pont Jehan Ango, Dieppe. Tel: 02 35 84 11 77.

i 113 Rue Alexandre le Grand, Fécamp. Tel: 02 35 28 51 01.

i 9 Place Maurice-

Guillard, Etretat. Tel: 02 35 29 96 73.

i 186 boulevard Clemenceau, Le Havre. Tel: 02 32 74 04 04.

i Quai Guilbaud, Caudebec-en-Caux. Tel: 02 35 96 20 65.

i 9 Arthur-Boudin, Honfleur. Tel: 02 31 89 23 30.

i 25 Place de la Cathédrale, Rouen. Tel: 02 32 08 32 40.

1 Varengeville-sur-Mer
Parc Floral des Moutiers
La Haie des Moutiers.
Tel: 02 35 85 10 02.
Open mid-Mar–mid-Nov daily 10–12, 2–6.
Manoir d'Ango
Town centre. Tel: 02 35 85 14 80.
Open Mar–Nov 10–12.30, 2.30–6.30.

2 Fécamp
Palais Bénédictine
110 rue Alexandre-le-Grand. Tel: 02 35 10 26 10.
Open daily 10–12, 2–5.
Musée des Beaux-Arts
21 rue Alexandre le Gros.
Tel: 02 35 28 31 99.
Open daily (ex Tue) 10–12, 2–5.30 (6.30 Jul–Aug).
Musée des Terre-Neuves et de la Pêche
27 boulevard Albert 1er.
Tel: 02 35 28 31 99.
Open daily (ex Tue Sep–Jun).

3 Etretat
Nungesser and Coli Museum
Tel: 02 35 27 07 47.
Open Easter–Oct.

4 Le Havre
Musée des Beaux-Arts André-Malraux
23 boulevard Clemenceau.
Tel: 02 35 42 33 97.
Open Wed–Mon 10–12, 2–6.
Musée de l'Ancien Havre
1 rue Jérôme Bellarmato.
Tel: 02 35 42 27 90.
Open Wed–Sun.

5 Caudebec-en-Caux
Musée de la Marine de Seine
Avenue Winston Churchill.
Tel: 02 35 95 90 13.
Open daily (ex Tue) 9–12.30, 2–6.30

i Tourist Information Office
12 Number on tour

6 La Haye-de-Routot
Four à Pain
Tel: 02 35 37 23 16.
Open Mar & Oct–Nov, Sun 2–6; Apr–Jun & Sep, Sat & Sun 2–6.30; Jul–Aug daily 1.30–6.30.
Musée du Sabotier
Tel: 02 35 37 23 16.
Open Mar & Oct–Nov, Sun 2–6; Apr–Jun & Sep, Sat & Sun 2–6.30; Jul–Aug daily 1.30–6.30.

8 Honfleur
Musée Eugene Boudin
Tel: 02 31 89 54 00.
Open daily (ex Tue), mid-Mar–Sep 10–12, 2–6; Oct–mid-Mar 2.30–5.
Musée de la Marine
Church of St Etienne.
Tel: 02 31 89 14 12.
Open daily (ex Mon).

9 Le Bec-Hellouin
Abbaye du Bec-Hellouin
Tel: 02 32 43 72 60.
Guided tours Mon & Wed–Sat from 10am summer; from 11am winter, Sun afternoons only.

10 Rouen
Musée Jeanne d'Arc
33 place du Vieux Marché.
Tel: 02 35 88 02 70.
Open daily, summer 9.30–7; winter 10–12, 2–6.30.
Musée des Beaux-Arts
Rue Jean Lecanuet. Tel: 02 35 52 00 62.
Open daily (ex Tue) 10–6.

For Children
Abbaye du Valasse
Gruchet le Valasse, 3km (2m) north of Lillebonne.
Tel: 02 35 31 55 97.
Performances Jun–Aug, Fri & Sat at dusk.

Back to Nature
Reserve de Faune
Cedena. Tel: 02 32 56 94 87.
Open all year, Mon–Fri 9–5.

Special to...
Maison de la Pomme
Sainte Opportune-la-Mare. Tel: 02 32 57 16 48.
Open weekends 2–6.30.

For Children
Chateau de Robert-le-Diable/Musée des Vikings
Moulineaux. Tel: 02 35 18 02 36.
Open Mar–Nov daily 9–7; Nov–Dec & Feb Sun only.

TOUR 3

i 11 rue St-Yves, Rennes. Tel: 02 99 67 11 11.

i Place St Yves, Vitré. Tel. 02 99 75 04 46.

i 1 Place Aristide-Briand, Fougères. Tel: 02 99 94 12 20.

i Corps de Garde des Bourgeois, Le Mont-St-Michel. Tel: 02 33 60 14 30.

i Esplanade St-Vincent, St Malo. Tel: 02 99 56 64 48.

i 2 Boulevard Féart, Dinard. Tel: 02 99 46 94 12.

i Tour Vauban, Cap Fréhel. Tel: 02 96 41 53 81.

i Boulevard de la Mer, Erquy. Tel: 02 96 72 30 12.

i 6 Rue de l'Horloge, Dinan. Tel: 02 96 39 75 40.

i Mairie, rue Nationale, Tinténiac Tel: 02 99 68 02 15.

1 Vitré
Musée de l'Abeille Vivante
18 rue de la Briqueteri
Vitré. Tel: 02 99 75 09 01.
Open Jul–Aug Mon 2–6, Tue–Sat 10–6.

2 Fougères
Château de Fougères
Place Symon. Tel: 02 99 99 79 59.
Open Feb–Mar & Oct–Dec, daily 10–12, 2–5; Apr–mid-Jun, daily 9.30–12, 2–6; mid-Jun–Sep daily 9–7.
Musée Emmanuel de la Villéon
51 rue Nationale. Tel Tourist Office: 02 99 94 12 20
Open weekends all year 11–12.30, 2.30–5; also weekdays mid-Jun–mid-Sep.

3 Le Mont-St-Michel
Abbaye, Archéoscope and Museums
Tel: 02 33 60 14 14.
Open May–Sep daily 9.30–11.30, 1.30–6; Oct–Apr daily (ex Tue) 9.30–4.30.
Museographie
Route de Roche Torin, Courtils. Tel: 02 33 60 11 01.
Open Apr–May & Oct–mid-Nov daily 12–6; Jun–Sep daily 10–7; winter Sun 2–6.

---

5 St-Malo
Musée de la Ville/Quic-en-Groigne waxworks
Château. Tel: 02 99 40 71 57.
Open Easter–Sep daily (ex Tue) 10–12, 2–6.
Château Solidar
Tel: 02 99 40 71 58.
Open daily 10–12, 2–6.

7 Cap Fréhel
Le Phare du Cap Fréhel
Tel: 02 96 41 40 03.
Open by appointment only.
Fort la Latte
Plevenon. Tel: 02 96 41 40 31.
Open daily Easter & Jun–Sep 10–12, 2.30–6.30; Oct–May 2–5.30.

9 Dinan
Château and museum
Porte de Guichet. Tel: 02 96 39 45 20.
Open Mar–mid-Nov daily 10–5.30 (closed lunchtime low season); mid-Nov–Feb daily (ex Wed) 1.30–5.
Tour de l'Horloge
Rue de l'Horloge.
Tel Tourist Office: 02 96 39 75 40.
Open Jul–Sep daily 10.45–1:15, 3–6.

10 Tinténiac
Musée de l'Outil et des Métiers
Quai de la Donac. Tel: 02 99 68 02 03.
Open Jun–Aug daily 10–12, 2.30–6.
Musée International de la Faune
Québriac. Tel: 02 99 68 10 22.
Open Jun–Aug daily 10.30–7; Apr–May & Sep–Nov, telephone for details.

For History Buffs
Musée Automobile de Bretagne
Loheac village, Rte Lieuron.
Tel: 02 99 34 02 32.
Open Tue–Sun 10–12, 2–7.

For Children
Reptilarium
Beauvoir. Tel: 02 33 68 11 18.
Open Feb–Dec daily 10–7.

Special to...
Oyster Museum
Cancale. Tel: 02 99 89 69 99.
Open daily; tours at 3pm.

TOUR 4

i 7 rue Déesse, Quimper. Tel: 02 98 53 04 05.

i 1 Rue du Docteur Mével, Douarnenez. Tel: 02 98 92 13 35.

i Boulevard de la Plage, Morgat. Tel: 02 98 27 29 49.

i Quai Kléber, Camaret-sur-Mer. Tel: 02 98 27 93 60.

i Landevennec. Tel: 02 98 27 72 65.

i Place de la Liberté, Brest. Tel: 02 98 44 24 96.

i Place Aristide-Briand, Huelgoat. Tel: 02 98 99 72 32.

2 Douarnenez
Le Port-Musée
Quai de Port-Rhu. Tel: 02 98 92 65 20.
Open Jun–Sep daily 10–7; Oct–Dec & May Tue–Sun 10–12.30, 2–6.

3 Morgat
Maison des Minéraux
Rte Cap de la Chevre
Morgat. Tel: 02 98 27 19 73.
Open daily 10–7.

5 Landévennec
Musée de l'Ancienne Abbaye
Tel: 02 99 27 35 90.
Open Jul Aug daily 10 7; Sep–Jun weekends 2–6.

6 Brest
Musée de la Marine
Château. Tel: 02 98 22 12 39.
Open Wed–Sun 9.15–12, 2–6.
Conservatoire Botanique National de Brest
52 Allée du Bot. Tel: 02 98 41 88 95.
Open Mon–Fri.
Océanopolis
Rue Alain-Colas au Port de Plaisance du Moulin Blanc. Tel: 02 98 34 40 40.
Open daily 9.30–5 or 6; closed Mon am during winter.

8 Ménez-Meur
Ménez-Meur Estate
Halvec. Tel: 02 98 68 81 71.
Open Jun–Sep daily 10–7; Oct–Dec & Feb–May Wed & Sun 10–7.

Practical information

ⓘ Tourist Information Office
⑫ Number on tour

Back to Nature
Réserve Ornithologique
Cap Sizun. Tel: 02 98 70 13 53.
Open Apr–Jun daily 10–12, 2–6; Jul–Aug daily 10–6.

Special to...
Les Moulins-de-Kerouat
Commana. Tel: 02 98 68 87 76; *telephone for details.*

For History Buffs
Maison des Pilhaouerien
Loqueffret. Tel: 02 98 26 44 50.
Open Jul–Aug daily (ex Mon) 10–12, 2–6.
Château de Trévarez
St Goazec. Tel: 02 98 26 82 79.
Open Apr–Jun & Sep daily 1–6; Jul–Aug daily 11–6.30; Oct–Mar Wed, Sat & Sun 2–5.30.

TOUR 5

ⓘ Place de la Victoire, Clermont-Ferrand. Tel: 04 73 98 65 00.

ⓘ Avenue Auguste Rouzaud, Place Allard, Royat. Tel: 04 73 35 81 87.

ⓘ Le Puy de Dôme. Tel: 04 73 62 21 46.

ⓘ Place de la République, La Bourboule. Tel: 04 73 65 57 71.

ⓘ Avenue de la Libération, Le Mont-Dore. Tel: 04 73 65 20 21.

ⓘ Place du Docteur-Pipet, Besse-en-Chandesse. Tel: 04 73 79 52 84.

ⓘ Les Grands Thermes, St-Nectaire. Tel: 04 73 88 50 86.

ⓘ Place de l'Hotel de Ville, Ambert. Tel: 04 73 82 61 90.

ⓘ Maison du Pirou, Thiers. Tel: 04 73 80 65 65.

⓵ Royat
Maison du Passé
Place Cohendy. Tel: 04 73 29 98 18.
Open all year Mon–Sat 3–6.

⓶ Puy de Dôme
Roman temple, exhibition, information centre
Tel: 04 73 62 21 45.
Open summer only.

⓸ La Bourboule
Musée de Geologie Botanique
Tel: 04 73 81 11 25.
Open Jul–Sep, Mon–Fri 10–12, 3–6

G Besse-en-Chandesse
Ski Museum
Tel: 04 73 79 57 30.
Open daily during school hols.

⓻ St-Nectaire
Maison du St-Nectaire
Route de Murol. Tel: 04 73 88 51 66.
Open Feb–Jun & Oct–mid-Nov daily 3–6; Jul–Aug daily 10–7; Sep daily 10–12, 2–6
Cornadore grotto
St-Nectaire Lebas. Tel: 04 73 88 51 66.
Open daily 10–12, 2–6; Jun–Mar, phone for times.

⓼ Ambert
AGRIVAP museum
Rue de la Gare. Tel: 04 73 82 60 42.
Open Mar–Oct daily 10–12, 2–6 (Jul–Aug daily 10–7).
Fourme d'Ambert Cheese museum
Place du Châtelet Ambert. Tel: 04 73 82 49 23.
Open Feb–Dec daily 9–12.30, 2–7 (6 in winter).

⓽ Moulin Richard-de-Bas
Valeyre. Tel: 04 73 82 03 11.
Open daily 9–12, 2–6 (9–8 Jul–Aug).

⓾ Thiers
Maison de Couteliers
23 & 58 rue de la Coutellerie. Tel: 04 73 80 58 86.
Open daily 10–12.30, 2–6.30 (all day Jul–Aug, ex Sun); closed Mon Oct–May.

Special to...
Vulcania
15km west of Clermont Ferrand on the D941b. Tel: 04 73 31 85 64.
Due to open during 2000.

For Children
Parc des Dômes
Route du Puy de Dôme, Orcines. Tel: 04 73 62 12 19.
Open daily 9–8 (times vary low season).

For Children
Parc Animalier et de Loisirs
Ardes-sur-Couze. Tel: 04 73 71 82 86.
Open daily 10–8.

TOUR 6

ⓘ Boulevard Fleurus, Limoges. Tel: 05 55 34 46 87.

ⓘ Chateau de Pompadour, Arnac-Pompadour. Tel: 05 55 98 55 47.

ⓘ Place de la Libération, Uzerche. Tel: 05 55 73 15 71.

ⓘ 2 Place Emil Zola, Tulle. Tel: 05 55 26 59 61.

ⓘ Place de la République, Treignac. Tel: 05 55 98 15 04.

ⓘ Rue Vieille, Aubusson. Tel: 05 55 66 32 12.

ⓘ 1 Av Charles de Gaulle, Guéret. Tel: 05 55 52 14 29.

⓶ Arnac-Pompadour
French National Stud
Tel Tourist Office: 05 55 98 55 47.
Guided tours every afternoon.

⓸ Tulle
Musée de la Cloitre
Place de la Cathédrale. Tel: 05 55 26 22 05.
Open daily (ex Wed) 9–12, 2–6 (pm only on Sat).
Musée de la Résistance et de la Déportation
2 quai Edmond Perrier. Tel: 05 55 26 24 36.
Open Mon–Fri 9–12, 2–6.

⓻ Treignac
Museum
Rue du Docteur Fieyssac. Tel: 05 55 98 35 26.
Open Jun–Sep 10–12, 3–5.

⓽ Aubusson
La Maison du Tapissier
Rue Vieille Aubusson. Tel Tourist Office: 05 55 66 32 12.
Open Mon–Sat 9.30–6.30, Sun & winter weekdays 10–12.30, 2.30–5.30.

⓾ Guéret
Musée de la Sematorerie
Avenue de la Sematorerie. Tel: 05 55 52 07 20.
Open mid-Jun–Oct daily 9–12, 2–6, winter pm only.
Musée de Presidial
Place du Marché Guéret. Tel: 05 55 52 10 44.
Open all year daily 2–6.

For History Buffs
Musée de la Porcelaine
Les Palloux, place Winston Churchill, Limoges. Tel: 05 55 33 08 50.
Open daily (ex Tue) 10–12.30, 2–5.45 (10–5.45 Jul–Aug).
La Tour de Zizim
Bourganeuf. Tel Tourist Office: 05 55 64 12 20.
Under restoration.

TOUR 7

ⓘ Place de la Petite Sirene, La Rochelle. Tel: 05 46 41 14 68.

ⓘ 5 bis, rue de la Blanche, Le Bois-Plage-en-Ré. Tel: 05 46 09 00 55.

ⓘ Quai de Sénac, La Flotte. Tel: 05 46 09 60 38.

ⓘ Avenue Sadi Carnot, Rochefort. Tel: 05 46 99 08 60.

ⓘ 2 rue du Québec, Brouage. Tel: 05 46 85 19 16.

ⓘ Route du Viaduc, Bourcefranc, Ile d'Oléron. Tel: 05 46 85 65 23.

ⓘ 62 cours National, Saintes. Tel: 05 46 74 23 82.

ⓘ 7 bis rue du Chat, Place des Halles, Angouleme. Tel: 05 45 95 16 84.

ⓘ Place de la Poste, Niort. Tel: 05 49 24 18 79.

ⓘ Place de l'Eglise, Coulon. Tel: 05 49 35 99 29.

ⓘ Quay Poëy d'Avant, Fontenay-le-Comte. Tel: 02 51 69 44 99.

⓵ Ile de Ré
Musée Ernest Cognac
Av Victor Bouthillier, St Martin. Tel: 05 46 09 21 22.
Open daily Jul–Aug 10–7; Sep 10–12, 2–6; Oct–Jun 10–12, 2–5 (closed Tue).
Phare des Baleines
Le Gillieux, St Clement des Baleines. Tel: 05 46 29 18 23.
Open all year (ex Jan) daily 10–12.30, 2–5 or 6 (open all day most of summer).

⓶ Rochefort
Corderie Royale – Centre International de la Mer
Tel: 05 46 87 01 90.
Open daily 9–6 (to 7 or 8pm in summer).
Maison Pierre Loti
141 rue Pierre-Loti. Tel: 05

46 99 16 88.
*Open Apr–Sep Mon & Wed–
Sat 10–12, 2–5, Sun 2–5;
Oct–Mar daily (ex Tue) 2–4.*

7 Niort
Château
Rue Duguesclin. Tel: 05 49
28 14 28.
*Open daily (ex Tue), 9–12,
2–5 (to 6pm Apr–Oct).*

8 Coulon
Musée Maraichin
Rue de l'Église. Tel: 05 49
35 94 09.
*Open irregular hours. Check
before visiting.*
Aquarium de la Venise
Verte
Place de l'Eglise. Tel: 05 49
35 90 31.
Open Apr–Oct daily 9–7.

9 Fontenay-le-Comte
Chateau de Terre-Neuve
Rue de Jarnigarde. Tel: 02
51 69 17 75.
*Open May–Sep daily 9–12,
2–6.*

For Children
L'Arche de Noé
Near Prés du Phare, St
Clement de Baleines, Ile de
Ré. Tel: 05 46 29 23 23.
*Open Apr–Sep daily 2–5
(10.30–6 Jun & school
summer hol); Oct Sun 2–6.*

For History Buffs
Maison de l'Empereur
Rue Napoléon, Aix. Tel: 05
46 84 66 40.
*Open daily 9.30–6; (closed
Tue and lunchtimes in winter.*

For Children
Petit Train
St-Trojan-les-Bains.
Tel Tourist Office: 05 46 76
00 86. *Open Jun–Sep daily.*

Special to...
Musée de Cognac
Boulevard Denfert-
Rochereau, Saintes. Tel: 05
45 32 07 25.
*Open daily (ex Tue), Jun–Sep
10–12, 2–6; Oct–May 2–5.30.*

Back to Nature
Zoorama
La Fourré de Chizé, Villiers
en Bois. Tel: 05 49 77 17 17.
*Open daily, Apr–Sep 9–8;
Oct–Mar 9–12, 2–6.*

Special to...
Oyster Bed Tours &
Museum
St-Trojan en Oléron.

Tel: 05 46 76 08 16.
*Open Apr–mid Jun & Sep
Tue–Sat 3 & 4.30; mid
Jun–Aug Tue–Sat 4 & 5.30.*

TOUR 8

i 7 rue Valmy, Nantes. Tel:
02 40 20 60 00.

i Place du Minage,
Clisson. Tel: 02 40 54 02 95.

i Place de Rougé,
Cholet. Tel: 02 41 49 80 00.

i Place du Champ de
Foire, Doué-la-Fontaine.
Tel: 02 41 59 20 49.

i Place de la Bilange,
Saumur. Tel: 02 41 40 20 60.

i au Château, Baugé. Tel:
02 41 89 18 07.

i Place Nicolay, Le Lude.
Tel: 02 43 94 62 20.

i Rue de l'Etoile, Le
Mans. Tel: 02 43 28 17 22.

i 1 Place du Président
Kennedy, Angers. Tel: 02 41
23 51 11.

2 Cholet
Musée d'Arts et
d'Histoire
Avenue de l'Abreuvoir.
Tel: 02 41 49 29 00.
Open Wed–Mon 10–12, 2–6.
Musée Paysan
Ferme de la Goubaudiere,
Lac de Ribou. Tel: 02 41 71
25 94.
Open daily (ex Tue) 3–5.
Musée du Textile Choletais
La Riviere Sauvageau.
Tel: 02 41 75 25 40.
Open daily (ex Tue) 2–6.
Musée de l'Industrie
Regionale de la Chaussure
6 rue Saint-Paul, St André
de la Marche. Tel: 02 41 46
35 65.
*Open Apr–Oct daily 2.30–6;
(also 10–12 Jul–Aug; closed
Sat, Sun & Mon afternoons);
Nov–Mar Sun 2.30–6.*
Parc Oriental
Maulévrier. Tel: 02 41 55 50
14.
*Open Mar–Jun & Sep–mid-
Nov daily (ex Mon) 2–6;
Jul–Aug 10.30–7.30.*

3 Doué-la-Fontaine
Parc Zoologique des
Minieres
Route de Cholet. Tel: 02 41
59 18 58

*Open daily, May–Sep 9–7;
Oct–Apr 9–12.30, 2–6*
Musée des Commerces
Anciens
Ecuries du Baron Foullon,
route de Soulanger. Tel: 02
41 59 28 23.
*Open May–Jun & Sep–Oct
daily (ex Tue) 9.30–12, 2–7;
Jul–Aug daily 9–7; Nov–Apr
daily 10–12, 2–6.*
Arènes
Rue des Arènes. Tel: 02 41
59 22 28.
Open Tue–Sun 10–12, 2–5.
Moulin Cartier
Tel: 02 41 59 20 49.
*Open Jul–mid-Sep Tue–Sun
10–12, 3–6.*

4 St-Hilaire
Musée du Champignon
Route de Gennes. Tel: 02
41 50 31 55.
Open Feb–Nov daily 10–7.
Ecole National d'Equitation
Petit Souper. Tel: 02 41 53
50 50.
Open Apr–Sep.

5 Saumur
Château de Saumur and
Museums
Tel. 02 41 40 24 40.
*Open Jul–Sep daily 9–6.30;
Oct–Jun daily 9–11.30, 2–
5.30 (closed Tue Nov–Apr).*
Musée de la Figurine-Jouet
Jun & Sep Wed–Mon 2–6;
Jul–Aug Wed–Mon 10–6.*

6 Baugé
Château/Musée de Baugé
Tel: 02 41 89 18 07.
*Open, Museum: Apr–Jun
weekends 2.30–6; mid-Jun–
Aug daily (ex Mon in Jun)
11–1, 2.30–6; Castle: closed
for renovation.*
La Girouardiere Convent
Rue Girouardiere. Tel: 02
41 89 12 20.
Open Wed–Mon 2.30–4.15.

7 Le Lude
Château du Lude
Place François-de-Nicolay.
Tel: 02 43 94 40 54.
*Open Apr–Sep daily 2–6;
park daily 9.30–12, 2–6 .*

8 Le Mans Circuit
Motor Museum
Tel: 02 43 72 72 24
*Open daily 10–6 (may vary
in Jan & Feb).*

9 Le Mans
Musée de la Reine
Bérengere

Rue de la Reine Bérengere.
Tel: 02 43 47 38 51.
*Open daily 9–12, 2–6
(closed Mon Nov–Apr).*
Abbaye Cistercienne de
l'Epau
Route de Changé (Paris
road). Tel: 02 43 84 22 29.
Open daily 9.30–12, 2–6.
Musée de Tessé
2 avenue de Paderborn.
Tel: 02 43 47 38 51.
*Open daily 9–12, 2–6
(closed Mon Nov–Apr)*

10 Angers
Château d'Angers
Place du Président-Kennedy.
Tel: 02 41 87 43 47.
Open daily 10–5 (7 Jul–Aug).

Special to...
Puy du Fou
Rue Georges Clémenceau,
Les Epesses. Tel: 02 51 64
11 11.
*Open May Sat & Sun;
Jun mid-Sep daily 10–7;
Cinéscénie Jun–Aug Fri &
Sat 10pm.*

Recommended Walks
Foyer Rural Musée
Jupilles. Tel: 02 43 79 48 69.
*Open Mon–Fri 9–12,
1.30–6.30.*

Special to...
La Distillerie Cointreau
Rue de la Crois-Blanche,
St-Barthélémy d'Angou. Tel:
02 41 31 50 50.
*Guided tours Jun–Sep week-
days from 10am, weekends
at 3 & 4.30; Oct–May Mon–
Sat at 3, Sun at 3 & 4.30.*

For Children
Aquarium Tropical
Murs-Erigné. Tel: 02 41 57
83 14.
*Open Mon–Sat 10–12, 2–7,
Sun 2–7.*

For History Buffs
Troglodyte Village
Louresse-Rochemenier.
Tel: 02 41 59 18 15.
*Open Feb–Mar & Nov
weekends 2–6; Apr–Nov
daily 9.30–7.*

TOUR 9

i 78 rue Bernard-Palissy,
Tours. Tel: 02 47 70 37 37.

i 233 quai Géneral-de-
Gaulle, Amboise. Tel: 02 47
57 09 28.

ℹ️ 2 avenue de la Résistance, Valençay. Tel: 02 54 00 04 42.

ℹ️ Place de la Paix, Romorantin-Lanthenay. Tel: 02 54 76 43 89.

ℹ️ Centre Anne de Beaujeu, Place Jean-Jaures, Gien. Tel: 02 38 67 25 28.

ℹ️ Place Albert 1er, Orléans. Tel: 02 38 24 05 05.

ℹ️ 3 avenue du Dr-Jean-Laigret, Blois. Tel: 02 54 74 06 49.

ℹ️ Rue Gambetta, Vouvray. Tel: 02 47 52 70 48.

1 Amboise
Château d'Amboise
Tel: 02 47 57 00 98.
Open daily, 9–12, 2–5 (to 6.30pm Apr–Jun; open throughout day Jul–Aug).
Musée de la Poste
6 rue Joyeuse. Tel: 02 47 57 00 11.
Open mid-Jan–mid-Dec, daily (ex Mon) 10–12, 2–5.30 (to 6.30pm Apr–Sep).
Chanteloup pagoda
3km (2 miles) south of Amboise, on Chenonceau road. Tel: 02 47 57 20 97.
Open Mar–Apr & Oct daily 10–12, 2–5; May–Sep daily 10–7 (to 8pm Jul–Aug); Nov–Feb Mon–Fri 2–5, weekends 10–12, 2–5.

2 Chenonceau
Château de Chenonceau
Tel: 02 47 23 90 07.
Open daily from 9am, closes between 4.30 and 7, depending on season.

3 Valençay
Château/Motor Museum
Tel: 02 54 00 15 69.
Open mid-Mar–mid-Nov daily 9–12, 2–dusk or 8pm; winter weekends 2–5.

4 Romorantin-Lanthenay
Carroir d'Orée archaeological museum
21 rue de la Pierre Centre-Ville. Tel: 02 54 76 22 06.
Open mid-Jun–mid-Sep daily (ex Thu & Sun) 2.30–6.30.
Musée de la Sologne
Moulin du Chapitre. Tel: 02 54 95 33 66.
Open daily (ex Tue & Sun mornings) 10–6.

L'Espace Matra Automobile
Faubourg d'Orleans. Tel: 02 54 94 41 53.
Open daily ex Tue & Sun mornings) 10–6; closed lunchtimes Nov–Mar.

5 Gien
Château and Musée International de la Chasse
Tel: 02 38 67 69 69.
Open daily, Apr–Oct 9.30–6.30; Nov–Mar 9–12, 2–5.

6 Orléans
Maison de Jeanne d'Arc
3 place du Général-de-Gaulle. Tel: 02 38 52 99 89.
Open Tue–Sun 10–12, 2–6 (afternoons only Nov–Apr).
Musée des Beaux-Arts
1 rue Ferdinand-Rabier. Tel: 02 38 53 39 22
Open daily (ex Tue) 11–6.
Hôtel Groslot
Place de l'Etape. Tel: 02 38 79 22 30.
Open daily, Jul–Sep 9–7; Oct–Jun 10–12, 2–6 (Sat 4.30–6).
Musée Historique et Archéologique
Place de l'Abbé-Desnoyers. Tel: 02 38 79 25 60.
Open Jul–Aug Tue–Sun 10–6; Sep–Jun Wed, Sat, Sun 2–6.

7 Chambord
Château de Chambord
Tel: 02 54 50 40 28.
Open daily 9.30–5.15.

8 Blois
Château de Blois
Tel: 02 54 74 16 06.
Open daily, Apr–Aug 9–6; Sep–Mar 9–12.30, 2–5.30.
Les Jacobins Natural History Museum
Rue Anne de Bretagne. Tel: 02 54 74 13 89.
Open daily (ex Mon) 2–6.

9 Vouvray
Ecomusée
24 rue Victor Herault. Tel: 06 15 74 89 81.
Open Apr–Oct daily (ex Tue) 9.45–12, 2–6.

Special to...
Le Clos Lucé
2 rue du Clos-Lucé. Tel: 02 47 57 62 88.
Open daily, Sep–Oct & Apr–Jun 9–6; Nov–Mar 10–5; Jul–Aug 9–7.

For Children
Zoo Parc de Beauval
St Aignan. Tel: 02 54 75 50 00. *Open daily, 9–dusk.*

For History Buffs
Musée de la Résistance et de la Déportation
Lorris. Tel: 02 38 94 84 19.
Open daily (ex Tue).

Special to...
Musée Dunois
Château, Beaugency. Tel: 02 38 44 55 23.
Open Apr–Oct daily (ex Tue) 10–12, 2–5.

For History Buffs
Château de Meung
Meung-sur-Loire. Tel: 02 38 44 36 47.
Open daily for guided visits, Apr–Oct daily 9.30–5; Nov–Mar daily 10.30–12, 2.30–4.30.

ℹ️ 12 cours du XXX Juillet, Bordeaux. Tel: 05 56 00 66 00.

ℹ️ 19 avenue du Mal de Lattre de Tassigny, Gujan-Mestras. Tel: 05 56 66 12 65.

ℹ️ Esplanade Georges Pompidou, Arcachon. Tel: 05 57 52 97 97.

ℹ️ 439 avenue de la Plage, Biscarrosse. Tel: 05 58 78 20 96.

ℹ️ 39 avenue Maurice Martin, Mimizan. Tel: 05 58 09 11 20.

ℹ️ 6 place du Général Leclerc, Mont-de-Marsan. Tel: 05 58 05 87 37.

ℹ️ Place Royal, Labastide-d'Armagnac. Tel: 05 58 44 67 56.

ℹ️ Maison du Curiste, Barbotan-les-Thermes. Tel: 05 62 69 52 13.

ℹ️ 11 rue Principale, Sauternes. Tel: 05 56 76 69 13.

1 Gujan-Mestras
Aqualand
145 route des Grands Lacs. Tel: 05 56 66 39 39.
Open Jun–mid-Sep daily 10–7.30.
Village Médiéval d'Artisans d'Art
Parc de Loisirs de la Hume. Tel: 05 56 66 16 76.
Open late Jun–Aug daily 10–7.

Musée de la Maquette Marine
19 boulevard du Général Leclerc. Tel: 05 57 52 00 03.
Open Easter–Jul & Sep weekends 2–6; Jul–Aug daily 10–12.30, 3–7.

2 Arcachon
Aquarium museum
2 rue Professeur Jolyet. Tel: 05 56 83 33 32.
Open daily Feb–Nov 10–12.30, 2–7 (to 11pm Jul–Aug).

3 Biscarrosse
Musée Historique de l'Hydraviation
332 avenue Louis Breguet. Tel: 05 58 78 00 65.
Open daily Apr–Sep 3–7 (from 10am Jul–Aug); Oct–Mar 2–6.
Musée de l'Histoire Populaire et Tradition
216 avenue Louis Bréguet. Tel: 05 58 78 77 37.
Open Jul–Aug daily 10–12, 3–7; Sep–Jun daily (ex Mon) 10–12, 2–6.

4 Mimizan
Mimizan Museum
8 rue de l'Abbaye. Tel: 05 58 09 00 61.
Open mid-Jun–mid-Sep Mon–Sat 10.30–7; other times, telephone for details.

5 Sabres
Ecomusée de Marqueze
Tel: 05 58 08 31 31.
Open Apr–Oct 10–12, 2–5 (closed Sun Apr, May & Oct).

6 Mont-de-Marsan
Musée Despiau Wlérick
6 place Marguerite de Navarre. Tel: 05 58 75 00 45.
Open Wed–Mon 10–12, 2–6.
Centre d'Art Contemporain
11 rue St Vincent de Paul. Tel: 05 58 75 55 84.

7 Labastide-d'Armagnac
Bastides exhibition
Tourist Office, place Royal. Tel: 05 58 44 67 56.
Open late Apr–late May, Mon–Sat 10–12.30, 2–6.40, Sun 2–6.
Musée du Vigneron
Chateau Garreau. Tel: 05 58 44 88 38.
Open daily 9–12, 2–6 (to 3pm Sun, Apr–Nov).

9 Nérac
Château de Nérac
Rue Henri IV. Tel: 05 53 65
21 11.
Open Wed–Sun 10–12,
2–6, Mon 2–6.

Back to Nature
Parc Ornithologique
RB250 Bordeaux–Arcachon
road. Tel: 05 56 22 80 93.
Open daily 10–6 (to 10pm
in summer).

For Children
Parc Animalier La
Coccinelle
La Hume, Gujan-Mestras.
Tel: 05 56 66 30 41.
Open late May–early Jul
daily 10–6.30; early Jul–Aug
daily 10.30–7.30.

For History Buffs
Musée du Pétrole
Route du Lac, Parentis-en-
Born. Tel: 05 58 78 40 02.
Open daily Jul–Aug.

For History Buffs
Musée Napoléon III
Mairie, Solférino. Tel: 05 58
07 21 08.
Closed for restoration.

Special to...
l'Atelier des Produits
Résineux
Luxey. Tel: 05 58 08 31 31
Open Apr–Oct, Sat 2–6, Sun
10–12, 2–6; Jun–Sep daily
10–12, 2–6.

TOUR 11

| i | 26 place Francheville,
Périgueux. Tel: 05 53 53 10
63. |

| i | Place de la Mairie, Les
Eyzies. Tel: 05 53 06 97 05. |

| i | Place Léo-Magne,
Montignac. Tel: 05 53 51 82
60. |

| i | Place de la Liberté,
Sarlat-la-Canéda. Tel: 05 53
31 45 45 |

| i | Boulevard Louis-Jean
Malvy, Souillac. Tel: 05 65 37
81 56. |

| i | Hospitalet,
Rocamadour. Tel: 05 65 33
62 59. |

| i | Place de la Halle,
Domme. Tel: 05 53 31 71
00. |

| i | 97 rue Neuve

d'Argenson, Bergerac. Tel:
05 53 57 03 11.

1 Grotte du Grand
Roc
Signposted from Les
Eyzies-de-Tayac. Tel: 05 53
06 92 70.
Open Feb–Dec daily 9.30–6
(7 Jul–Aug).
Musée de Spéléologie
Tel: 05 53 35 43 77.
Open mid-Jun–Aug, daily (ex
Sat) 10–6.

2 Les Eyzies
Musée National de la
Préhistoire
Follow signs for Grotte du
Grand-Roc. Tel: 05 53 06
45 45.
Open Jul–Aug daily 9.30–7
(10 on Fri);Sep–Jun daily (ex
Tue) 9.30–12, 2–5 or 6.
Abri Pataud
Tel: 05 53 06 92 46.
Open daily 9–12, 2–6.
Abri de Cap Blanc
Marquay Les Eyzies. Tel: 05
53 59 21 74.
Open Apr–Jun & Sep–Oct
daily 10–12, 2–6; Jul–Aug
daily 9.30–7

3 Lascaux II
Off route Montignac–Les-
Eyzies. Tel: 05 53 35 50 10.
Open daily 10–12, 2–5.30
(ex Mon out of season).
Régourdou Caves and
Museum
Montignac. Tel: 05 53 51 81
23.
Open Apr–Sep daily 10–6;
Oct–Mar school hols 2–6.

4 Sarlat-la-Canéda
Musée Aquarium
3 rue du Commandant-
Maratuel. Tel: 05 53 59 44
58.
Open Jun–mid-Sep daily
10–7; mid-Sep–Oct &
Apr–May 10–12, 2–6.

5 Souillac
Musée de l'Automate
Place de l'Abbaye. Tel: 05
65 37 07 07.
Open Apr–Oct 10–12, 3–6
(Jul–Aug 10–7); closed Mon
Apr–May; Nov–Mar Wed–
Sun 2–5.

6 Gouffre de Padirac
Tel: 05 65 33 64 56.
Open Apr–Sep 9–12, 2–6.

7 Domme
Museum
Place de la Halle. Tel Tourist

Office: 05 53 31 71 00.
Open Apr–Jun & Sep–Oct
daily (ex Sat) 10.30–12,
2.30–6; Jul–Aug daily 10–7.
Caverns
Place de la Halle. Tel Tourist
Office: 05 53 31 71 00.
Open Apr–Sep daily 9.30–
12, 2–6; Mar & Oct daily
2–6.

9 Les Milandes
Castle/Falconry Museum
Tel: 05 53 59 31 21.
Open daily, Apr–Sep 9.30–
12, 2–6; Mar & Oct daily 2–6.

10 Bergerac
Musée du Tabac
10 rue de l'Ancien-Pont.
Tel: 05 53 63 04 13.
Open Tue–Sat 10–12, 2–5
or 6, Sun 2.30–6.30.
Musée du Vin de la Batel-
lerie et de la Tonnellerie
5 rue des Conferences.
Tel: 05 53 57 80 92
Open mid-Mar–mid-Nov
Tue–Fri 10–12, 2–5.30, Sat
10–12, Sun 2.30–6.30.

For History Buffs
La Roque-St-Christophe
Peyzac le Moustier. Tel. 05
53 50 70 45.
Open daily, Apr–Oct 10–
6.30; Nov–Mar 11–5.

For History Buffs
Préhisto-Parc
Tursac. Tel: 05 53 50 73 19.
Open Mar–mid-Nov daily
10–6 (9.30–7 Jul–Aug).

For Children
La Féerie du Rail
Rocamadour. Tel: 05 65 33
71 06.
Open Apr–Oct daily at 11,
2.15 & 4.30.

Back to Nature
Parc Animalier
Route de Cajarc, Gramat.
Tel: 05 65 38 81 22.
Open all year daily,
Easter–Sep 9–7, Oct–Easter
10–6.
Forêt des Singes
Rocamadour. Tel: 05 65 33
62 72.
Open Apr–Oct daily 10–12,
1–6.
Rocher des Aigles
Rocamadour. Tel: 05 65 33
65 45.
Open Apr–Oct daily.

For History Buffs
Château de Castelnaud
Tel: 05 53 31 30 00.

Open Mar–mid-Nov daily
from 10am; Dec–Feb daily
(ex Sat) 2–5.

TOUR 12

| i | Havas Voyages, Place
Clemenceau, Pau. Tel: 05 59
11 86 86. |

| i | 3 cours Gambetta,
Tarbes. Tel: 05 62 51 30 31. |

| i | 3 allées Tournefort,
Bagnères-de-Bigorre. Tel:
05 62 95 50 71. |

| i | Les Olivetains, St-
Bertrand-de-Comminges.
Tel: 05 61 83 32 07. |

| i | Allées d'Étigny,
Bagnères-de-Luchon. Tel:
05 61 79 21 21. |

| i | Maison du Parc
National, Gavarnie. Tel: 05
62 92 49 10. |

| i | Pl Beyramalu, Lourdes.
Tel: 05 62 42 77 40. |

1 Tarbes
Musée Massey
Jardin Massey. Tel: 05 62 36
31 49.
Open Wed–Sun 10–12, 2–6.
Haras Stables
Avenue de Regiment de
Bigorre. Tel: 05 62 56 30 80.
Open Jul–mid Sep Mon–Fri
10–12, 2–5.

2 Bagnères-de-
Bigorre
Musée Bigourdan
Rue de Hount Blanque.
Tel: 05 62 91 07 33.
Open Tue–Fri 10–12, 2–6.
Musée Salies.
Tel: 05 62 91 07 26.
Open mid-May–Nov daily
(ex Mon) 3–6.

3 St-Bertrand-de-
Comminges
Museum
Batiment des Olivetains,
Parvis de la Cathédrale.
Tel: 05 61 88 31 79.
Open Mon–Fri 8–12, 1.30–5.

4 Bagnères-de-
Luchon
Musée du Pays de Luchon
18 allée de T'Etigny. Tel: 05
61 79 29 87.
Open Apr–Oct daily 9–12,
2–6.

6 Gavarnie
Pyrenees National Park

Information Centre

Village centre. Tel: 05 62 92
49 10
Open all year, Mon–Fri 9–6.

❼ Cauterets

Pyrenees National Park
Information Centre
Tel: 05 62 92 52 56.
*Open daily, Jun–Sep 9.30–12,
2.30–7; Oct–May 3–6.30.*
Museum
Tel: 05 62 92 52 56.
*Open daily, Jun–Sep 9.30–12,
2.30–7; Oct–May 3–6.30.*

❽ Lourdes

Grotto
*Open after morning masses,
at about 10.30am.*
Pavilion Notre-Dame,
Musée Bernadette, Musée
d'Art Sacré du Gemmail
72 rue de la Grotte. Tel: 05
62 94 13 15.
*Open daily 9.30–11.45,
2.30–6 (closed Tue Dec–Jun).*
Musée Pyrénéen
Château, 25 rue du Fort.
Tel: 05 62 94 02 04.
*Open daily (ex Tue from
mid-Oct–Easter) 9–12, 2–7.*

❾ Grottes de Bétharram

Saint Pe de Bigorre. Tel: 05
62 41 80 04.
*Open Jan–Mar Mon–Fri, one
tour at 2.30; Apr–Oct daily
8.30–12, 1.30–5.30.*

For History Buffs

Marshal Foch Museum
Tarbes. Tel: 05 62 93 19 02.
*Open daily 10–12, 2–5.30
(closed Mon, Tue Sep–Jul).*

Back to Nature

Observatoire et Institut
de Physique du Globe
Pic du Midi. Tel: 05 62 95
19 69.
Closed for restoration.

For Children

The Animated Crib
21 quai Saint Jean, Lourdes.
Tel: 05 62 94 71 00.
*Open Apr–Oct daily 9–12,
1.30–7.*

For History Buffs

Musée de Lourdes
Parking de l'Egalité. Tel: 05
62 94 28 00.
*Open Apr–Oct daily 9–12,
1.30–6.45.*
Musée du Petit Lourdes
68 avenue Peyramale. Tel:
05 62 94 24 36.
Open Apr–Oct daily 9–7.

TOUR 13

ⓘ 4 la Canebiere,
Marseille. Tel: 04 91 13 89
00.

ⓘ Place Baragnon, Cassis.
Tel: 04 42 01 71 17.

ⓘ Allées Vivien, Bandol.
Tel: 04 94 29 41 35.

ⓘ Place des Riaux, Toulon.
Tel: 04 94 18 53 00.

ⓘ Rotonde, Jean-Salusse,
Hyères. Tel: 04 94 65 18 55.

ⓘ Quai Jean-Jaures, St-
Tropez. Tel: 04 94 97 45 21.

ⓘ 1 boulevard des
Aliziers, Grimaud. Tel: 04 94
43 26 98.

ⓘ Avenue Antide Boyer,
Aubagne. Tel: 04 42 03 49
98.

❶ Cassis

Museum
Place Baragnon. Tel: 04 42
01 88 66.
*Open Wed, Thu & Sat,
Apr–Sep 3.30–6.30;
Oct–Mar 2.30–5.30.*

❸ Bandol

Jardin Exotic Zoo
Commune de Sanary.
Tel: 04 94 29 40 38.
*Open daily, Mon–Sat 8–12,
2–6, Sun 10–12, 2–7.*

❹ Toulon

Musée de la Marine
Place Monsenergue. Tel: 04
94 02 02 01.
Open daily 10–6.30.
Zoo de Toulon
Mont Faron. Tel: 04 94 88
07 89.
*Open Easter–Sep daily
10–6 (closes on rainy days).*
Musée de Debarquement
de Provence
Route de Faron. Tel: 04 94
88 08 09.
*Open Tue–Sun 9.30–11.30,
2–5.30.*

❺ Hyères

Museum
Place Lefebvre. Tel: 04 94
35 90 42.
*Open daily (ex Tue), week-
days 10–12, 3–6, weekends
3–6.*

❼ St-Tropez

Musée de l'Annonciade
Place Georges Grammont.

Tel: 04 94 97 04 01.
*Open daily (ex Tue) 10–12,
3–7 (10–12, 2–6 Oct–May).*
Musée de la Marine
Citadelle. Tel: 04 94 97 59
43.
Open daily, (ex Tue) 10–5.

❿ Chartreuse de la Verne

Route de Collobriers.
*Tel Tourist Office: 04 94 48
08 00.*
*Open daily (ex Tue) 11–5 (6
Jun–Aug).*

⓫ Aubagne

Musée de la Légion
Etrangère
Caserne Viénot. Tel: 04 42
18 82 41.
*Open Jun–Sep Tue–Sun
9–12, 2–5; Oct–May Wed,
Sat & Sun 10–12, 2–6.*

For Children

OK Corral
Cuges le Pins, on the N98.
Tel: 04 42 73 80 05.
*Open all year; days and
times vary; phone for details.*

TOUR 14

ⓘ Palais des Festivals, 1 la
Croisette, Cannes. Tel: 04
93 39 01 01.

ⓘ 11 place du Général-
de-Gaulle, Antibes. Tel: 04
92 90 53 00.

ⓘ 6 place de la Chapelle,
Biot. Tel: 04 93 65 05 85.

ⓘ 22 cours Honoré-
Cresp, Grasse. Tel: 04 93 36
03 56.

ⓘ Place de l'Eglise,
Gourdon. Tel: 04 93 09 68
25.

ⓘ 8 rue Nationale, Castel
lane. Tel: 04 92 83 61 14.

ⓘ Place Marcel Paslorelli,
St-André-les-Alpes. Tel: 04
92 89 02 39.

ⓘ 4 allée Louis Gadiol,
Riez. Tel: 04 92 77 82 80

ⓘ Rue du Seigneur de la
Clue, Moustiers-Ste-Marie.
Tel: 04 92 74 67 84.

ⓘ 9 boulevard
Clémenceau, Draguignan.
Tel: 04 94 68 63 30.

ⓘ Place St-Sébastien,
Mons. Tel: 04 94 76 39 54.

❶ Cap d'Antibes

Musée Naval et
Napoléonien
Batterie du Grillon, avenue
Kennedy. Tel: 04 93 61 45
32.
*Open Mon–Fri 9.30–12,
2.15–6, Sat 9.30–12.*
Jardin Thuret
Boulevard du Cap. Tel: 04 93
67 88 00.
*Open Mon–Fri 8.30–12,
2.30–5.30.*

❷ Antibes

Archaeological Museum
Bastion St-André, prome-
nade de l'Amiral-Grasse.
Tel: 04 92 90 54 35.
*Open daily (ex Mon) 9–12,
2–6; closed Nov.*
Musée Picasso
Château Grimaldi. Tel: 04
93 90 54 20.
*Open daily (ex Tue) Jun–Sep
10–6; Oct–May 10–12, 2–6.*

❸ Biot

Musée National Fernand
Léger
Chemin du Val de Pomme.
Tel: 04 92 91 50 30.
*Open Wed–Mon 10–12.30,
2–5.30 (to 6pm Apr–Sep).*
Verrerie de Biot
5 chemin des Combes.
Tel: 04 93 65 03 00.
*Open daily, Mon–Sat 9–6.30,
Sun 10.30–1, 2.30–6.30.*

❹ Grasse

Musée International de la
Parfumerie
8 place du Cours. Tel: 04
93 36 80 20.
*Open Jun–Sep daily 10–7;
Oct–May Wed–Sun 10–12,
2–5.*
Maison Fragonard
23 boulevard Fragonard.
Tel: 04 93 36 02 71.
*Open daily, Jun–Sep 10–7;
Oct–May 10–12, 2–5.*
Musée d'Art et d'Histoire
de Provence
2 rue Mirabeau. Tel: 04 93
36 01 61.
*Open Mon–Sat 10–12, 2–5
(to 6pm Apr–Oct).*
Musée de la Marine
2 boulevard du Jeu de
Ballon. Tel: 04 93 40 11 11.
*Open daily 10–6 (ex May);
closed lunchtimes Oct–May); closed
1st 2 weeks Nov.*

❺ Gourdon

Château de Gourdon
Le Bar sur Loup. Tel: 04 93

09 68 02.
*Open daily Jun–Sep 11–1,
2–7; Oct–May (ex Tue) 2–6.*

[10] **Moustiers-Ste-Marie**
Musée des Faïences.
Tel: 04 94 77 80 72.
Open Jul–mid Sep daily 3–7.

[12] **Draguignan**
Musée des Arts et
Traditions Populaire
15 rue Joseph Roumanille.
Tel: 04 94 47 28 80.
*Open Tue Sat 9 12, 2 6,
Sun 2–6.*
Musée du Canon et des
Artilleurs
Ecole d'Application de
l'Artillerie, Quartier Bona-
parte. Tel: 04 94 60 23 85.
*Open mid-Jan–mid-Dec daily
8.15–11.30, 2.15–5.30.*

[14] **Mons**
Les Maison des Peintres
22 rue Jean Vadon. Tel: 04
94 76 36 66..
*Open Tue–Sun 2–7 (also
occasional mornings).*

For Children
Marineland
Route Nationale 7. Tel: 04
93 33 49 49.
*Open daily 10 6 (midnight
Jul–Aug; phone for closing
times Sep–Mar).*

Special to...
Maison de l'Abeille
Rte de Manosque, Valen-
sole. Tel: 04 92 74 85 28.
*Open Jul–Aug daily 8–12,
1.30–6; Sep Wed 2.30–6.*

Back to Nature
Lapidaire Pierres de
Provence
Cartier St-Benoit, Digne-
les-Bains. Tel: 04 92 36 70 80
*Open daily 9–12, 2–5
(closed weekends Nov–Mar).*

[i] Avenue Thiers, Nice.
Tel: 04 93 87 07 07.

[i] 59 avenue Denis
Seméria, St-Jean-Cap-
Ferrat. Tel: 04 93 76 08 90.

[i] 2 boulevard des
Moulins, Monte Carlo. Tel:
(377) 92 16 61 66.

[i] Palais e l'Europe,
avenue Boyer, Menton. Tel:
04 92 41 76 76.

[i] Le Pont Vieux, Sospel.
Tel: 04 93 04 15 80.

[1] **Cap Ferrat**
Musée Ephrussi de
Rothschild
Tel: 04 93 01 33 09.
*Open daily 10–6 (7 Jul–Aug;
2–6 on weekdays Nov–Feb).*

[2] **Monaco**
Palais du Prince and
Musée Napoléon
Tel: (377) 93 25 18 31.
*Open Jun–Oct daily
9.30–6.30.*
Musée Océanographique
and Aquarium
Avenue St-Martin.
Tel: (377) 93 15 36 00.
Open daily 9.30–6 or later.

[3] **Menton**
Jardin de la Serre de la
Madone
74 route de Gorbia.
Open 1st & 3rd Fri of month.
Musée Jean Cocteau
Bastion du Port, 2 quai
Napoléon-III. Tel: 04 93 57
72 30.
Open Wed–Mon 10–12, 2–6.

[5] **Sospel**
Musée de la Résistance
Fort St Roch. Tel: 04 9 04
00 09.
*Open Jun–mid Sep, daily (ex
Mon) 2–6; mid Sep–Oct &
Easter, weekends 2–6.*
Orient Express Museum
Gare du Sospel. Tel: 04 93
04 14 79.
Open Feb–Oct daily 10–6.

For Children
Cap Ferrat Zoo
117 avenue Général de
Gaulle. Tel: 04 93 76 04 98.
Open all year daily.

For History Buffs
Villa Kérylos
Beaulieu. Tel: 04 93 01 60 71.
*Open mid-Feb–mid-Nov
daily 10.30–6 (7 Jul–Aug);
phone for winter opening.*

Back to Nature
Jardin Exotique
Boulevard du Jardin
Exotique. Tel: (377) 93 30
33 65.
*Open daily 9–7 (but phone
to check Oct–Mar).*
Grotte de l'Observatoire
Boulevard du Jardin
Exotique. Tel: (377) 93 15
29 80.
Open Jan–Nov daily 10–6.

[i] 6 rue Auguste, Nimes
Tel: 04 66 67 29 11.

[i] 24 cours Gambell,
Beaucaire. Tel: 04 66 59 26
57.

[i] 59 rue des Halles,
Tarascon. Tel: 04 90 91 03
52.

[i] 41 cours Jean-Jaures,
Avignon. Tel: 04 90 82 65
11.

[i] Place Jean-Jaures, St-
Rémy-de-Provence. Tel: 04
90 92 05 22.

[i] Hôtel de Manville, Les
Baux de Provence. Tel: 04
90 54 34 39.

[i] Boulevard des Lices,
Arles. Tel: 04 90 18 41 20.

[i] 5 avenue van Gogh,
Saintes-Marie-de-la-Mer.
Tel: 04 90 97 82 55.

[i] Porte de la Gardette,
Aigues-Mortes. Tel: 04 66
53 73 00.

[2] **Beaucaire**
Musée Municipal Auguste
Jacquet
Château de Beaucaire.
Open daily.
Château/Falconry Centre
Tel Château: 04 66 59 26
72; Falconry: 04 66 59 58 33.
Open Apr–Oct Thu–Tue.

[3] **Tarascon**
Maison de Tartarin de
Tarascon
55 bis boulevard Itam.
Tel: 04 90 91 05 08.
*Open daily, summer 10–12,
2–7; winter 10–12, 1.30–5.*
Château
Tel: 04 90 91 01 93.
*Open daily 9–12, 2–6
(all day Jul–Aug, pm only
Oct–Mar).*

[4] **St-Michel-de-Frigolet**
Tel: 04 90 95 70 07.
Open all year daily 7–7.

[5] **Avignon**
Palais des Papes
Place du Palais. Tel: 04 90
27 50 73.
*Open daily, Apr–Oct 9–7;
Nov–Mar 9–12.45, 2–6.*

[6] **St-Rémy-de-Provence**
Musée des Alpilles
1 place Favier. Tel: 04 90 92
70 14.
*Open Mar–Sep daily
10–12, 2–6 (5 Jul–Aug).*
Nostradamus Museum
Rue Nostradamus, Salon
de Provence. Tel: 04 90 56
64 31.
*Open daily, Mon–Fri 9–12,
2–6, weekends 2–6.*
Monastère de St-Paul-de-
Mausolée
Tel: 04 90 92 77 00.
Open daily 8–5 or later.
Centre Archéologie
Antique
Hôtel de Sade, rue du
Parage. Tel: 04 90 92 64 04.
*Open Jun–Sep daily 9–12,
2–6; Apr–May & Oct Mon–
Sat 3–6, Sat & Sun 10–12.*
Glanum Roman Site
Avenue Vincent Van Gogh.
Tel: 04 90 92 23 79.
Open daily, 9–12, 2–5.

[7] **Les Baux-de-Provence**
Château and Museum
Tel: 04 90 54 37 37.
Open daily 9 6 or later.
Théâtre des Images
Carrier St Just (1km/½ mile
north). Tel: 01 90 54 38 65.
*Open late Mar–Dec daily
10–7 (also Fri evening Jul–
Aug); Jan–Mar weekends.*

[8] **Arles**
Arènes
Rond-Point des Arènes.
Tel: 04 90 96 03 70.
*Open daily, Nov–Mar 9–
4.30, Apr–Oct 9–6.30 or 7;
closed lunchtime ex Jun–Sep.*
Théâtre Antique
Rue du Cloître. Tel: 04 90
96 93 30.
*Open daily, Nov–Mar 9–
4.30, Apr–Oct 9–6.30 or 7;
closed lunchtime ex Jun–Sep*
Fondation Vincent Van
Gogh
Palais de Luppé, 24 bis,
Rond Point des Arènes. Tel:
04 90 49 94 04.
Open daily 10–7.

[10] **Musée Camarguais**
Mas du Pont de Rousty
Albaron. Tel: 04 90 97 10 82.
Open all year daily.

[11] **Maison du Parc**
Tel: 04 90 97 10 82.
Open all year daily.

Parc Ornithologique
North of Saintes-Maries-de-la-Mer. Tel: 04 90 97 82 62.
Open daily 8–dusk (from 10am Nov–Feb).

12 Saintes-Marie-de-la-Mer
Musée Baroncelli
Rue Victor Hugo. Tel: 04 90 97 87 60.
Open Apr–mid-Nov daily 10–12, 2–6.

13 Aigues-Mortes
Tour de Constance
Place Anotole-France. Tel: 04 66 53 61 55.
Open daily, Apr–Oct 9–7; Nov–Mar 9.30–12, 2–5.30.

For History Buffs
Moulin de Daudet
D33, outskirts of Fontvieille. Tel: 04 90 54 60 78.
Open Apr–Oct daily 9–12, 2–7; Nov–Dec & Feb–Mar daily 10–12.

For Children
Tiki III cruises
Pier, Saintes-Maries-de-la-Mer. Tel: 04 90 97 81 68.
Cruises Apr–Oct daily at 10, 2 and 4.

TOUR 17

i 14 place Stanislas, Nancy. Tel: 03 83 35 22 41.

i Porte Haute, Liverdun Haut. Tel: 03 83 24 40 40 or 03 83 24 46 76.

i Place d'Armes, Metz. Tel: 03 87 55 53 76.

i Place de la Nation, Verdun. Tel: 03 29 86 14 18.

i Rue de Palais de Justice, St-Mihiel. Tel 03 29 89 06 47.

i Parvis de la Cathédrale, Toul. Tel: 03 83 64 11 69.

1 Parc de Haye
Velaine en Haye. Tel: 03 83 23 24 99. *Open daily.*
Motor Museum
Zone de Loisirs, Velaine-en-Haye. Tel: 03 83 23 28 38.
Open all year weekends 2–6; Jun–Aug daily 2–6.30.

3 Metz
La Cour d'Or Musée d'Art et d'Histoire

2 rue du Haut-Poirier. Tel: 03 87 75 10 18.
Open daily 10–12, 2–5.

5 Verdun: Champs de Bataille
Fort de Douaumont
10km (6 miles) north of Verdun. Tel: 03 29 84 54 81.
Open daily, Apr–Sep 9–12, 2–5, 5.30; May–Aug 9–6 or 6.30.

6 Verdun
Underground Citadel
Avenue du 5ème RAP.
Open daily, Apr–Sep 9–5 or later; winter 10–5 (pm only Jan–mid-Feb); closed lunchtime ex high season.
Musée Hôtel de la Princerie
11 rue de la Belle Vieige. Tel: 03 29 86 10 62.
Open Apr–Oct daily (ex Tue) 9.30–12, 2–6.

7 St-Mihiel
Benedictines' Library
Rue du Palais de Justice. Tel: 03 29 89 02 87.
Open Apr–Jun & Sep weekends 2–6; Jul–Aug daily (ex Tue) 2–6.

For History Buffs
Schuman Museum
Rue Robert Schuman, Scy-Chazelles. Tel: 03 87 66 54 01.
Open all year.
Musée Militaire
Gravelotte. Tel Town Hall: 03 87 60 92 56.
Open Wed 2–6, Sat & Sun 10–12, 2–6.

Special to...
Maison du Polyculture
Lucey. Tel: 03 83 63 85 21.
Open May–Sep Thu–Sat 2–6, Sun 2.30–6.30.
Centre du Promotion
Bruley. Tel: 03 83 64 55 09.
Open Mar–Dec daily (ex Mon) 2–5.

TOUR 18

i Place Bellecour, Lyon. Tel: 04 72 77 69 69.

i 3 place Hôtel de Ville, Villars-les-Dombes. Tel: 04 74 98 06 29.

i Place du Champ de Foire, Châtillon-sur-Chalaronne. Tel: 04 74 55 02 27.

i Place de l'Hôtel de

Ville, Amplepuis. Tel: 04 74 89 01 71.

i 1 cours de la République, Roanne. Tel: 04 77 71 51 77.

i 6 place Jean-Baptiste Galland, Chazelles-sur-Lyon. Tel 04 77 94 22 15.

i 18 avenue Charles de Gaulle, Charbonnières-les-Bains. Tel: 04 78 87 04 21.

0 Musée Henri Malartre
Roche Gaillée Château. Tel: 04 78 22 18 80.
Open daily (ex Mon) 9–6.

3 Parc des Oiseaux
Off N83 near Villars-les-Dombes. Tel: 04 74 98 05 54.
Open daily 9–7.

5 Châtillon-sur-Chalaronne
Apothecairerie
Place St Vincent de Paul. Tel Tourist Office: 04 74 55 02 27.
Open summer Sun & Mon.

7 Amplepuis
Musée Barthélémy Thimonnier
Place de l'Hôtel de Ville. Tel: 04 74 89 08 90.
Open daily 2.30–6.30.

8 Roanne
Ecomusée
Impasse Général Giraud. Tel: 04 77 71 31 88.
Open Mon–Fri 2–6.
Musée Déchelette
22 rue Anatole France. Tel: 04 77 23 68 77.
Open daily 10–12, 2–6 (10–6 Fri, 2–6, Sun).
Maison des Métiers d'Art
Place de Lattre de Tassigny. Tel: 04 77 23 20 00.
Open for special exhibitions.

9 Chazelles-sur-Lyon
Musée du Chapeau
Place Jean-Baptiste Galland. Tel: 04 77 94 23 29.
Open daily (ex Tue, but open Tue Jul–Aug) 2–6.

For Children
Parc de la Tête d'Or
Masséna Parc Zoologie. Tel: 04 78 89 53 52.
Open daily 6am–11pm (9pm winter).

For Children/For History Buffs
Musée Maison d'Ampere
Poleymieux. Tel: 04 78 91 90 77.
Open Wed–Mon 9–12, 2–6.

For History Buffs
Maison Monsieur Vincent
Place des Halles, St Vincent de Paul. Tel: 04 74 55 26 64.
Open daily 10–6.

For Children
Musée d'Allard
Boulevard de la Préfecture, Montbrison. Tel: 04 77 96 08 69.
Open daily (ex Tue) 2.30–6.

Back to Nature
Parc de Courzieu
Montmain la Côte, Courzieu. Tel: 04 74 70 96 10.
Open Mar–Oct daily 10–7.

TOUR 19

i 14 rue de la République, Grenoble. Tel: 04 76 42 41 41.

i 24 boulevard de la Colonne, Chambéry. Tel: 04 79 33 42 47.

i Place Maurice Mollard, Aix-les-Bains. Tel: 04 79 35 05 92.

i Centre Bonlieu, 1 rue Jean-Jaurès, Annecy. Tel: 04 50 45 00 33

i Parc de l'Eglise, La Clusaz. Tel: 04 50 32 65 00.

i On the D925, Beaufort. Tel: 04 79 38 37 57 or 04 79 38 15 33.

i Place de la Gare, Bourg-St-Maurice. Tel: 04 79 07 12 57.

i Modane. Tel: 04 79 05 24 75.

i Maison de Val-d'Isere, Val-d'Isere. Tel: 04 79 06 06 60.

i Place de la Cathédrale, St-Jean-de-Maurienne. Tel: 04 79 83 51 51.

0 La Grande Chartreuse
Musée de la Correrie
Near road to monastery. Tel: 04 76 88 60 45.
Open Easter–Oct daily 9.30–12, 2–6.

2 Chambéry

Château
Rue Basse du Château.
*Tours May–Sep daily 10.30,
2.30 (also 3.30, 4.30, 5.30
Jul–Aug), weekend pm only
Mar–Apr & Oct–Nov.*
Musée des Beaux-Arts
Place du Palais de Justice.
Tel: 04 79 33 75 03.
*Open Wed–Mon 10–12,
2–6.*
Musée Savoisien
Square Lannoy-de-Bissy.
Tel: 04 79 33 44 48.
*Open Wed–Mon 10–12,
2–6.*
Galerie Eurêka
Tel: 04 79 60 04 25.
*Open Jul–Aug daily 2–6;
Sep–Jun Tue, Thu & Fri 5–7,
Wed & Sat 2–6 (Tue–Sat
2–6 during school holidays).*

3 Aix-les-Bains

**Temple of Diana and
Museums**
Place Mollard. Tel: 04 79
35 05 92.
*Open daily 9–12.15, 2–6
(closed Sun Oct–Mar).*
Musée Faure
10 boulevard des Côtes.
Tel: 04 79 61 06 57.
*Open daily (ex Tue) 10–12,
1.30–6.*

4 Annecy

Castle Museum
Place du Château. Tel: 04
50 33 87 31.
*Open daily (ex Tue) 10–6;
(closed lunchtime Oct–May).*
Palais de l'Ile and Museum
3 passage de l'Ile. Tel: 04
50 33 87 30.
*Open daily (ex Tue) 10–6;
(closed lunchtime Oct–May).*

5 Beaufort

Cheese Co-operative
Avenue du Capitaine
Bulle. Tel: 04 79 38 33 62.
*Open daily 8–12, 2–6.30
(closed Sun Oct–May).*

6 Bourg-St-Maurice

Musée des Minéraux
Avenue du Maréchal
Leclerc. Tel: 04 79 07 12 74.
*Open Jul–Aug Tue–Sat
10–12, 3–7, Sun–Mon 3–7.*
**Beaufort Cheese Co-
operative**
Zone Artisanale des
Colombières. Tel: 04 79 07
08 28.
Open Mon–Sat 9–12.
Costume Museum

Hauteville-Gondon. Tel: 04
79 07 09 01.
Open afternoons (ex Tue).

10 Modane

Fort St-Gobain
*Tel: 04 79 05 01 50.
Open May–Nov daily 10–7
(may close lunchtime).*

11 St-Jean-de-Maurienne

Musée de Costumes
Place de la Cathédrale.
Tel Tourist Office: 04 79 83
51 51.
*Open Wed 4–6; Jul–Aug
Mon–Sat 10–12, 2–6.*
Opinel Knife Museum
Avenue H Falcoz. Tel: 04
79 64 04 78.
Open Mon–Sat 9–12, 2–7.

For Children
Luge d'Été
Téléphérique de Beau-
regard, La Clusaz. Tel: 04
50 02 40 09.
*Open mid-Jun–early Sep
daily 10–12.30, 2–6.30 (also
8.30pm–10.30pm on Thu).*

For Children
Funicular railway
Bourg St Maurice. Tel: 04
79 41 55 18.
Open late Jun–early Sep

For History Buffs
**Museum of the French
Revolution**
Vizille Château. Tel: 04 76
68 07 35.
Open daily, (ex Tue) 10–5.

TOUR 20

i 17 place de la
Cathédrale, Strasbourg.
Tel: 03 88 52 28 28.

i Place du Prensureux,
Ste-Marie-aux-Mines. Tel:
03 89 58 80 50.

i 6 place Joffre, Thann.
Tel: 03 89 37 96 20.

i 9 avenue du Maréchal-
Foch, Mulhouse. Tel: 03 89
45 68 31.

i 73 rue de la
République, Guebwiller.
Tel: 03 89 76 10 63.

i 4 rue Unterlinden,
Colmar. Tel: 03 89 20 68
92.

i 38 rue du Général de
Gaulle, Kaysersberg. Tel: 03
89 78 22 78.

i 2 rue de la 1ere
Armée, Riquewihr. Tel: 03
89 49 08 40.

i 10 boulevard Leclerc,
Sélestat. Tel: 03 88 58 87
20.

2 Ste-Marie-aux-Mines

St Bartélemy Mine Tour
Tel: 03 89 58 72 28.
*Open Jul–Aug daily
9.30–12, 2–6.*
**Maison du Pays and
Musée Minéralogique**
Place du Prensureux.
Tel: 03 89 58 56 67.
Open daily 10–12, 2–6.

3 Thann

Musée des Amis de Thann
Halle aux Blés. Tel: 03 89
37 02 31.
*Open mid-May mid-Oct
Tue–Sun 10–12, 2–6.30.*

4 Mulhouse

Musée des Beaux-Arts
4 place Guillaume-Tell.
Tel: 03 89 45 43 19.
*Open daily (ex Tue) 10–12,
2–5 (to 6pm Jun–Sep).*
**Musée Français du
Chemin de Fer**
2 rue Alfred-de-Glehn.
Tel: 03 89 42 25 70.
Open daily 9–5 or 6.
**Musée du Sapeur-
Pompier**
2 rue Alfred de Glehn.
Tel: 03 89 42 25 67.
Open daily 9–5 or 6.
**Musée National de
l'Automobile**
192 avenue de Colmar.
Tel: 03 89 33 23 23.
Open daily (ex Tue) 10–6.

5 Écomusée de Haute Alsace

8km (5 miles) southeast of
Guebwiller via D430.
Tel: 03 89 74 44 74.
*Open daily, summer 9–6 or
7, Mar–May & Oct–Nov 10
or 11–5.*

6 Guebwiller

Musée du Florival
1 rue de 4-Février. Tel: 03
89 74 22 89.
*Open Mon & Wed–Fri 2–6,
Sat & Sun 10–12, 2–6.*

7 Colmar

Musée d'Unterlinden
1 rue Unterlinden. Tel: 03
89 20 15 50.
Open daily 9–5 or 6; closed

*Tue & lunchtimes
Nov–Mar.*
Musée Bartholdi
30 rue des Marchands.
Tel: 03 89 41 90 60.
*Open Apr–Dec, daily (ex
Tue) 10–12, 2–6.*

8 Kaysersberg

**Albert Schweitzer
Birthplace Museum**
126 rue du Général de
Gaulle. Tel: 03 89 47 36 55.
*Open May–Oct daily
9–12, 2–6.*

9 Riquewihr

Musée Dolder
Rue Général de Gaulle.
Tel: 03 89 47 92 15.
*Open Apr–Oct weekends
9–12, 1.30–6 (daily
Jul–Aug).*
Tour des Voleurs
Rue des Juifs. Tel: 03 89 47
92 15.
*Open mid-Apr–mid-Nov
daily 9.15–12, 1.30–6.*
**Musée d'Histoire des
PTT d'Alsace**
Cour du Château. Tel: 03
89 47 93 80.
*Open Easter–mid-Nov
daily, (ex Tue) 10–12, 2–6.*

10 Sélestat

Bibliothèque Humaniste
1 rue de la Bibliothèque.
Tel: 03 88 92 03 24.
*Open Mon–Fri 9–12, 2–6,
Sat 9–12; Jul–Aug also Sat
& Sun 2–5.*

For Children
Luge d'Été
La Vue des Alpes, Villar sur
Thur, Le Grand Ballon.
Tel: 03 89 76 14 40.
Open May–Aug 10–6.

Special to...
**Centre de
Réintroduction des
Cigognes**
Hunawihr. Tel: 03 89 73
72 62.
*Open Apr mid-Nov daily
10–12, 2–4 (later in high
season).*

For Children
Montagne des Singes
Kintzheim. Tel: 03 88 92
05 94.
*Open Apr–mid-Nov daily
10–12, 1–4 (later in high
season).*
Volerie des Aigles
Kintzheim. Tel: 03 88 92
84 33.

*Open Easter–mid-Nov daily
2.30–4 (later in high season).*

For History Buffs
Château de Haut-
Koenigsbourg
Tel: 03 88 92 11 46.
*Open daily, Jun–Sep 9–6;
Oct–May 9–12, 1–4 or later.*
Musée de l'Abri
Hatten. Tel: 03 88 80 14 90.
*Open Mar–Nov Thu–Sun
10–12, 1.30–6;daily Jul,Aug.*

TOUR 21

ⓘ 12 bd Clemenceau,
Calais. Tel: 03 21 96 62 40.

ⓘ Rte Nationale, Sangatte.
Tel: 03 21 34 97 98. i

ⓘ Forum Jean-Noël, quai
de la Poste, Boulogne. Tel:
03 21 31 68 38.

ⓘ Palais de l'Europe, place
de l'Hermitage, Le Touquet.
Tel: 03 21 06 72 00.

ⓘ 1 rue Carnot, Le
Crotoy. Tel: 03 22 27 05 25.

ⓘ 21 rue Carnot, Mont-
reuil. Tel: 03 21 06 04 27.

ⓘ Rue Jean Macé, Des-
vres. Tel: 03 21 87 69 23

2 Cap Blanc-Nez
Musée du Transmanche
Mont Hubert Escalles.
Tel: 03 21 85 57 42.
*Open Apr–Sep Tue–Sun
10–5.15 (daily Jul–Aug).*

3 Boulogne
Château-Musée
Rue de Bernet. Tel: 03 21
10 02 20.
*Open daily 10–12.30, 2–7,
(to 5.30pm Sun).*

**5 Domaine du
Marquenterre**
Parc Ornithologique de
Marquenterre
Tel: 03 22 25 03 06.
Open Apr–mid Nov daily.

6 Le Crotoy
Steam Train Rides
Tel: 03 22 26 96 96.
*Open May–Jun Wed, Sat &
Sun; Jul–Aug Tue–Sun depart
3.30, return 6.30.*

9 Desvres
Maison de la Faïance
Rue Jean Macé. Tel: 03 21
83 23 23.
Open Tue–Sun (daily Jul–

*Aug) 10–1, 2–6.30; Nov–
Mar 2–6.30.*

For History Buffs
Colonne de la Grande
Armée
Off Calais road, outskirts of
Boulogne. Tel: 03 21 80 43
69.
Open Thu–Mon 9–12, 2–5.

For Children
Aqualud
Boulevard de la Mer, Le
Touquet seafront. Tel: 03 21
05 90 96
Open daily 10–6 or 7.

For Children
Bagatelle Fun Park
D940, south of Le Touquet.
Tel: 03 21 89 09 99.
Open Apr–Sep daily 10–7.

TOUR 22

ⓘ 6 bis rue Dusevel,
Amiens. Tel: 03 22 71 60 50.

ⓘ Place du Général de
Gaulle, Picquigny. Tel: 03 22
51 46 85.

ⓘ Place des Héros, Arras.
Tel: 03 21 51 26 95.

ⓘ 70 place d'Armes,
Douai. Tel: 03 27 88 26 79.

ⓘ Place du Parvis, Laon.
Tel: 03 23 20 28 62.

ⓘ Place de l'Hôtel-de-
Ville, Pierrefonds. Tel: 03 44
42 81 44.

ⓘ Place de l'Hôtel-de-
Ville, Compiègne. Tel: 03 44
40 01 00.

ⓘ 1 rue René de
Girardin, Ermenonville. Tel:
03 44 54 01 58.

ⓘ 1 rue Beauregard,
Beauvais. Tel: 03 44 45 08 18.

1 Samara
La Chaussée Tirancourt.
Tel: 03 22 51 82 83.
Open Apr–mid-Nov daily.

2 Grottes de Naours
Tel: 03 22 93 71 78.
*Open Feb–mid-Nov daily
9–12, 1.30–6.*

**3 Battlefields of the
Somme**
Historial de la Grande
Guerre
Château de Peronne.
Tel: 03 22 83 14 18.

*Open mid-Jan–mid-Dec
daily (ex Mon) 10–6 (also
Mon May–Sep).*

4 Arras
Musée des Beaux-Arts
20 rue Paul-Doumer. Tel:
03 21 71 26 43.
*Open daily (ex Tue) 10–12,
2–5.30 (6 Apr–mid-Oct).*

6 Douai
Belltower and Hôtel de
Ville
Rue de la Mairie. Tel: 03 27
87 26 63.
*Guided tours daily on the
hour from 2pm (3 Sun); Sun
& Jul–Aug also at 10 & 11am.*

**7 Centre Historique
Minier**
Fosse Delloyer. Tel: 03 27
95 82 82.
*Open daily 10–4 (from
noon weekdays Nov–Feb).*

8 Laon
Musée d'Art et
d'Archéologie de Laon
32 rue Georges-Ermant.
Tel: 03 23 20 19 87.
*Open daily (ex Tue) 10–12,
2–5 (to 6pm Apr–Sep).*

9 Blérancourt
Museum of Franco-
American Co-operation
Off D939. Tel: 03 23 39 60
16.
*Open daily (ex Tue)
10–12.30, 2–5.30.*

10 Pierrefonds
Château
Tel: 03 44 42 72 72.
*Open daily 10–5 or 6 (may
close for lunch low season).*

11 Compiègne
Palace and Museums
Place du Général-de-
Gaulle. Tel: 03 44 38 47 00.
*Open daily (ex Tue) 9.15–6
(to 3.45pm Oct–Mar).*
Musée Antoine Vivenel
2 rue d'Austerlitz. Tel: 03
44 20 26 04.
*Open Tue–Sat 9–12, 2–6,
Sun 2–6.*
Musée de la Figurine
28 place de l'Hôtel de Ville.
Tel: 03 44 40 72 55.
*Open Tue–Sat 9–12, 2–6,
Sun 2–6 (to 5pm Nov–Feb).*

12 Ermenonville
Zoo Jean-Richard
La Mer de Sable. Tel: 03 44
54 00 96.
Open Apr–Sep.

Abbey of Chaalis
Fontaine-Chaalis. Tel: 03 44
54 04 02.
Open daily 10–12.30, 2–5.

N Beauvais
Galérie Nationale de la
Tapisserie
1 rue St-Pierre. Tel: 03 44
05 14 28.
*Open Tue–Sun, Apr–Sep
9.30–11.30, 2–6; Oct–Mar
10–11.30, 2.30–4.30.*
Musée Départementale
de l'Oise
1 rue du Musée. Tel: 03 44
11 43 83.
Open Wed–Mon 10–12, 2–6.

For Children
Parc Astérix
10km (6m) south of Senlis.
Tel: 08 36 68 30 10.
*Open Apr–mid-Oct daily 10–
6; otherwise Wed, Fri, Mon.*

TOUR 23

ⓘ 2 rue Guillaume de
Machault, Reims. Tel: 03 26
77 45 25.

ⓘ 3 quai des Arts,
Châlons-en-Champagne.
Tel: 03 26 654 17 89.

ⓘ Maison du Meunier,
Valmy. Tel: 03 26 60 27 19
or 03 26 60 41 24.

ⓘ 5 place Général
Leclerc, Ste-Menehould.
Tel: 03 26 60 85 83

ⓘ Place du Château,
Sedan. Tel: 93 24 27 73 73.

ⓘ 22 place Ducale,
Charleville-Mézières. Tel: 03
24 56 06 08.

ⓘ Mairie, avenue
Gambetta, Rethel. Tel: 03
24 39 51 44.

**2 Châlons-en-
Champagne**
Musée du Cloître Notre-
Dame-en-Vaux
Rue Nicolas Durand. Tel: 03
26 64 03 87.
Open daily.

**5 Varennes-en-
Argonne**
Musée d'Argonne
9 rue Louis XVI. Tel: 03 29
89 71 01.
*Open Apr–Jun, Sep–Oct Sat,
Sun 3–6 (daily May–Jun); Jul–
Aug daily 10.30–12, 3–6.*

6 Parc de Vision de Belval
Belval Bois-des-Dames.
Tel: 03 24 30 01 86.
Open May–Aug. Wed–Mon 12.30–6 (from 10.30 Sun).

7 Sedan
Château-Fort and Military Museum
Tel: 03 24 27 73 75.
Open daily 10–5 or later; closed Mon in winter.
Rug-making Workshops
13 boulevard Gambetta.
Tel: 03 24 27 73 73.
Open Mon–Sat.

8 Charleville-Mézières
Musée de l'Ardenne
31 place Ducale. Tel: 03 24 32 44 60.
Open Tue–Sun 10–12, 2–6.

9 Musée de l'Ardennes
Tel: 03 24 54 82 66.
Open Jul Aug daily 9 7; Sep–May daily 9–12, 2–5.

10 Rethel
Musée Verlaine
Juniville. Tel: 03 26 55 23 40.
Open May–Oct Thu–Sun 2–6.

For Children
Karting Centre
Lonny. Tel: 03 24 54 99 82.
Open mid Jan–mid Dec daily 11–8.

TOUR 24

i Boulevard de la République, Chalon-sur-Saône. Tel: 03 85 48 37 97.

i Rue de l'Hôtel-Dieu, Beaune. Tel: 03 80 26 21 30.

i 2 place Gaveau, Semur-en-Auxois. Tel: 03 80 97 05 96.

i 4 rue Bocquillot, Avallon. Tel: 03 86 34 14 19.

i Rue St Pierre, Vézelay. Tel: 03 86 33 23 69.

i Maison du Parc, St-Brisson. Tel: 03 86 78 79 00.

i Place Notre Dame, Château-Chinon. Tel: 03 86 85 06 58.

i 2 avenue Charles de Gaulle, Autun. Tel: 03 85 86 80 38.

1 Beaune
Hôtel-Dieu
Rue de l'Hôtel-Dieu. Tel: 03 80 24 45 00.
Open daily 9–5.30 (closes lunchtimes mid-Nov–Mar).
Musée du Vin de Bourgogne
Rue d'Enfer. Tel: 03 80 22 08 19.
Open all year daily 9.30–6 (closed Tue Dec–Mar).
Musée Marey
Hôtel de Ville. Tel: 03 80 24 56 98.
Open Apr–Oct daily (ex Tue) 2–6.

2 Flavigny-sur-Ozerain
Crypt Tours
Abbaye de Flavigny. Tel: 03 80 96 20 88.
Open daily 8.30–11.30, 2–5.

3 Semur-en-Auxois
Château de Flée
Tel: 03 80 97 17 07.
Open all year daily.

4 Avallon
Musée de l'Avallonnais
Place de la Collégiale. Tel: 03 86 34 03 19.
Open May–Oct daily (ex Tue) 10–12, 2–6.
Collection of Limousines
Le Château Montjalin, Sauvigny le Bois. Tel: 03 86 34 46 42.
Open Apr mid-Nov, weekends 9–7.

6 St-Brisson
Maison du Parc du Morvan
Tel: 03 86 78 79 00.
Open Apr–mid-Oct daily 10.30–6.
Musée de la Résistance
Maison du Parc du Morvan. Tel: 03 86 78 79 06.
Open daily, 10.30–6.

7 Château-Chinon
Musée du Costume
6 rue du Château. Tel: 03 86 85 18 55.
Open Feb–Dec daily (ex Tue) 10–12, 2–6.
Musée du Septennat
6 rue du Château. Tel: 03 86 85 19 23.
Open Feb–Dec daily (ex Tue) 10–12, 2–6.

8 Autun
Musée Rolin
5 rue des Bancs. Tel: 03 85 52 09 76.

Open Wed–Sun 10–12, 2–4 or later (also Mon Apr–Sep).

For History Buffs
Époisses Château
Tel: 03 80 96 40 56 or 03 80 96 42 65.
Open Jul–Aug Wed–Mon 10–12, 3–6; park & garden all year daily.

TOUR 25

i Place de la Cathédrale, Chartres. Tel: 02 37 21 50 00.

i 8 place de la Libération, Rambouillet. Tel: 01 34 83 21 21.

i 60 rue Jean Cocteau, Milly-la-Forêt. Tel: 01 64 98 83 17.

i 55 Grande-Rue, Barbizon. Tel: 01 60 66 41 87.

i 4 rue Royale, Fontainebleau. Tel: 01 60 74 99 99.

i 4 bis Place de Samois, Moret-sur-Loing. Tel: 01 60 70 41 66.

i Mail-Ouest, Gare Routière, Pithiviers. Tel: 02 38 30 50 02.

1 Rambouillet
Château
Tel: 01 34 83 00 25.
Open daily (ex Tue).
Bergerie Nationale and Museum
Château. Tel: 01 34 94 28 00.
Open Wed–Sun 2–5.
Wildlife Reserve
Southeast on the D27.
Tel: 01 34 83 05 00.
Open Wed–Mon, Apr–Oct 9–6; Nov–Mar 10–5.

2 Milly-la-Forêt
Conservatoire National Route de Nemours. Tel: 01 64 98 83 77.
Open mid-Apr–mid-Oct, Mon–Fri 9–5 (also weekends 2–6 May–mid-Sep).

3 Barbizon
Rousseau's House
55 Grande-Rue. Tel: 01 60 66 22 38.
Open Wed–Mon 10–5 (ex lunchtime on weekdays).
Auberge du Père Ganne and Museum
92 Grande-Rue. Tel: 01 60

66 22 27.
Open daily 10–12.30, 2–5.

4 Fontainebleau
Palace
Tel: 01 60 71 50 60.
Open daily (ex Tue) 9.30–5; gardens till dusk.
Musée Napoléonien d'Art et d'Histoire
88 rue St Honoré. Tel: 01 60 74 64 89.
Open Tue–Sat 2–5.

5 Moret-sur-Loing
La Grange Batelière
Via rue du Peintre-Sisley.
Tel: 01 60 70 51 21.
Open Easter–mid-Nov Sat & Sun 3–6.

7 Pithiviers
Musée Municipal
17 rue de la Couronne. Tel: 02 38 30 10 72.
Open daily (ex Mon) 10–12, 2–5 or 6.
Steam Railway
rue Carnot. Tel: 02 38 30 50 02.
Open May–Oct Sun and holidays 2–6.

Special to...
Musée des Vieux Métiers
Route de Nemours.
Tel: 01 64 98 83 77.
Open mid-Apr–mid-Oct, Mon–Fri 9–5 (also weekends 2–6 May–mid-Sep).

For Children
Tacot des Lacs
Grez-sur-Loing. Tel: 01 64 28 67 67.
Open Mar–mid-Nov daily, from 2.30 (3.30 weekends).

For History Buffs
Château de Malesherbes
Tel: 02 38 34 80 18.
Open Wed–Sun afternoons.
Château de Rouville
Malesherbes. Tel: 02 38 34 78 25.
Open daily 9–12, 2–6.

INDEX

Index & Acknowledgments

The Automobile Association
wishes to thank the following libraries and photographers for their assistance
in the preparation of this book.

MICHELLE BUSSELLE front cover, main picture
BARRIE SMITH 77, 79, 80
SPECTRUM COLOUR LIBRARY 65, 81
TONY STONE IMAGES front cover, main picture

The remaining photographs are held in the Association's own library (AA PHOTO LIBRARY) with
contributions from:

P ATTERBURY 140, 142; A BAKER 83, 86, 87, 88/9, 91, 93, 95, 96, 98, 104; P BENNETT 76; S DAY 22, 23, 24/5,
84; J EDMANSON 20, 58, 59, 61; P KENWARD 32, 41, 42, 43, 44, 49, 62, 63, 66, 67, 68, 71, 73, 75, 78; R MOORE
5, 9, 11, 14, 17, 19, 33, 37, 51, 52/3, 54, 55, 57, 82, 106/7, 115, 117, 118, 120; R MOSS 15; D NOBLE 155, 156; T
OLIVER 34, 35, 38, 45, 101, 108, 109, 111, 114, 128, 130, 131, 132, 137, 138, 139, 143, 154; N RAY 99; D
ROBERTSON 110, 113, 133, 135, 141; C SAWYER back cover (a), 6, 7, 8, 10, 12, 13, 16, 18; M SHORT 134, 150,
151, 152, 153; B SMITH inside flap, back cover (b), 21, 30, 36, 39, 46, 47, 56, 60, 64, 69, 70, 74, 85, 94, 100, 103,
112, 116, 119, 122, 123, 124/5, 127, 129, 144, 146/7, 148, 149, 157; R STRANGE 2, 26, 27, 28, 29, 50, 90, 92, 97,
105, 126; R VICTOR 31.

Contributors
Verifier: Penny Phenix **Copy editors:** Audrey Horne, Dilys Jones **Indexer:** Marie Lorimer